Wang Fuzhi's Reconstructic

"Professor Tan explores the sophisticated bread   _ uzm's
thought, which syncretizes Zhu Xi's philosophy (_.. (*uxue*), Zhang Zai's
philosophy of material force (*qixue*) and Wang Yangmin's philosophy of mind
(*xinxue*). Professor Tan's comprehensive study of Wang's thought, both its tradi-
tionalist and innovative features, thus reveals in great and convincing detail what
may justly be called a *summa philosophica* of later traditional Chinese thought."
—Richard John Lynn, *Professor Emeritus of Chinese Thought and Literature,*
University of Toronto

"Professor Mingran Tan presents us here with his comprehensive study of one of
the Confucian masters, Wang Fuzhi. The enormous significance of Wang Fuzhi in
the Confucian tradition has been set in a sharp contrast with the scarcity of studies
of his philosophy in both English and Chinese. Professor Tan's work contributes
greatly to filling up this gap by revealing the underlying structure of Wang's philosophy and highlighting the intention of Wang's reconstruction of Confucianism."
—Yong Huang, Professor, *Department of Philosophy, Chinese University of*
Hong Kong, Editor-in-Chief of Dao: A Journal of Comparative Philosophy.
yonghuang@cuhk.edu.hk. tel. (852) 3943-9678
Shatin, New Territories, Hong Kong

"II. Wang Fuzhi pondered such existential questions of his time as the collapse of
the Ming, and the harmony between humanity and Nature. Professor Tan shows
that Wang's answers still resonate and are worth pondering in our time: a stable,
flourishing state depends on the leaders remaining mindful of their purpose and
responsibility. If humanity practiced the cultivation of observing ritual propriety and
reducing desires, social harmony would be secured and resonate with natural harmony among Heaven, Earth and the Myriad Things."
—Kirill O. Thompson, Professor, *Department of Foreign Languages and*
Literatures National Taiwan University; Roosevelt Road, Sec. 4, No. 1 Taipei
106-16 TAIWAN Email: ktviking@gmail.com Tel. +886-987-992-045

"In this learned book, Mingran Tan is committed to a Confucian moralist interpretation of the neglected seventeenth-century thinker Wang Fuzhi. Although Wang Fuzhi analyzed the fall of the Ming through his uncompromising lens which he insisted barbarians stay on the frontier and remained staunchly anti-Manchu, Tan shows how Wang's views have inspired both anti-Manchu critics at the turn of the twentieth century, and proponents of "harmonious society" in the people's republic of China today."

—Paul R. Goldin, Professor, *University of Pennsylvania, prg@sas.upenn.edu, tel. 215-898-7466*

Mingran Tan

Wang Fuzhi's Reconstruction of Confucianism

Crisis and Reflection

Mingran Tan
College of Philosophy
Nankai University
Tianjin, China

ISBN 978-3-030-80265-3   ISBN 978-3-030-80263-9   (eBook)
https://doi.org/10.1007/978-3-030-80263-9

This Palgrave Macmillan imprint is published by the registered company Springer Nature Switzerland AG.
The registered company address is: Gewerbestrasse 11, 6330 Cham, Switzerland

This manuscript explores a Ming scholar Wang Fuzhi's reconstruction of Neo-Confucianism from political, moral and cosmological perspectives and his criticism of other philosophical schools of his time.

ACKNOWLEDGMENTS

This book is a development of my doctoral dissertation, *Crisis and Hermeneutics: Wang Fuzhi's Interpretation of Confucian Classics in a Time of Radical Change from the Ming to the Qing Dynasty*, completed at the University of Toronto in 2010. In the process of its composition, I have greatly benefited from my supervisor, Vincent Shen, both in terms of methodology and of the way that I interpret Wang Fuzhi and other early Chinese scholars' thought. I am grateful to him for training me in the context of English writing and thinking, as well as during the process of revising my dissertation.

I have been working on this book for nearly ten years and have incurred many debts in the process. I have consulted Yong Huang and Graham Sanders on how to restructure the book and how to write and submit a book proposal. I express my thanks to David Chai, Kyle Muntz, and Kirill O. Thompson for taking the time to read the draft and to provide their comments. In particular, with his meticulous copy-editing, Kirill has turned this manuscript into an appealing piece for readers.

I would like to thank Burke Gerstenschlager for his acceptance of my book proposal and encouragement to publish it. I am greatly appreciative of Phil Getz and Amy Invernizzi's assistance and support. Over the years, Phil has responded to the many issues of this manuscript with professionalism and has managed to guide my book into print. Finally, Arun Prasath has maintained a consistent and creative oversight of the many details which attended its publication.

I would like to acknowledge the support which I have received from Chiang Ching-kuo Foundation for International Scholarly Exchange (USA) and the Center of Zhouyi and Ancient Chinese Philosophy of Shandong University.

Mingran Tan

BRIEF DESCRIPTION

This project is a comprehensive review of a Ming loyalist's, Wang Fuzhi (1619–1692), understanding of historical events and his interpretation of Confucian classics. It aims to explain what kind of Confucian system Wang Fuzhi was trying to construct under the urge of his motto, "The Six Classics spur me to initiate something new," and his attempt to find solutions for both cultural and political crises of his time. It indicates that Wang Fuzhi tried to establish a syncretism which melded the three branches of Neo-Confucianism, that is, the philosophy of principle proposed by Zhu Xi (1130–1200), the philosophy of mind by Wang Yangming (1472–1529), and the philosophy of *qi* (vital force) by Zhang Zai (1020–1077). Politically, he proposed ethnic separation and the enlightened monarchy. Morally, he resorted to Confucian self-cultivation and the change of one's physical embodiment. Cosmologically, he believed that all things are in the same flux of *qi* and can influence each other. In order to prevent the rise of conflicts and disasters, everyone should preserve the peace of mind and return the universe a mass of harmonious *qi*. In this way, Wang Fuzhi elevated self-cultivation and political governance to the cosmological level and prescribed the meaning of life for all sentient beings. Yet, Wang Fuzhi reduced political problems to moral cultivation and thus could not prescribe a true remedy for dynastic China although his moral teachings and universal harmony are still appealing to the improvement of social atmosphere.

Reading this book, a reader will be able to grasp the main theme of Wang Fuzhi's sophisticated arguments in his voluminous works and understand his goal of influencing natural and social process through human effort and moral cultivation. With Wang Fuzhi's criticism of previous Neo-Confucian scholars, the reader will be able to delve deeper into Zhu Xi's and Wang Yangming's thoughts and see the influence of Buddhism on Neo-Confucianism. Moreover, the reader will understand Wang Fuzhi's role in Chinese intellectual history, in particular his influence on Mao Zedong and present-day China.

CONTENTS

CHAPTER 1

Introduction

The writings of Wang Fuzhi 王夫之 (Wang Chuanshan 王船山 1619–1692), a Ming loyalist, have attracted sustained scholarly attention ever since their publication in 1866. However, the sheer volume of his commentaries and wide scope of his writings make it difficult to offer a summation of his thought. Ji Wenfu 嵇文甫 sketched an overview titled *A Discussion on Wang Chuanshan's Academics* (Ji 1962). Chen Lai 陳來 edited a collection of his notes and reflections on Wang's works (Chen 2004). And, Zeng Zhaoxu 曾昭旭 mounted a systematic study of Wang Fuzhi's thought but overlooked the pivotal role of *qi* 氣 in his system (Zeng 2008).

In the English-speaking world, **Ian McMorran** insightfully points out that Wang Fuzhi was influenced by Wang Yangming in his attempts to modify and criticize the Cheng-Zhu School, and thus showed similarity to Wang Yangming in his emphasis on action (McMorran 1973). But it is untenable for McMorran to conclude that Wang Fuzhi could be distinguished from Wang Yangming by saying, "Wang Fuzhi sought the moral through reality" (McMorran 1973), for Wang Fuzhi was regulating reality with a priori nature rather than seeking it from reality. Wang Fuzhi differed from Yangming in his belief that, after one awakened to a priori nature, one should verify and enhance it through compliance with ritual propriety, and gradually approach sagehood. In another essay, Ian McMorran addresses Wang Fuzhi's life and analyzes the factors that influence the formation of Wang's thought. He gives

M. Tan, *Wang Fuzhi's Reconstruction of Confucianism*, https://doi.org/10.1007/978-3-030-80263-9_1

the reason that Wang Fuzhi changed his dream of restoration to the dream of cultural preservation. However, his understanding of the relation among the supreme ultimate (*taiji* 太極), the supreme void (*taixu* 太虛), and the Supreme Harmony (*taihe* 太和) needs to be revisited (McMorran 1975). In her book *Man and Nature in the Philosophical Thought of Wang Fu-chih*, **Alison Harley Black** mainly interprets ideas from Wang Fuzhi's *Zhouyi Wai Zhuan* (周易外傳) and emphasizes the epistemological aspects of the relationship between man and nature. She is right to indicate that the main difference between Wang and his contemporaries lay in his deep interest in the broadly defined philosophical task of articulating and integrating his ideas into a comprehensive world view (Black 1989: 164–165). But she is unaware that Wang Fuzhi's main concern was to promote the Way of humaneness, which leads Wang to prefer knowledge from virtue and nature 德性所知 to the knowledge from hearing and seeing 聞見之知. Thus, she incorrectly concludes that in Wang Fu-chih, there is a considerable blurring of the boundaries between two kinds of knowledge (Black 1989: 182). **Liu Jeeloo** clearly understands that Wang Fuzhi regarded *qi* to be the fundamental element of the universe. *Qi* is self-sufficient, self-propelling, self-regulating, and, above all, good. It is regulated with its own internal logic which he calls "*li* 理" or principle. Principle is the inherent logic or pattern of the distribution as well as the development of *qi*. Therefore, principle does not have any transcendent status; it is also not logically prior to *qi*. However, Liu seems to misinterpret Wang Fuzhi when she says, "Wang separated the *li* that is the natural order of things and the *li* that is the ultimate moral completion in the human world" (Liu 2010), for the *li* in the human world is the concretization of the *li* that is the natural order of things. Moreover, Liu does not realize that Wang Fuzhi acknowledged the existence of evil human nature when he claimed, "When there are both alternation (*bian* 変) and conjoining (*he* 合), not all can be good" (Liu 2010; Wang 1996: 6:1052). At this point, it is untenable for Liu to say, "Daily renewal is also a progression towards perfection," or "There are smarter or stupider people by birth, but there are no moral or immoral people by birth" (Liu 2010).

The present book will incorporate McMorran and other scholars' insights on Wang Fuzhi and explore Wang Fuzhi's cosmology, moral cultivation, and political theory in detail. It aims to examine Wang Fuzhi's purpose in producing his vast corpus of writings, and presents an account of structure of his thought. It will also address Wang Fuzhi's evaluation of Wang Yangming and Zhuxi and his criticism of heterodox teachings. And all of these undertakings will start from a clear understanding of Wang Fuzhi's authorial purpose.

1.1 Wang Fuzhi's Authorial Purpose

Wang Fuzhi dedicated himself to preserving and transmitting Confucianism for future generations through his scholarship and writing. Revering Confucianism as the standard bearer of civilization, the expression of humanism, and the ethical core of Chinese culture, his deepest fear was that the Manchu regime would undermine Chinese culture and condemn the Chinese to a brutish way of life, vying for food and spouse unleavened by decorum or a sense of decency. Wang thus sought to invigorate and transmit Confucianism to imbue society with civility and humanity. In the spirit of Immanuel Kant's dictum, "Only the human being, and with him every rational creature, is an end in itself" (Kant 2002: 112). Wang enjoined people to love and respect one another and cherish life. Opposing society's tendency to honor people according to their worldly achievements, Wang advocated honoring people by a moral standard: their practice of Confucian humaneness 仁, righteousness 義, and ritual propriety 禮. By this standard, he praised the scholar Guan Ning 管寧 (158–241 CE) for his efforts to preserve the sprouts of humanity, righteousness, and ritual propriety in society during the chaotic Three Kingdoms period, observing that "Chinese society in the late Han and the Three Kingdoms period was not held together by the warlords Liu Bei 劉備, Sun Quan 孫權 and Cao Cao 曹操, nor by the ministers Xun Yue 荀悅 and Zhuge Kongming 諸葛孔明. It was held together by [the propriety of] Guan Ning" (Wang 1996: 10:345–346).[1]

Wang Fuzhi's faith was that a harmonious society was held together, not by power, but by the people's humaneness and love; consequently, it was Guan Ning's efforts to establish humaneness that held society together.

---

[1] "Wang" stands for Wang Fuzhi; "1996" for publication year; "10" for volume 10; "345–346" for page numbers.

If a powerful warlord were to conquer the world by force and stratagems but failed to govern by humaneness and ritual propriety, his rule would not be lasting. Wang Fuzhi thus urged the rulers to restore Confucianism and promote humaneness and righteousness, and criticized the founders of the Ming dynasty for having failed to restore Confucian ritual propriety once they had driven out the Mongols; for it was this failure that weakened political loyalty and social cohesion, giving the Manchus the opportunity to conquer China later.

> Alas, ritual propriety is crucial to proper governance. The neglect of ritual propriety results in the invasion of nomads, however maintaining ritual propriety is a vital measure for protecting the people from harassment by the nomads. If a ruler or a general were to drive off the nomads but failed to realize the necessity to uphold ritual propriety, the nomads would return. Regrettably, this is why the Ming founders Liu Ji 劉基, Song Lian 宋濂, Tao An 陶安 and Zhan Tong 詹同 could not match the feats of Guan Zhong 管仲, and were a far cry from the Duke of the Zhou. (They were not qualified to stand in the dust of Duke of the Zhou's chariot.) (Wang 1996: 5:146)

While issuing his vow to restore Confucian humaneness and ritual propriety, Wang Fuzhi lived in poverty and was surveilled and harassed by the Manchus. Even after the passing of his wives and children, he continued his studies and writing, hoping to bequeath a light of humaneness to future generations, to guide them to practice the humane Confucian Way and ward off future barbarian assaults. At this point, like Huang Zongxi 黃宗羲 (1610–1695) who wrote "*Waiting for the Dawn*" to place his hope on the future, Wang Fuzhi wrote:

> During a deeply chaotic time, one should not fear one is alone in guiding the people along the path of compassion, shame, and honor. Assuredly, one must continue one's efforts until they succeed… This reflects the regenerative movement of the mind of Heaven and Earth, an unceasing movement in the world. (Wang 1996: 10:1099)

Wang Fuzhi described the work of preserving humaneness as "storing it up for future use (*chu tianxia zhi yong* 儲天下之用)." He had no expectation that his ideals would be adopted by the Manchu regime of the time. He denied the legitimacy of Manchu rule, calling the Manchus bandits and usurpers, confident he was serving the Way of the late sage kings 先聖王之道—the Yellow Emperor 黃帝, Shen Nong 神農, Shun 舜, and Yu 禹

who had warded off bandits, thieves, birds, and beasts. In this, Wang displayed the moral courage of Mencius 孟子 (371–289 BCE) and stayed dedicated to the Way of the late sage kings during the period of Manchu rule. In this spirit, he ridiculed Zhuangzi 莊子 (c. 399–295 BCE) for not upholding the Way of the sages in facing the dangers and risks of the Warring States period, saying, "Zhuang Zhou 莊周 was horrified by the chaos of his time and just wished to be a useless tree. He advocated being useless and did not uphold the things that would be most useful in the future" (Wang 1996: 10:69).

Wang Fuzhi's commitment to Confucianism and his resistance to the Manchu regime are expressed in a couplet that hangs in his study: "The Six Classics spur me to initiate something new. My five-foot body accepts its destiny even if to be buried alive (by the Manchu regime)" (Wang 1996: 15:717). He was committed to renewing and transmitting the Confucian tradition, reviving the Ming, and resisting the Manchus. He maintained this staunch commitment for the rest of his life.

Taking Confucian humaneness and righteousness as his standard, he weighed and assessed the scholars and heroes of antiquity, criticized doctrinal heterodoxy, and rectified interpretations of the Six Classics. In particular, besides criticizing Zhuangzi's fear of facing the chaos, he did not accept Zhuangzi's teaching of transcending right and wrong and life of detachment. He feared Zhuangzi's teachings would weaken people's loyalty to the Ming and lessen their hatred to the Manchu. He likened a minister's loyalty to his ruler to a wife's devotion to her husband; having made such a commitment, one should accept it as one's destiny, to share in life through thick and thin together, without thought of separating (Wang 1996: 3:318). Angered by the positive reception of the Manchu emperor Kangxi 康熙 and the popularity of Manchu drama in Suzhou in 1684 (Zhou and Peterson 2002: 407), Wang Fuzhi cast the common people as no better than birds and beasts, devoted solely to "seeking food, spouse, and shelter," over which they would fight lest threatened by the death penalty (Wang 1996: 12:478). Such reflections strengthened Wang Fuzhi's resolve to reject Zhuangzi's teaching of transcending right and wrong and the Buddhist doctrines of emptiness and illusion. He feared that such amoral teachings could justify anybody's becoming the emperor and legitimize the Manchu conquest of China.

Wang Fuzhi's ideal politics is the Kingly Way 王道 or humane governance 仁政 according to which only those who practice humaneness, observe ritual propriety, and cannot bear the suffering of others are qualified to rule. By this standard, Wang Fuzhi ranked Liu Xiu 劉秀 (5 BCE–57 AD) and Zhao Kuangyin 趙匡胤 (927–976) as second only to the Three Sage Kings of the Xia, Shang, and Zhou dynasties. Liu Xiu continued to observe ritual propriety even while fighting other warlords, and he practiced humane governance in ruling the state. Zhao Kuangyin practiced humaneness and was kind to his brother, the ex-emperor's family, and scholars around the state. Seeing no potential rulers of this moral caliber in his day, Wang insisted that the reins of rulership be passed to strong ministers or even bandits, anyone who was capable, rather than to barbarians and nomads who devalued humaneness, neglected ritual propriety, and conducted themselves like birds and beasts. While admitting that the Manchus and other nomadic peoples could adopt the Confucian Way and practice ritual propriety, Wang Fuzhi insisted that it would be a pretense. Their donning the robes of Confucianism would be like a monkey wearing a human cap.

1.2   THE STRUCTURE OF WANG FUZHI'S THOUGHT

Wang Fuzhi's thought is structured around three main facets: political governance, moral cultivation, and cosmic harmony. Wang asserted, "When an exemplary person instructs others, he traces human nature 性 back to the heavenly endowment 天命, elevates learning to the sagely achievement, and governs the state by the Kingly Way" (Wang 1996: 8:750). He sought to connect moral cultivation and humane governance with cosmic harmony in his system. Besides these three facets, he sought to correct errors in earlier scholars' interpretations of the Confucian Classics and critiqued teachings that he regarded as heterodox, such as Buddhism, Daoism, and Legalism.

As to political governance, Wang Fuzhi advocated implementing the Kingly Way based on Mencius' notion of humane governance. In Wang's view, when the Kingly Way prevailed during the Three Dynasties, the kings and ministers loved each other and cooperated naturally without orders or remonstrations. He compared their loving, symbiotic relationship to that between raindrops and plants; the rain falls on plants and the plants receive the moisture naturally without coercion or demand (Wang 1996: 3:396). In practicing the Kingly Way, the ruler should regard the throne as public property, fill his mind with humaneness, and master himself with ritual propriety. With humaneness filling his mind, his practical measures would ensure humane governance and transform the people into moral subjects. This approach involved moral charisma: when the people observed the sage king's pure demeanor they would feel a compelling preference for goodness; when they observed the king's regal bearing their inner sense of shame and honor would be stirred. How would such a rule need to control the people by reward and punishment (Wang 1996: 8:843)?

At the same time, Wang Fuzhi knew that the Kingly Way of the Three Dynasties had been practiced only in the remote past. Like his contemporary Huang Zongxi, Wang ascribed the chaos and disasters of the empire to the rulers' selfishness and suspicions, since they regarded the throne as their private property and feared overthrow. Wang instead upheld humane governance by kingly ruler as the remedy. He praised Liu Xiu and Zhao Kuangyin for their policies of tolerance, observance of ritual propriety, and treating scholars and others with respect and leniency. In contrast, he noted the Ming emperors' selfishness, suspiciousness, meanness, and cruelty. In one example, he criticized the low salary policy of the Ming dynasty (Wang 1996: 12:565). In another example, he condemned the Ming emperor's ordering flogging a minister at court, arguing that the order was solely to make officials lose their sense of shame and honor and be pawns of the throne. He said, this scholar-official, now loved and coddled by the emperor, now seized and thrown into a dungeon, then fettered and shackled, then disrobed and beaten …. In this fashion, even if the scholar-official didn't feel ashamed about being beaten at court, how could he possibly share the emperor's issues above, and still care about the common people's complaints below (Wang 1996: 10:106)? Ironically, while Wang Fuzhi recognized the evil of tyrants, he, like Hobbes, still regarded a powerful ruler as a necessary evil for controlling social conflict. He would not consent to the overthrow of a tyrant; he preferred keeping a tyrant in place to risking the collapse of ritual propriety and social order. In this way, his silver cloud of humaneness concealed a dark lining of abiding tyrants.

Wang Fuzhi still advocated a set of measures to remedy the misrule of the Ming court, ranging from limiting imperial power, empowering prime ministers, and disciplining officials, to nurturing and educating the people. He also showed insight in identifying the feelings of the people as the eyes of Heaven and advocating for securing the people's basic needs and improving their morals. Also, as to realizing humane governance, unlike earlier Confucians, Wang held that setting the world in order and transforming the people had to be done in stages, following *The Great Learning*. He did not trust in the transformative power of moral exemplars on the people, but stressed the implementation of political measures and arts (*shu* 術), such as reducing taxes and nurturing the people. He also did not believe that sagely rule in and of itself would induce the moral transformation of the people spontaneously; it would just pacify the people and make them content with their lot but wouldn't incline them to cultivate and become exemplary people themselves. In other words, Wang advocated that the people needed a proper education, then to cultivate themselves to shed bad habits and make moral and practical progress (Wang 1996: 7:136).

As to moral cultivation, Wang Fuzhi advocated that the ruler's being humane minded was a prerequisite of his practicing the Kingly Way or humane governance. Only a ruler whose mind could not bear to see the suffering of others could lead a government that could not bear to accept the suffering of the people. By the same token, only a common person who treated his fellows with humaneness and love could lead his fellows to be upright and live in harmony. Wang Fuzhi had two practical considerations for advocating that a society of exemplary people could be realized only by a leader who sincerely observed ritual propriety and followed his conscience. First, following Confucius, he stressed the ruler's influence as a moral model on the people. A ruler's displays of humane mindedness would incline the people to goodness just as the wind inclines the grass to one side. He expressed this idea in his comments on Song Xing 宋鈃 dissuading the kings of the states of Qin 秦 and Chu 楚 from going to war, which was discussed in the *Mencius*. Wang argued that if Song Xing had told the kings not to go to war because it would be unprofitable, it would give people the impression that seeking profit itself was the path to being safe and staying alive. Thereafter, the people would seek profit regardless of filial piety or loyalty and the state would not last. If Song Xing had counseled not going to war because it was not humane or righteous, it would impress the people it was humaneness and righteousness that had made them safe and kept them alive. It would also incline them to be compassionate and moderate their anger and greed. Thereafter, the kings and ministers, fathers and sons, and elder and younger brothers would love and respect each other and not prioritize considerations of profit and loss (Wang 1996: 8:771–772).

Second, following the *Great Learning* teaching that "when a single family is humane, the whole country will be stirred toward humaneness," Wang Fuzhi held that a common person's practice of humaneness and righteousness could move his fellows to be righteous as well. Concerning how to set this in motion, he advocated a method of cultivating oneself internally and externally, that is, to discipline one's conduct by ritual propriety without while arousing one's conscience within. For example, he argued that if a mourner were to wear mourning clothes, eat simple food, and live in a hutch, he would seldom forget his sense of loss and respect for his parent due to losing himself in finery and temptations; since his environment would be controlled, his mind would not go astray. On the contrary, if a mourner were to wear fine silk attire, eat meat, and live in a palace, it would be difficult for him not to forget his loss and love for his departed parent; since his environment would be full of temptations, his desires would be constantly aroused. Wang Fuzhi concluded that while exemplary and filial people express their love and respect through ritual propriety and keep their mind sincere, the common people must control their behavior by observing ritual propriety, which stirs their love and respect (Wang 1996: 10:422–423). In this way, everyone would be stirred to practice humaneness and righteousness and live in harmony.

Wang Fuzhi argued that all people were born with a compassionate mind and able to practice ritual propriety because humaneness and compassion were characteristics of the mind of Heaven and Earth that produced the myriad things, including human beings. Following *The Book of Changes* teaching that "The successive movement of yin and yang is the Way. What issues from the Way is good, and that which embodies it is the individual nature," Wang added that, as the endowment of Heaven in each person, the human nature was precisely the principle of Heaven and Earth that produced the myriad things. For him, this notion was evidenced in the reality of humaneness and the mind that could not bear to see the suffering of others, that is, in the fact that every human being is born with a humane mind and can become good. Wang also made the case that people become evil because of bad habits. Ingrained bad habits change not only a person's temperament but also their nature.

How could one restore their original good nature? Wang Fuzhi advocated working to form and develop good habits. He called this "changing one's physical embodiment (*bianhua qizhi* 變化氣質)" or conducting sustained "practice to remake one's nature (*xi yu xing cheng* 習與性成)" (Wang 1996: 6:962). He stressed that forming good habits and practices lay in observing ritual propriety as a means to regulate the desires, since ritual propriety was the concrete reflection of heavenly principle in proper human conduct.

Wang Fuzhi sought to avoid the flaws he noticed in Zhu Xi's 朱熹 (1130–1200) teachings. For example, he criticized that Zhu's teaching of "extinguishing the desires to realize principle" would make practitioners become passive and alienate them from society. He implicitly accepted Wang Yangming's teaching of inborn knowledge of the good 良知 and stressed knowing the fundamentals and having moral self-mastery. He described inborn knowledge of the good as the attainment of one's nature (*xing zhi de* 性之得), and instructed his students to awaken to this attainment and draw on it to guide their behavior. A person with such attainment and practice could deal with the myriad things in response to their principles, and his behavior would always be in compliance with the Way. Notably, this teaching was inconsistent with Wang Fuzhi's other teaching that one could form a second nature by developing good habits.

Wang Fuzhi had stressed the discipline of ritual propriety in view of the shortcomings of Wang Yangming's disciples who had not practiced ritual propriety and lacked discernible attainment but still claimed they followed their inborn knowledge of the good in conduct. He criticized Wang Yangming's disciples Wang Gen 王艮 and Li Zhi 李贄, in particular, for regarding the desires themselves as inborn knowledge of the good. In response, Wang Fuzhi divided the mind into two sections—the Way mind 道心 and the humanly mind 人心. The former was rooted in inborn knowledge of the good, observed ritual propriety, practiced righteousness, and distinguished right from wrong, while the latter was rooted in natural instincts and perceptions. In Wang Fuzhi's view, Wang Yangming and his disciples had mistaken the humanly mind of man as rooted in inborn knowledge of the good, so they mistook the desires as principle of Heaven. Wang Fuzhi argued that Wang Yangming himself was able to observe ritual propriety after awakening to inborn knowledge of the good because he had been observing ritual propriety all along. However, his disciples who lacked such cultivation could not express the Confucian Way in word or deed by depending solely on their awakened inborn knowledge of the good. Consequently, Wang Fuzhi faced a dilemma between his teachings of following one's attainment originating from the nature and reshaping the nature by practicing ritual propriety. At the same time, this dilemma reflected Wang Fuzhi's attempt to synthesize the teachings of the Cheng-Zhu School and the Wang Yangming School.

As to method of moral cultivation, Wang Fuzhi redefined the relationships between the nature (*xing* 性) and the emotions (*qing* 情), principle (*li* 理) and desire (*yu* 欲), the Way (*dao* 道) and objects (*qi* 器), and the Way mind and the humanly mind to rectify what he took to be misinterpretations in the previous Neo-Confucian readings of the Six Classics. For example, he rejected Li Ao's 李翱 (772–841) notion of recovery of the nature by eliminating the emotions, but advocated calming the nature by appropriately expressing the emotions, instead. He did not accept Zhu Xi's notion of extinguishing the desires to realize principle but advocated discovering principle right in the expression of desires. He compared extinguishing the desires to realize principle to draining water to farm fish, an impossible approach.

In fact, Wang Fuzhi's redefinitions were based on his rearrangement of the relations between principle (*li* 理) and *qi* 氣. Unlike Zhu Xi's ontological distinction between principle and *qi*, Wang Fuzhi advocated the unity of principle and *qi*. In his view, principle is the pattern of *qi*'s flow; it depends on *qi* and cannot exist apart from *qi*. By the same token, the Way exists in objects and is manifested as the pattern of objects. Without objects, the Way would not be manifested. Because feelings and desires were expressions of a person's *qi* or bodily temperament, Wang Fuzhi also held that the nature and principle could not exist apart from them, either.

Wang Fuzhi's emphasis on *qi*, objects, and desires reflected a new trend and pattern of thinking at the late Ming. It not only healed Zhu Xi's opposition of principle and desire and his estrangement of principle and *qi*, but it also restored the pre-Qin view of the emotions, as described in the *Doctrine of the Mean*: to hit due measure and degree in expressing the emotions. Wang's emphasis on *qi*, objects, and desires helped to pave the way for Dai Zhen 戴震 (1723–1777) to affirm that principle itself is the lines and patterns of blood, vital force, the mind, and intelligence. "Nature (principle) refers to an allotment of yin and yang and the Five Elements, which forms the very blood, vital force, the mind, and intelligence, by which the myriad things are differentiated" (Dai 1961: 25). "Principle consists of unerring expressions of the emotions, hitting the mark. Principle can never prevail when the emotions are not expressed in due measure and degree" (Dai 1961: 1; Chan 1963: 712).

As to cosmology, Wang Fuzhi advocated each person's assisting Heaven by cultivating their allotment of harmonious *qi*. This was the ultimate goal of practicing both the Kingly Way and personal self-cultivation and the way to avert political and social conflicts and natural disasters. On the one hand, the essential benefit of humaneness laid in inducing harmony. The practice of humane governance and the Kingly Way involved extending the ruler's humaneness to the world and inducing harmony in society. On the other hand, the mind of Heaven and Earth itself consisted in humaneness; and the great virtue of Heaven and Earth lay in their producing and nourishing the myriad things. The harmonious *qi* of Heaven and Earth and human beings, the humaneness of Heaven and of human beings were the same in kind and they mingled and nurtured each other. Therefore, a person's thought and action could influence the harmonious *qi* of the cosmos at any moment. Each person needed to have faith that his mind of humaneness could arouse harmony and love in the world, just as a single spark may arouse a conflagration. Wang Fuzhi thus advocated that everyone strive to reduce improper customs in society by cultivating themselves and assisting in the transforming and nourishing of Heaven and Earth. He foresaw the rise of a wondrous world in which each person could fully cultivate his harmonious *qi*:

> If a person were to cultivate and preserve both (spirit and body) without loss, he would thereby knead the pure, clear *qi* of Heaven and earth. When [such a person passes on,] his body and spirit disperse and return to primal *qi*, their purity and clarity will wondrously identify with the Great Void. The sun, moon, and stars above will be brighter, and all things below will receive nurture and flourish. Their primal *qi* will become the breeze animating Heaven and Earth, and the principle of life will attract positive *qi* in the formation of new persons. In this way, even though a person's body may change and decompose, his pure, clear harmonious *qi* will not change but will induce goodness and blessings and benefit every living thing in the world. In this way, such a person would assist in the transformations of Heaven, exist eternally, spread around the cosmos, and mingle with the myriad forms. No benefit could be greater than this. It is to this end that the utmost person keeps devoted to cultivating his life. (Wang 1996: 13:293)

As to practical measures, besides moral cultivation, Wang Fuzhi recommended that people take care in choosing food, shelter, as well as timing actions. He also noted that the sage kings of antiquity had used music and dance to rouse the harmonious *qi* of the disabled so they too would cherish their lives. He recommended acting in accordance with the change of seasons and avoiding exposure to storms, blizzards, and extreme heat. Such measures were intended to modify the people's behavior by ritual propriety and to harmonize their blood and *qi*, that is, to transform their physical embodiment by moral cultivation (*bianhua qizhi* 變化氣質).

Overall, Wang Fuzhi advocated assisting Heaven through cultivating harmonious *qi* to instill the sense of having a mission in life in people so their lives would be settled and their destiny fulfilled. Indeed, this sense of being settled and having a destiny stirred Wang to carry on after the fall of the Ming. To him, the sustainability of society lay not in wealth, power, and institutions, but in the spirit of humaneness, righteousness, ritual propriety, and wisdom. In the absence of humaneness, ritual propriety, and wisdom, a society where people lived by the law of the jungle would not be valued even though it might be prosperous and bolstered by strict laws.

This was Wang's key consideration in denying the legitimacy of the Manchu conquest and its promotion of Neo-Confucianism. Anticipating the revival of Chinese rituals and music, he preserved the seeds of humaneness and righteousness for later generations.

1.3 WANG FUZHI'S CRITIQUE OF HETERODOX TEACHINGS

Wang Fuzhi attributed the fall of the Ming dynasty largely to the spread of heterodox teachings. He said, "In recent times, Wang Yangming based teaching of inborn knowledge of the good on Buddhist ideas. It included transcending words and thought, leaving no trace or bit of dust, and attaching no ideas or opinions … As the spread of Lu Zijing's 陸子靜 (Lu Jiuyuan 陸九淵 1139–1193) teachings led to the ruin of the Song dynasty, so too the spread of Wang Yangming's incurred the fall of the Ming" (Wang 1996: 12:370–371). Wang Fuzhi sharply criticized earlier Neo-Confucians for adding Buddhist, Daoist, and Legalist ideas into Confucianism and sought to purge Confucianism of heterodox elements. He devoted himself to writing fresh commentaries on the Six Classics and producing a pure Confucian doctrine for the education of the people.

In response to the Buddhist teaching of emptiness, Wang proposed the idea of true being (*shi you* 實有). He argued that, because the Buddhists saw all things as empty and illusory, they tended to abandon human relationships and overlook the dichotomy between good and evil such that even a thief or a prostitute could become a Buddha by awakening to the emptiness of all dharmas. Influenced by the Buddhist teaching of emptiness, Zhu Xi regarded principle as forming "a pure, vast, and empty realm" (Li 1994: 3) and asserted that "the principle of Heaven will prevail only after the annihilation of human desires" (Zhu 1983: 130).

Besides critiquing the teaching of emptiness, Wang Fuzhi criticized the idea of sudden awakening, a direct intuition of the empty and impermanent nature of all things. He also rebuked Wang Yangming for appealing to this Chan Buddhist idea in discussing the Confucian comprehension of utmost principle and for pronouncing "there is no distinction of good and evil in the original substance of the mind" (Chan 1963: 688), a teaching that could have the same destructive impact as Buddhist emptiness. In Wang Fuzhi's view, Wang Yangming's account of the original substance of the mind not only undermined the virtue of humaneness but it rendered the practice of ritual propriety unnecessary. Wang Yangming's disciples indeed considered ritual propriety as unnecessary; for he taught them that a person who acted on his inborn knowledge of the good would spontaneously observe ritual propriety. A few of his disciples went so far as to discard moral norms, identify their selfish desires with the principle of Heaven, and rationalize their actions, whether bad or simply absurd, by appealing to the inborn capacity to carry out the good.

Wang Fuzhi's criticism of Wang Yangming was echoed in Yan Yuan's 顏元 (1635–1704) further attack. Yan Yuan argued that if the substance of the mind transcended the distinction between good and evil, it would unable to ground the inborn knowledge of the good, which enabled people to distinguish good from evil, just as realization of Buddhist emptiness would not assure the realization of compassion. Yan Yuan criticized the popular view that Confucianism was like Buddhism in fundamentals but they differed in practice, claiming this was as absurd as saying a sprout of wheat could emerge from a root of hemp. Confucians viewed human nature as humaneness, righteousness, ritual propriety, and wisdom, while Buddhism regarded the nature as empty and inherently detached. Moreover, while the former notion supported loyalty and filial piety, the latter implied alienation and fostered disloyalty and impiety. How could they be the same in fundamentals and only differ in practice (Yan 2000: 177–178)?

Buddhism, Daoism, and Legalism were regarded by Wang Fuzhi as the three calamities of Chinese culture. He criticized Laozi, the founder of Daoism, for propounding treacherous and crafty ideas, like, "In order to grasp, one must first give" (Chan 1963: 157). He held that Laozi had evinced a calculating mind, alert for opportunities to manipulate the world, and inclined people to become opportunists. He criticized Zhuangzi for lacking any sense of social responsibility, as evidenced in Zhuangzi's arguments against the distinction of right and wrong and quest for personal freedom. Wang Fuzhi's criticism stressed that Laozi's ideas ran counter to humaneness, loyalty, and fidelity while Zhuangzi's thought lacked any sense of national pride and would not support Wang's anti-Manchu mission.

Wang Fuzhi criticized Legalism for its excessive harshness and lack of kindness as well as for its severity and discrimination. In his view, a government that deployed such harsh and discriminative measures would drive the people to be evasive, irresponsible, and contentious. To a certain extent, Wang Fuzhi was casting aversion at the Ming regime by alluding to its legalist-style measures, such as flogging a minister at court, low salary, high taxes, and concentration of land ownership. He thought that such Ming measures disheartened the scholar-officials, and pushed them to be corrupt, selfish, irresponsible, and ungrateful.

Wang Fuzhi saw relations among the three big calamities of China. Based on his study of the course of Chinese, he concluded that the popularization of Buddhism and Daoism would lead to the state adopting legalist measures. When a ruler attained utmost vacuity and maintained pure quietude, he would discard all plans and efforts, and simply decide all affairs according to one fixed principle or law. Conversely, if a ruler were to rule the state by legalist measures, the people would embrace the teachings of Buddhism and Daoism, for if a government were to cause the people to feel fear and anxiety, they would withdraw and embrace the teachings of emptiness and nothingness, to soothe their conscience and justify their shunning responsibility and blame. Facing strict laws and harsh punishments, the people would hold their superiors responsible for the situation, betray their rulers and fathers, and accept the Buddhist teaching that a person who acts without intentions will incur no blame. Wang Fuzhi appealed to this consideration when explaining why the teachings of Wang Ji 王畿 and Li Zhi 李贄—both of whom advocated Chan Buddhism in the guise of Confucianism—had become so popular after Prime Minister Zhang Juzheng 張居正 (1525–1582) repressed the people with strict laws and harsh regulations (Wang 1996: 10:653).

Besides leveling criticisms at heterodox teachings, Wang Fuzhi tried to purge the influence of heterodox teachings on the previous Confucian commentaries on the Confucian Classics. For example, he criticized the Buddhist influence on Zhu Xi, saying, "To seek principle beyond desires is only a Buddhist teaching, which ignores the rules of things and abandons human relations" (Wang 1996: 6:911). Then, he criticized Wang Yangming's teaching of the unity of knowledge and action by noting that Wang Yangming sought to replace action with knowledge and mistook non-intentional action as action (Wang 1996: 2:312). In response to Wang Yangming's view that "Once a person has an idea, he is already acting" (Wang 2012: 198), Wang Fuzhi countered, "There are mountains in Yue 越, but it cannot be said that Yue had no mountains before I arrived there and saw them. It cannot be said either that my arriving there or my act of seeing the mountains is the mountains" (Wang 1996: 2:378). In other words, Wang Fuzhi did not think that subjective consciousness was identical with action, nor that human activity was identical with objective entities. In this way, he deftly refuted Wang Yangming's tacit acceptance of the Buddhist idea that "The three worlds are only mind, and all things are just consciousness 三界唯心, 萬法唯識," a summation of the themes of the School of Flower Ornament and the School of Conscious Only.

Besides the three big calamities, Wang Fuzhi criticized Mohism and the Jesuits for advocating universal love. He argued that since Heaven and Earth were the origin of all things, we should love them and regard all creatures as our companions. As Heaven and Earth produce us through our parents and distinguish us from other creatures, we should love our parents and siblings first. We should not ignore our parents to love Heaven and Earth without distinction (Wang 1996: 12:352). Therefore, when the Mohist loved his son and his neighbor's son equally, or the Jesuits worshipped Heaven as "the Heavenly Lord," Wang Fuzhi criticized them for disrespecting their ancestral spirits and betraying parents without scruple (Wang 1996: 1:1015). On his view, love among close kin was spontaneous and real while so-called universal love was just a pretense. One should extend one's kin love to his neighbors and strangers, not love them equally.

1.4   WANG FUZHI'S ORIGINALITY AND HIS TIMES

Although Wang Fuzhi had a profound reflection upon the crises of his time, he nevertheless shared many common features with his peers. Like his peers, he promoted practical studies, embraced the unity of human desires and heavenly principle, criticized Neo-Confucianism, and rejected the distinction between the nature of heavenly endowment (天命之性 *tianming zhi xing*) and the nature of physical embodiment (氣質之性 *qizhi zhi xing*), but he showed more moderation than them, in particular in the criticism of Neo-Confucianism. In order to prevent people from identifying Wang's original contributions with the common features of his time, it is necessary to compare Wang Fuzhi with his peers before analyzing his Confucian system.

First, Wang Fuzhi was a recluse and was not involved in initiating any new academic trend, such as evidential learning. Although he had discussed some practical concerns in his works, he was still limited to shortsighted utility. He did not have a positivistic or empirical approach, and often fell into speculation. In contrast, his peer Gu Yanwu "denounced the subjective learning Wang Yangming School advocated, as not amounting to true learning; and indicated many research methods for investigating the objective world. As a result, the academic atmosphere was completely refreshed. During the following 200–300 years, people followed the way that he had opened" (Liang 2004: 65).

Second, Wang Fuzhi criticized the monarchy and raised the idea that the monarch should be unselfish and regard the world as belonging to all people. But he did not know how to accomplish this ideal, instead resorting to hopes for the emergence of sagely kings and emperors. Moreover, Wang Fuzhi rejected overthrowing a tyrant or replacing an incompetent monarch, and had not yet transcended the institution of the monarchy. In contrast, Huang became completely disillusioned with the function of the monarchy, proposed the establishment of the Imperial Academy as a political body, and conclude that "What brings the world great disasters is none other than the monarch himself" (Huang 2012: 1:2).

Third, Wang Fuzhi, as a friend and colleague of Fang Yizhi, disagreed strongly with the latter's attitudes toward both Western culture and Buddhism. Fang Yizhi earnestly accepted Western culture, integrated it into the investigations of things of the Cheng-Zhu School, and proposed a new doctrine, the investigation of physical things (質測 *zhice*) so as to grasp the ultimate principles (通幾 *tongji*). By contrast, Wang Fuzhi still limited his theory of investigating things to the traditional understanding of Xun Zi 荀子 and Zhu Xi 朱熹, restricting it to a near-sighted practical service for immediate human needs and moral cultivation, and did not elevate it to a level where it would be suited for grasping general scientific principles. Although Wang Fuzhi came into contact with Western astronomy, he opposed them based upon his ethnic and cultural prejudices, rather than studying them sympathetically.

Contrasted with Yan Yuan 顏元[2] and Chen Que 陳確,[3] Wang Fuzhi seemed to have been more conservative in his criticism of Neo-

[2] Yan Yuan flatly denied the legitimacy of Neo-Confucianism due to his belief that it was adulterated with Buddhism and was lacking practical utility. He accused Neo-Confucians of betraying the Duke of Zhou and Confucius' practical concerns. In his view, they were fond of abstruse debate, quiet-sitting, and abstract speculation, but did not know that great feats and achievements must be done through social practices (Yan 2000: 395). "Only if a piece of Cheng Yi and Zhu Xi's thought is stripped can a piece of Confucius and Mencius' learning be recovered" (Yan 2000: 774). "Before Cheng and Zhu's doctrines had disappeared, the Duke of Zhou and Confucius's teachings would not prevail" (Yan 2000: 398).

[3] Chen Que tried to overthrow Neo-Confucianism both ontologically and practically. First, he regarded the division of the original nature and the nature of material endowment as a distorted interpretation of Mencius' view of human nature, one that was plagiarized from the Buddhist division between thusness and phenomena. With this adulteration of Confucianism with Buddhist ideas, Neo-Confucians had ruined Confucianism and misled the human mind. Second, Chen Que denied the separation of heavenly principle from human desires, and instead regarded desires as the basis of heavenly principle. He realized the fatalistic conse-

Confucianism. Yan and Chen had aimed to overthrow Neo-Confucianism completely and replace it with the pragmatic doctrines espoused by Confucius and Mencius, but Wang Fuzhi instead tried to reconstruct Neo-Confucianism based upon Zhang Zai's doctrines, while adding some important elements of the Cheng-Zhu and Wang Yangming Schools. He incorporated their doctrines of mind and nature into his new system based on *qi*-monism. In practice, he was not as practical as Yan Yuan had been, did not have a clear doctrine of the unity of profit and righteousness, and still followed the tradition of giving preference to righteousness over profit. In theory, he had aimed to purify Confucianism of Buddhist and Daoist elements, yet he never reached the sharpness and clarity of Chen Que's insight—Neo-Confucianism had instead wrapped the essence of Buddhism in the appearance of Confucianism.

The present comparison shows that Wang Fuzhi was far from a revolutionary scholar or innovator in the Ming-Qing transition period. His unique contribution lay in his construction of a relatively consistent and synthetic Confucian system through the acceptance of critical Neo-Confucian ideas. His synthesis could be summarized as starting from a correction of the Ming polity with the Kingly Way, passing through the cultivation of humaneness, and ending in assisting Heaven and preserving the Great Harmony. Humaneness was to be the thread running through all three levels. With humaneness as his main concern, he unfolded his doctrines on various topics and tried to solve the problems arising from previous theories and practices. Wang Fuzhi was original in his synthesis; that is, he corrected Zhu Xi's *li-qi* dualism with Zhang Zai's *qi*-monism, he criticized Zhu Xi's rigid compliance with ritual propriety from the perspective of Wang Yangming's inborn knowledge of the good, and he supplemented Wang Yangming's doctrine of inborn knowledge of the good with the compliance with ritual propriety. Although Wang's doctrines, such as "nature renews and completes itself daily" and "one can transform one's own physical embodiment," are acclaimed as novel, they seldom go through a careful examination.

---

quences of repressing desires and excluding petty persons. He argued, "Even in a sage's court, it was impossible to drive petty persons away completely. What the sage did was to transform them into noblemen. Even the sage could not eliminate human desires, what he did was to convert human desires into heavenly principles" (Chen 1979: 425).

1.5   Conclusion

The Ming's collapse and the Manchu conquest resulted from the combined effect of many factors. The superficial factors were the Ming's misadministration and corruption, heavy taxes, and peasant rebellion. In Wang Fuzhi's view, all these could be subsumed under maladministration and the degenerative ethos. He first attempted to dig out the true administrative measures in the Confucian Classics and hoped that future rulers would put them into practice. However, he was more concerned about the correction of the human mind and the cultivation of an honest social ethos. He thus went further to develop a healthy and vigorous Confucian doctrine, hoping to protect the Chinese people from conquest in the future. At this point, he liquidated Neo-Confucianism, including the Cheng-Zhu School and the Wang Yangming School, and aimed to purify Confucianism from the Buddhist elements they brought in. His uniqueness lies in his synthesis and comprehensive examination of Neo-Confucianism, yet he seldom shared Huang Zongxi and Chen Que's revolutionary ideas. In the following chapters, we will analyze his insight on political, moral, and universal reconstructions based on his voluminous works.

Bibliography

Early Chinese Texts

Dai, Zhen 戴震, *Mengzi Ziyi Shuzheng* 孟子字義疏證 (*Correction of Exegesis on the Mencius*), Beijing: Zhonghua Shuju 北京: 中華書局, 1961
Huang, Zongxi 黃宗羲, *Huang Zongxi Quanji* 黃宗羲全集 (1–22 冊) (*The Complete Works of Huang Zongxi*), Volume 1–22, Hangzhou: Zhejiang Guji Chubanshe 杭州:浙江古籍出版社, 2012
Kant, Immanuel, *Critique of Practical Reason*, trans. by Werner S. Pluhar, Hackett Publishing Co., 2002
Li, Jingde, ed. 黎靖德, *Zhu Zi Yu Lei* 朱子語類 (*Conversations of Master Zhu, Arranged Topically*), Beijing: Zhonghua Shuju 北京: 中華書局, 1994
Wang, Yangming 王陽明, *Chuan Xi Lu Zhushu* 傳習錄注疏 (*Instructions for Practical Living*), annotated by Deng Aimin 鄧艾民, Shanghai: Shanghai Guji Chubanshe 上海: 上海古籍出版社, 2012
Wang, Yu 王敔, *Daxing Fujun Xingshu* 大行府君行述 (*A Brief Biographical Sketch of my Diseased Father*), in *Chuanshan Quanshu* 船山全書16 (*The Complete*

Works of Chuanshan), Volume 16, Changsha: Yuelu Shushe 長沙: 岳麓
書社, 1996
Yan, Yuan 顏元, *Xi Zhai Si Cun Bian* 習齋四存編 (*The Collection of the Four
Preservations at Xizhai*), Shanghai: Shanghai Guji Chubanshe 上海: 上海古籍
出版社, 2000
Zhu, Xi 朱熹, *Sishu Zhangju Jizhu* 四書章句集注 (*A Collected Commentary on the
Four Books*), Beijing: Zhonghua Shuju 北京: 中華書局, 1983

SECONDARY SOURCES

Black, Alison Harley, *Man and Nature in the Philosophical Thought of Wang
Fu-chih*, Seattle: University of Washington Press, 1989
Chan, Wing-tsit, *A Source Book in Chinese Philosophy*, Princeton: Princeton
University Press, 1963
Chen, Lai 陳來, *Quanshi yu Chongjian: Wang Chuanshan de Zhexue Jingshen* 詮釋
與重建: 王船山的哲學精神 (*Interpretation and Reconstruction: The Spirit of
Wang Chuanshan's Philosophy*). Beijing: Peking University Press, 北京:北京大
學出版社, 2004
Chen, Que 陳確, *Chen Que Ji* 陳確集 (*A Collection of Chen Que's Writings*),
Beijing: Zhonghua Shuju 北京: 中華書局, 1979
Ji, Wenfu 嵇文甫, *Wang Chuanshan Xueshu Luncong* 王船山學術論叢 (*A
Discussion on Wang Chuanshan's Academics*), Beijing: Sanlian Bookstore, 北京:
三聯書店, 1962
Liang, Qichao 梁啟超, *Zhongguo Jin Sanbainian Xueshu Shi* 中國近三百年學術史
(*Chinese Intellectual History from 1623 to 1923*), Beijing: Dongfang Chubanshe
北京: 東方出版社, 2004
Liu, Jeeloo, Wang Fuzhi's Philosophy of Principle (li)Inherent in Qi, in *Dao
Companion to Neo-Confucian Philosophy*, J. Makeham ed., Springer Science and
Business Media B.V., 2010
McMorran, Ian, Wang Fuzhi and the Neo-Confucian Tradition, In Debary, Wm.
Theodore, ed., *The Unfolding of Neo-Confucianism*, New York: Columbia
University Press, 1975
McMorran, Ian, Late Ming Criticism of Wang Yangming: The Case of Wang
Fuzhi, *Philosophy East & West*, 1973, vol.23, no.1&2, pp91–102
Zeng, Zhaoxu 曾昭旭, *Wang Chuanshan Zhexue* 王船山哲學 (*Wang Chuanshan's
Philosophy*) Taiwan: Liren Chubanshe 台灣: 里仁出版社, 2008
Zhou, Zhiping 周質平 & Peterson, Willard J., eds., *Guoshi Fuhai Kaixin Lu* 國史
浮海開新錄 (*A New Collection of Chinese History in Overseas*), Taipei: Lian jing
Chuban Shiye Youxian Gongsi 臺北: 聯經出版事業有限公司, 2002

CHAPTER 2

Wang Fuzhi's Life and Dreams

Wang Fuzhi was born in Hengyang 衡陽, Hunan in October 1619. His honorific name was Chuanshan Master 船山先生, since he had lived on Shi'chuanshan 石船山 (Stone Boat Mountain). His courtesy name was Ernong 而農, and his poetic name was Jiangzhai 薑齋. He was the descendent of a low-ranking Ming general who had led a thousand troops. Wang's father passed the national examination as a supplemental candidate, but he rejected the path of officialdom after awaiting official appointment at the Imperial Academy. Unwilling to bribe officials at the Ministry of Personnel Affairs to secure a post, he returned home to study and teach Neo-Confucianism privately. In 1642, Wang Fuzhi, tutored by his father, placed first in the Hunan provincial examination, on the *Spring and Autumn Annals*, and departed for Beijing to take the civil examination only to return to Hengyang due to a peasant uprising the following year. In 1648, Wang raised an army to defend against Manchu forces at Hengshan Mountain, but met with defeat. He then fled to Zhaoqing 肇慶 to assist the Ming Yongli court there. After joining a factional struggle between the Wu 吳 and the Chu 楚 parties, he had to resign from the court and return to Hengyang in 1650. He had two opportunities to serve in the court later, but he declined them after consulting the *Book of Changes*, which augured that a return to the court would be inauspicious. In 1662, after the Yongli court collapsed, Wang became depressed and then vowed to preserve Ming culture. He would write records in honor of martyrs for the Ming cause and new commentaries on the Confucian

M. Tan, *Wang Fuzhi's Reconstruction of Confucianism*, https://doi.org/10.1007/978-3-030-80263-9_2

classics. He brooded over the failures of the Ming court, rectified errors in the earlier commentaries on the Confucian classics, and produced a vast corpus of writings, totaling eight million words of text. However, because Wang was an unrepentant Ming loyalist, his writings were blacklisted by the Manchus and remained inaccessible to Chinese scholars until 1866 when Zeng Guofan 曾國藩 published them all under the title, Chuanshan's Extant Works (*Chuanshan Yishu* 船山遺書).

Wang Fuzhi, like his peers, witnessed the fall of the Ming and the Manchu conquest of China. They exhibited different responses to these traumatic events: resistance to the Manchus, acceptance of the reality of the Manchu conquest, and brooding over the misrule of the Ming regime vis-à-vis the success of the Manchus. Some remained steadfast in their resistance. One Ming loyalist, Wu Zhongluan 吳鍾巒, vowed: "My will is set on restoring the Ming dynasty. I will confine myself to this one room and never betray my ancestor's orders; in that way, at least one room of territory will be recovered. The Manchus may hold the entire empire, but my spirit remains indomitable … This is the meaning of the adage that a state will survive so long as one loyal subject lives" (Quan 1965: 607). Others loyalists devoted themselves to preserving Ming culture. Huang Zongxi wrote *Waiting for the Dawn* and compiled a series of intellectual biographies of eminent Ming Neo-Confucians. Wang Fuzhi devoted himself to preserving and practicing humaneness and ritual propriety in an age in which bandits, birds, and beasts dominated. While many diehard restorationists went mad from the hopelessness of their cause, others who adapted and found new dreams survived to leave their mark.

2.1   Wang Fuzhi's Dream of Ming Restoration

As descendants of a low-ranking general in the army of the Ming founder, Zhu Yuanzhang 朱元璋 (1329–1398), Wang Fuzhi's clan had privileges and a sterling reputation, for which they were proud and remained loyal to the Ming imperial family. Additionally, since the Wangs stressed the *Spring and Autumn Annals* in their family learning, the text's call to "honor one's ruler and banish the barbarians"[1] bolstered Wang Fuzhi's

[1] In the fourth year of Xigong 僖公, the Gongyang commentary says, "Duke Huan of Qi 齊桓公 saved Chinese states, banished barbarians, and finally subjected the State of Chu. This is the king's mission" (Chen 2017: 1103). In the fifth year of Xigong, the Guliang commentary says, "Duke Huan of Qi respected the Heir Apprentice of the Zhou, in order to express his honor of the King's order" (Ke 2020: 151).

loyalty and resolve. It also fed his disdain for peasant rebel leaders and galvanized his resistance against the Manchu conquest and acculturation of China.

The Ming Empire was in turmoil in 1619, the year Wang Fuzhi was born. Internally, a perfect storm of heavy taxes, widespread poverty, concentration of farm ownership, and natural disasters spurred peasant uprisings in central and western China. The peasant rebels coalesced into two main forces led by Zhang Xianzhong 張獻忠 (1606–1647) and by Li Zicheng 李自成 (1605–1645), respectively. In 1643, Zhang Xianzhong occupied Wang's hometown, Hengyang, capturing him and his father. Zhang wished to appoint his captives as officials; however, Wang's father threatened to commit suicide and Wang mutilated himself to demonstrate their unwillingness to cooperate. Eventually, the Wangs were freed owing to the quiet efforts of kin while staying loyal to the Ming regime.

Wang's hatred for the peasant rebels and the Manchus and loyalty to the Ming peaked during the fall of the Ming. In May 1644, upon hearing that Ming emperor Chong Zhen 崇禎 (1611–1644) had hung himself when Li Zicheng's forces entered the capital, Beijing, Wang wept and fasted for days, and wrote *Poem of Anger and Grief* (*beifen shi* 悲憤詩), condemning Li Zicheng. He erected a hut on remote Hengshan 衡山 mountain, christened "Refuge for Continuing Dreams (*Xu meng an* 續夢庵)," where he dreamt of Ming restoration. Two years later, he wrote *Second Supplement to the Poem of Anger and Grief* (*Zai Xu Beifen Shi* 再續悲憤詩), expressing his sorrow over the execution of Ming prince Zhu Yujian 朱聿鍵.

Before the Manchu army entered Hengyang in 1646, Wang Fuzhi sent an urgent missive to a Ming general proposing they raise and coordinate several loyalist armies, but his proposal was ignored. For a while, Wang consulted the *Book of Changes* to predict the right time through divination to attack Manchu forces. In 1648, during a Ming imperial family uprising in Leiyang 耒陽, Wang organized a force to attack the Manchus at Hengshan. His attack was repulsed and he fled to join the court of Ming prince Yongli in Zhaoqing, Guangdong.

Wang Fuzhi languished at the Yongli court for several years. Since he was only a provincial graduate (*juren* 舉人), he was appointed the prince's messenger and lacked authority, Later, he joined the factional struggle between the Wu 吳 and Chu 楚 factions in 1650. The Wu faction members were Confucian scholar-officials who, in Donglin tradition, despised court eunuchs and their followers and deemed it a shame to work with them. The Chu faction members were eunuchs and their followers who had vied for power at court to manage national affairs and bolster their positions. Wang favored the Wu faction. When the Wu faction member Jin Bao 金堡 (1614–1680) and others were arrested after having improperly impeached the eunuch Wang Huacheng 王化澄 (?–1652), Wang stood up in their defense. When he was about to be killed by the eunuchs' henchmen, a military officer appeared on the scene and saved him. Unnerved by the danger, Wang Fuzhi left the Yongli court on the pretext of mourning for his deceased mother. The threat of death disinclined him from returning to the Yongli court. After two years, however, he did consider such a return. Rather than making his decision based on the military and political situation, he consulted the *Book of Changes*. In one divination, he obtained hexagram 38, Kui 睽 (Estrangement), changing into hexagram 54, Gui Mei 歸妹 (Marrying Maiden). Wang later reported that this divination result made him realize a dilemma; that is, if he stayed at home and accepted Manchu rule he would no longer live in a pure land, but if he returned to serve the Yongli court, which was led by the evil general Sun Kewang 孫可望, he would have to sacrifice his principles. Soon afterward, General Li Dingguo 李定國 recovered the Hengyang area for the Ming court and invited Wang Fuzhi to return. Wang again consulted the *Book of Changes*. Surprisingly, he obtained the same result: the Kui hexagram, changing into the Gui Mei hexagram, indicating that he should stay home. Wang's hesitancy reflected his superstitions and feeling of helpless, on the one hand, and his inability to cope with the military and political crises, on the other. As a Neo-Confucian scholar, he had been trained to conduct peace time official affairs and was not equipped to deal with rebellion and conflict.

In 1662, when the Yongli prince was killed and Ming regime decisively fell, Wang Fuzhi regretted his hesitancy to act and yet his desire for Ming restoration ceased. He lost all spiritual support for the Ming restoration as displayed in his *Third Supplement to Poems of Anger and Grief* (*San Xu Beifen Shi* 三續悲憤詩). He also expressed his despair in *Sao Shou Wen* (*Scratch my Head and Ask* 搔首問):

It is not the way of a loyal minister to prolong his life for the future restoration of the Ming because that goal, which once seemed achievable, gradually became unachievable, and what's worse, I had no place to settle. (Wang 1996: 12:627)

Wang Fuzhi expressed this attitude in his comment on the recovery of the Yan-Yun 燕雲 region from the Liao 遼 (916–1125) during the Northern Song: "Thus, an ambitious scholar-official urgently chases an opportunity, fearing he is too late. How could he bear to wait even a moment longer" (Wang 1996: 11:59)? As the Manchus consolidated their conquest, Wang's dream of Ming restoration and a place to settle was shattered and his pure land vanished from the horizon.

2.2 Wang Fuzhi's Dream of Cultural Preservation

For Wang Fuzhi and his peers, the fall of the Yongli court quashed any real hope of a Ming restoration. To carry on, they needed a new dream to pursue or else accept the reality of Manchu rule. In Wang's words, "The old dream is no more, one had better awaken to new dreams" (Wang 1996: 15:341). His new dream was to preserve Ming culture.

To most of Wang's peers, accepting Manchu rule was out of the question. One reason for this was their Chinese complex. Taking pride in their assumed cultural superiority to the Manchus, as well as for expelling the Mongols, they felt humiliated by the Manchu conquest. Another reason was their outrage at the massacres in Yangzhou and Jiangyin by Manchu troops and being pressed to adopt Manchu attire and hairstyles, which made them feel the threat of ethnic and cultural extinction. Wang Fuzhi thus declared it would be better to offer the throne to Chinese bandits or rebels than to these barbarians.

In their resistance to Manchu acculturation, Ming loyalist scholars made efforts to preserve Ming culture as symbolic of the Ming dynasty. As Wu Zhongluan 吳鐘巒 stated:

Although I could not prevent the Manchu military conquest, I can still maintain my will for restoration. If I will restoration, the place I dwell will be the place I have restored. The Manchus may have conquered the whole world, but they will never conquer my heart and soul. They may have subjected the masses, but they will never subject us, the Ming loyalists. (Quan 1965: 607)

Wang Fuzhi shared Wu's dream that by preserving Ming culture they could awaken the Chinese to their cultural roots and inspire later generations to restore their culture. Wang Fuzhi and Li Yong 李顒 (1627–1705) continued to wear Ming attire and hairstyles, and never adopted Manchu ways to the end of their lives. Wang further documented the Ming loyalists who faced death rather than give up their Ming hairstyles in Record of the Yongli Court (Yongli Shilu 永歷實錄).

As to Ming culture, Ming loyalist scholars attempted to preserve Ming Confucianism, institutions, attire, and hairstyles, everything symbolizing Ming life. Among them, Huang Zongxi's Record of *My Old Acquaintances* (*Si Jiu Lu* 思舊錄) and Wang Fuzhi's *Record of the Yongli Court* recorded Manchu brutality and memorialized martyrs for the Ming cause. Gu Yanwu's *Record of Daily Accumulated Knowledge* (*Ri Zhi Lu* 日知錄) and Wang Fuzhi's *Huang Shu* 黃書 documented Ming institutions. While commenting on Chen Xian's 陳咸 efforts to preserve the laws, regulations, ceremonies, and records of the Former Han during Wang Mang's 王莽 (45 BC–23 AD) usurpation, Wang Fuzhi compared himself to Chen Xian and queried:

> Could it just be that he kept them waiting for the need of Han restoration? Truly, he could not bear the loss of the Han institutions. If a son longs for his parents, he loves their personal articles; if a minister adores his ruler, he cherishes his institutions. In the old institutions, the spirits of preceding emperors reside. That is why Chen Xian could not bear [to accept this loss]. Alas, while Gong Sheng 龔勝 (68–11 BC) died to maintain his purity, Chen Xian preserved the Han institutions by surviving to make the effort. These two felt deep commiseration [the root of humaneness]. Besides these two gentlemen, with whom could I abide? (Wang 1996: 10:209)

Continuing, Wang asserted that as a dedicated scholar who had born witness to the collapse of the rites and music, he could preserve the Confucian teachings dwelling alone atop a remote mountain in Hunan. He believed, later when another dynasty intended to revive these institutions and culture, its ministers would come to learn them from him or his followers, nobody else (Wang 1996: 11:61).

In practice, when the Ming loyalists witnessed Ming institutions, attire, and hairstyle being supplanted by Manchu ways, they focused on preserving Ming Confucianism, for it was the Confucian spirit, virtues, and rituals that distinguished the Chinese from the barbarians. Their deepest fear was that the Confucian rituals would be defiled by Manchu political measures and no longer stand as potent symbols of the Ming. Consequently, Huang Zongxi composed *Biographies of the Ming Confucian Scholars* (*Ming Ru Xue An* 明儒學案), and Wang Fuzhi annotated and wrote commentaries on the *Six Classics* and the *Four Books*. When expounding on why several ministers[2] had been unwilling to leave the last emperor and mourn the end of the Chen dynasty 陳 (557–589), Wang attributed such steadfastness to their Confucianism, the teaching of (correct) names.[3] These ministers could not bear to see the sacred cultural objects and institutions of previous dynasties perish from the world in the wake of the chaos of the Yongjia period 永嘉 (307–312) (Wang 1996: 10:694–695).

To Wang Fuzhi, the teaching of (correct) names, or Confucianism, was the nucleus of Chinese civilization, which distinguished it decisively from the surrounding barbarian cultures. However, Wang feared that under Manchu rule the Chinese would shed their Confucian culture and adopt nomadic customs. In *Extended Commentary on the Book of Odes* (*Shi Guang Zhuan* 詩廣傳), Wang Fuzhi expressed this worry in comments on the Song people's adoption of Liao customs in the Yan-Yun 燕云 area (present-day Beijing and northern areas in Hebei and Shanxi). He observed:

> In the beginning, the Song felt astonished when they first saw such conduct, so contrary to ritual propriety and common sense; naturally, they did nothing about it since there was nothing they could do. However, after doing nothing about it for a long time they simply forgot that their elders had considered such conduct contrary to ritual propriety and common sense. (Wang 1996: 3:377)

Similarly, Wang feared that over time the Chinese would forget Ming culture and adopt Manchu attire and hairstyle.[4] He continued:

---

[2] They were Yuan Xian 袁憲, Xu Shanxin 許善心, and Zhou Luohou 周羅睺 of the Chen Dynasty.

[3] Confucianism is called the teaching of (correct) terms (*mingjiao* 名教) based on Confucius' doctrine of the rectification of names.

[4] Wang Fuzhi's worry proved right in the manner in which the Suzhou people welcomed the Manchu emperor Kang Xi 康熙 (1654–1722). In 1684, Kangxi received a very hospitable welcome from the Suzhou people. The people enjoyed the Manchu drama enthusiastically, and seemed to have completely forgotten their Ming ancestors. (Zhou 2002: 407).

Alas, I fear that after practicing barbarian customs for many days and months, having practiced them for a long time, nobody will feel 'melancholy and longing (*yunjie* 蘊結)' for the old customs. (Wang 1996: 3:377)

This feeling of "melancholy and longing" is precisely the pain of witnessing the extinction of one's culture and ethnicity, hence Wang advocated that his peers accept the mission of promoting the teaching of (correct) terms and strive to preserve the old ways, even at risk of life and limb.

Wang Fuzhi praised Guan Ning 管寧 (158–241) for instructing Confucianism in remote Liaodong (present Liaoyang) during the transition between the Later Han 東漢 (25–220) and the Cao Wei dynasty 曹魏 (220–265). In praising Guan, he signaled his own aim to preserve Confucian culture while dwelling on a remote mountain: "I strive to fully extend my humaneness. Though the time is not ripe to realize the Way [in the world], I practice the Way in my daily life" (Wang 1996: 10:404). Notably, Wang intended to reinterpret the Confucian classics in the light of the Manchu invasion and the Ming fall, to provide later generations with an upright teaching that would aid the people in warding off future invasions. In his words, "The Six Classics require me to initiate something new" (Wang 1996).

Why didn't the Ming loyalists concede defeat and cooperate with the Manchus, who were promoting Song Neo-Confucianism? In fact, the Manchus were using Neo-Confucianism to win over the people and enhance their rule while the Ming loyalists advocated (Neo-) Confucianism as symbolic of the Ming and to distinguish between the Ming and the Manchu cultures. They denied they had any common ground for cooperation with the Manchus, noting that while Confucian propriety holds that filial sons maintain a full head of hair, the Manchus shaved their foreheads. The Ming loyalists considered that such cultural disparities revealed that the Manchus could not appreciate or practice Confucianism. Wang further expressed this view in comments on Tuoba Hong 拓跋宏 (467–499), a Xianbei emperor who adopted Confucianism. In Wang's view, Tuoba Hong only practiced Confucian rituals but did not grasp their essence, namely, humaneness, sincerity, and deference. He compared Tuoba Hong's observances of Confucian ritual to a monkey's wearing a hat or an actor's playing a role (Wang 1996: 10:617). In summary, Wang held that the Manchu promotion of Neo-Confucianism was false and hypocritical.

One factor in the Manchus' selection of Song Neo-Confucianism for their state orthodoxy was a time lag in the spread of Neo-Confucianism between China and the Manchu and Korean regions. For example, when Yi T'eogye 李退溪 (1501–1570) was developing and promoting Zhu Xi's teachings in Korea, Wang Yangming's teachings had already eclipsed Zhu Xi's and raised Neo-Confucianism to a new level in China. The Manchus were familiar with the Song Cheng-Zhu School but had not yet accepted the teachings of Wang Yangming and his followers. By adopting Cheng-Zhu thought as state orthodoxy, the Manchu regime *ipso facto* stymied the development of Neo-Confucianism and was ridiculed as monkeys wearing human hats by the Ming loyalists.

2.3 WANG FUZHI'S STRUGGLE BETWEEN DREAM AND REALITY

When Wang first erected his hut, "The Refuge of Continuing Dreams," atop remote Hengshan in 1644, his dream had been to restore the Ming dynasty. Although he had advised leaders and generals on matters of defense and even organized an offensive against Manchu forces at Hengshan, his efforts never met with success. His mounting failures made him realize the gulf between ideal and reality. Moreover, his brief, checkered career at the Yongli court disillusioned him about the possibility of ideal Confucian governance. He had witnessed first-hand that it was no simple matter to work with generals and administer the court. Finally, when his savior General Gao Bizheng 高必正 was ambushed and killed by Sun Kewang 孫可望 in 1651, Wang lost his faith that righteousness would always prevail over self-interest. He began to view righteousness as an adjustment of self-interest and desires, and began to feel sympathy for the peasant rebels of the late Ming. This change in attitude was reflected in new directions he took in interpreting the Confucian classics. He began to stress the importance of administrative and policy measures in realizing the Kingly Way and rejected the notion of spontaneous moral transformation advocated by earlier Neo-Confucians, Wang Yangming in particular.

When the Manchus captured the Yongli prince and consolidated control in 1662, Wang fell into deep despair. He lost his will to live but did not consider suicide. In order to go on living, he settled on another dream: to preserve Ming culture. As an old diehard who insisted on wearing Ming attire and hairstyle, he was surveilled and harassed by Manchu agents. He survived these hard times by keeping to himself and concentrating on reinterpreting the Confucian classics and other classical texts. Generally, his works before 1662 were direct and forceful while his later writings waxed nostalgic and tolerant. For example, in early works, such as *An Unofficial Commentary on the Book of Changes (Zhouyi Waizhuan* 周易外傳*)* and *Extended Comments on the Laozi (Laozi Yan* 老子衍*)*, Wang stressed the firmness and resolution associated with the first hexagram Qian 乾, and Laozi's homage to passivity and water, finding astute tactics in the *Laozi* and proper timing in the *Changes* for his anti-Manchu activities.

The tolerance and nostalgia of his later works reflected his compromise with the harsh reality. He began to appreciate Zhuangzi's survivalist approach and affirmed that Zhuangzi would have accepted Confucianism if the times had not been so chaotic. Wang also broke his intellectual taboo on Buddhism and composed *Annotations on the Faxiang Sect (Xiangzong Luosuo* 相宗絡索*)*, despite issuing earlier warning to learners to avoid Buddhist texts. Because his depression affected his health, he started to practice alchemical Daoism. This practice and intellectual tolerance opened Wang to seek a synthesis between Daoism and Confucianism, for instance, by linking the Daoist "assisting Heaven (nature)" (*xiangtian* 相天) with the Confucian "assisting in the transformation and nourishment of Heaven and Earth" (nature; *zan tiandi zhi huayu* 贊天地之化育), and praised Zhuangzi for grasping the principle of darkness and light, life and death (Wang 1996: 13:291). Wang also synthesized Zhuangzi's "harmony of Heaven and Earth" with Zhang Zai's 張載 (1020–1077) "Great Harmony" (*taihe* 太和) in *Zhengmeng* 正蒙 in proposing his own teaching of universal harmony. Afterward, Wang envisioned a harmonious cosmos free of war or disasters, which showed his refusal to resign himself to the harsh reality.

Wang Fuzhi did not confine his efforts to his studies nor did his peers give up the dream of a Ming restoration even though they realized that prospects for success were remote after the Manchus had consolidated their rule. Wang's colleague and friend, Fang Yizhi 方以智, escaped capture by masquerading as a Buddhist monk in 1650 and continued his Ming restoration activities until he was arrested in 1671. Wang stayed in touch with Fang and rose to action in 1673 when Wu Sangui 吳三桂 (1612–1678) fled to Hunan after rebelling against the Manchus. Although Wang was disinclined to cooperate with this Ming renegade, he still enjoyed visiting old friends, generals, and colleagues, and once even began to plan an uprising. He gave up this plan for lack of leadership and General Zhang Yongming's 張永明 reluctance to cooperate. He expressed his despondency in a poem:

The frightened goose cries to the clouds, but the sky does not clear.
At eventide one autumn day it flies, alone, to a remote place, weeping.
(Wang 1996: 15:376)

Word that Wang had suggested an uprising put him in danger, so he withdrew to his mountain retreat. This would be the last uprising that he contemplated.

Over time, life grew more unbearable. In poetry and comments on historical figures, Wang expressed deepening sadness and nostalgia while affirming that he remained staunchly Confucian, practicing humaneness and righteousness. He described his different states of mind before and after the fall of the Ming. Before the fall, as the loyal ministers disputed over the best way to advise the emperor and preserve the empire, they began to quarrel fiercely as if they were fighting enemies and supplicating the gods and spirits. In the aftermath of the slaying of the Ming princes and the fall of the Ming court, the loyal ministers grew forlorn, as if their parents had passed away. At this moment, they would have cherished their ruler as if he were a Yao 堯 or Shun 舜, if only he had survived. They would have had no time for anything else, let alone voicing criticisms and remonstrances (Wang 1996: 3:321).

Wang Fuzhi also came to regret his involvement in the factional struggle at the Yongli court, which forced him to resign; since he left the court he did not die with the emperor but just lived in limbo, lacking even a reason to die. This feeling of regret left a mark on his later writings, such as in his sharp criticisms of factionalism and empty bravado. He expressed this sense of regret in his comment on the capture of the Song Emperor Qinzong 宋欽宗 (1100–1156). He reflected that a scholar was unfortunate to have survived an imperial crisis and collapse with the emperor captured, the imperial ancestral shrine ruined, the occupants of the six palaces abused, and the princes killed. Every loyal minister was at the mercy of the barbarians while the traitors and villains who supported renegades as their new leaders flourished—how could the loyal scholar bear to go on living (Wang 1996: 11:212)!

Wang Fuzhi had to find a reason to carry on. On the one hand, he preferred dying righteously to staying alive; he would honor his interpersonal relationships, uphold humaneness and righteousness, maintain his reputation, and courageously face the barbarian hoards. On the other hand, he held up hope for the future. He held that the regenerative movement in the cycle of history offers solace to the philosopher who is trapped in an era when power and politics are ruthless and out of alignment with the Confucian ideals. Faith in the regenerative movement in history underwrites the significance of personal action in the course of events (McMorran 1979). As Wang affirmed:

> In the world when disaster has reached its nadir, a single person stands up to help people awaken their sense of compassion, shame and honor. He should not worry about being alone, for others will rise to complete his mission …This is the activity of the Mind of Heaven and Earth, which never ceases. (Wang 1996: 10:1099)

The Mind of Heaven and Earth supports the cyclic cosmic movement by which misfortune transforms into fortune and chaos into order.

This faint hope perhaps sustained Wang's spirit and helped him in facing hardship throughout life. However, the bitter truth was that neither his old dream nor his new dream would be fulfilled during his lifetime, for the old dream vanished with the death of the Yongli prince and the new dream was unraveled by the incoming Manchu customs and distortions of Confucianism. Consider the bitter tone of a poem Wang composed on his seventieth birthday:

> Holding a mirror to look at my face, I cannot recognize who this person is.
> Asking others, they say this is you, Mr. Jiangzhai 薑齋.
> After a tortoise rots, it will freely be used by people for divination.
> Before my dreams are realized, do not attempt to guess who I am. (Wang 1996: 15:717)

Jiangzhai was Wang Fuzhi's poetic name. The setbacks in Wang's life eventually made his visage unrecognizable—even to himself. He felt powerless to cease or even slow the Manchu adulteration of Chinese customs. Lamenting the disappearance of Ming culture and regretting his inability to resist Manchu rule, Wang passed away, expressing regret even in his gravestone epitaph:

> I have nursed the solitary wrath of Liu Yueshi 劉越石 (270–317) but found no avenue of self-sacrifice; I have inquired into the true doctrines of Zhang Hengqu 張橫渠 (張載 1020–1077) but have not been strong enough to realize them. Fortunate as I am to arrive safely to this grave, I vow to carry my sorrow with me through the ages. (Liu 1996; McMorran 1975; McMorran's translation, amended)

Wang admired Liu Yueshi who fought for the Western Jin dynasty (265–312) to his final breath while regretting that his own resignation from the Yongli court had let him survive the Manchu conquest, unable to die righteously and fulfill his loyalty to the Ming. He admired Zhang Zai's teachings, which clearly differed from Buddhism and upheld Confucianism, but he feared he lacked the energy and talent to carry it out. All he could do was hope for the sympathetic understanding of future generations. In this, Wang shared this hope with Huang Zongxi,[5] namely, that later generations would appreciate his works.

Wang Fuzhi's dream of cultural preservation began to come to fruition when Zeng Guofan 曾國藩 published his complete works under the title *Chuanshan Yishu* (*The Extant Works of Wang Chuanshan*), in 1866. Zeng had two goals in publishing Wang's writings. One was to enhance the reputation of Hunan province as a cultural center. The other was to lend this Confucian spiritual support to the Hunan provincial army in fighting the Taiping rebels. In the years that followed, Wang's works were widely read by the intelligentsia of the late Qing, and they greatly influenced Tan Sitong (1865–1898), Liang Qichao (1973–1929), Yang Changji, and other prominent scholar-reformers of the late Qing. Mao Zedong 毛澤東 cited Wang Fuzhi's works in his writings of the 1940s and 1950s. Moreover, with the support of other scholars from Hunan, such as Guo Songtao 郭嵩燾 and Zeng Guoquan 曾國荃, Wang Fuzhi, Gu Yanwu, and Huang Zongxi were worshiped as Confucian worthies in Confucian temples in 1908. However, Wang Fuzhi's dream of restoration was not fulfilled until 1911, when the Republic of China was established and replaced the Qing dynasty. Not until 219 years after Wang's death did the Chinese finally shed their Manchu attire and pigtails.

2.4   CONCLUSION

The fall of the Ming and the Manchu conquest posed a great challenge to the surviving Ming loyalists. Unlike common subjects, they felt dynastic loyalty and spiritual pride and regarded Manchu attire and hairstyle as a humiliation. However, their high-minded non-cooperation with the Manchu policies led to their being mistrusted, surveilled, harassed, and

[5] Huang Zongxi's *Waiting for the Dawn* (*Mingyi Dai Fang Lu* 明夷待訪錄) meant that he was waiting for being consulted in the future although he was in unfavorable situation at present because of the Manchu conquest.

forced to live in poverty. Trained solely as a scholar, Wang knew little about household management or agriculture, and his resulting impoverishment led to the deaths of his two wives and three children. Only through the charity of Buddhist monks did his clan get by. At the same time, Wang upheld the honor of a true Confucian scholar: "He cannot be led into excesses when wealthy and honored, or deflected from his purpose when poor and obscure, nor can he be made to bow before superior force. That is what I call a great man" (Mencius 3B.2). With a determined will despite his poverty, Wang carried out his mission, declaring, "The Six Classics require me to initiate something new."

The Manchu conquest and the fall of the Ming raised a host of issues for the Ming loyalists to ponder. Just as scholars criticized Confucianism and the patriarchal family system after China's defeats in the Opium War and the 1894 Sino-Japanese War, the Ming loyalists criticized the factional struggles in the Ming court, the concentration of farm ownership, the levy of heavy taxes, the pedantic official Cheng-Zhu School, and the neglect of moral norms by Wang Yangming's followers in the late Ming. Huang Zongxi expressed doubts about the justice of the system of imperial rule in *Waiting for the Dawn*. Wang Fuzhi came to feel sympathy for the peasant rebels, and began to advocate that the emperor act as a caretaker rather than the owner of the empire. Moreover, Wang Fuzhi and his peers appreciated the theological arguments and Western technology that Jesuit missionaries had introduced into China in the late Ming. Apart from his fondness of physical investigation (*zhi ce* 質測), Wang also revealed the influence of Jesuit thinking in his discussions on objects (*qi* 器) and the Way (*dao* 道). As the Jesuit had argued, "An object determines the existence of its principle. Without this object, there wouldn't be its principle, either. If an empty principle is assumed to be the origin of objects, it would be no different from the Buddhist and Daoist teachings [that being arises from non-being] … Please answer me: can the principle of cart produce a cart, without having movement or substance" (Ricci 2000: 35)? Obviously, when Wang claimed that "Without an object, its Way would not exist … Without bows and arrows, there would not be the Way of shooting. Without horses and chariots, there would be not the Way of charioteering" (Wang 1996: 1:1028). Wang surely had been influenced by both the Jesuit's arguments and physical investigations.

Wang's motto underscores that he did not preserve the Ming culture by rote but aimed to renew it through his reinterpretations of the classics and history. Therefore, unlike Huang Zongxi's *Biographies of the Ming Confucians*, Wang attempted to reinterpret the classics and criticized and corrected the earlier commentaries because he attributed collapse of the Ming in part to the degenerate social ethos released by the spread of unsound Neo-Confucian teachings. Wang's approach was to recover the original Confucian Way, and he revisited the Confucian classics for solutions for practical problems of the day. The following chapter examines how Wang developed his unique commentaries on the classics and history by pondering and criticizing late Ming culture and institutions.

BIBLIOGRAPHY

EARLY CHINESE TEXTS

Chen, Li 陳立, Gongyang Yishu 公羊義疏 (*Commentary and Annotation on the Gongyang Tradition of the Spring and Autumn Annals*), Beijing: Zhonghua Shuju, 2017

Quan, Zuwang 全祖望, *Ji Qi Ting Ji* 鮚琦亭集 (*Collection in Jie Ji Pavilion*) Taipei: Taiwan Shangwu Yinshuguan 台北: 台湾商务印書館, 1965

Ricci, Matteo, *Tianzhu Shiyi* 天主實義 (*The True Meaning of Catholicism*). Zheng Ande 郑安德, ed. Beijing: Institute of Religions, Beijing University, 2000

Wang, Yu 王敔, *Daxing Fujun Xingshu* 大行府君行述 (*A Brief Biographical Sketch of my Diseased Father*), in *Chuanshan Quanshu* 船山全書16 (*The Complete Works of Chuanshan*), Volume 16, Changsha: Yuelu Shushe 長沙: 岳麓書社, 1996

SECONDARY SOURCES

Ke, Shaomin 柯劭忞, *Chunqiu Guliang Zhuan Zhu* 春秋穀梁傳注 (*Annotation of the Guliang Tradition of the Spring and Autumn Annals*), Beijing: Zhonghua Shuju, 2020

Liu, Yusong 劉毓崧, *A Chronicle of Mr. Wang Chuanshan* (*Wang Chuanshan Xiansheng Nianpu* 王船山先生年譜), in *Complete Works of Chuanshan* (Chuanshan Quanshu 船山全書 16), Volume 16, Changsha: Yuelu Shushe, 1996

McMorran, Ian, The Patriot and the Partisans: Wang Fuzhi's Involvement in the Politics of the Yongli Court. In *From Ming to Qing: Conquest, Region and Continuity in the Seventeenth Century China*, ed. Jonathan D. Spence and John E. Wills, Jr., New Haven and London: Yale University Press, 1979

McMorran, Ian, Wang Fuzhi and the Neo-Confucian Tradition, In Debary, Wm. Theodore, ed., *The Unfolding of Neo-Confucianism*, New York: Columbia University Press, 1975

Zhou, Zhiping 周質平 & Peterson, Willard J., eds., *Guoshi Fuhai Kaixin Lu* 國史浮海開新錄 (*A New Collection of Chinese History in Overseas*), Taipei: Lian Jing Chuban Shiye Youxian Gongsi 臺北: 聯經出版事業有限公司, 2002

CHAPTER 3

Political Reconstruction

The fall of the Ming and the Manchu conquest provided a number of issues for the Ming loyalists to ponder. According to Wang Fansen, most of the loyalists began to feel remorse for their free lifestyles and irresponsible conduct in the late Ming after they realized there would be no Ming restoration. Averse to Manchu rule, these scholars no longer entered major cities, lectured in public, attended parties or clubs, as they were wont to do during the Ming. Feeling remorseful some exiled themselves from their hometowns and avoided social occasions (Wang 2004: 201). In these ways, they sought to atone for their past heedlessness and irresponsibility, and they scrupulously avoided the Manchu-dominated elite society. Wang Fuzhi too showed remorse, particularly sense of ineffectuality when the Yongli prince died. He belatedly offered a proposal to segregate the Chinese from the northern nomads to stymie Manchu influence.

Wang Fuzhi identified some major administrative problems that had infected military affairs, taxation, and the recruitment of officials during the Ming, and advocated political reform based on reorganizing the imperial court. He sought to ensure that noble people would be appointed to office while the petty minded would be excluded. In fact, not knowing how to deal with the petty minded directly, he proposed measures to contain and employ them to positive effect. He wrote extensively on how to improve the role of the emperor and prime minister and how to discipline wayward officials and educate the people. While noting that the emperors had been responsible for public welfare in antiquity, Wang lamented that

M. Tan, *Wang Fuzhi's Reconstruction of Confucianism*, https://doi.org/10.1007/978-3-030-80263-9_3

emperors had turned increasingly despotic since the Qin-Han, propped up by Confucian ritual propriety and social hierarchy. He sought to reform the role of the emperor and prime minister with the political ideal of the Kingly Way (*wang dao* 王道), as first espoused by Mencius, holding that "a noble person's discourses on rulership should be in accord with the Kingly Way" (Wang 1996: 8:750). Unpersuaded that the emperor's humaneness and righteousness, in and of themselves, could induce a spontaneous moral transformation of the people, Wang insisted that the ruler and prime minister had to implement practical policies and measures and not just manifest humaneness as a way to instill harmony in the empire. In this fashion, he disavowed the naïve political idealism of Mencius and earlier generations of Neo-Confucians, and envisioned the Kingly Way on a more practical basis.

3.1   WANG FUZHI'S REFLECTIONS ON THE FALL OF THE MING

As noted, Wang Fuzhi focused on the administrative factors that conduced to the fall of the Ming, notably problems with the administration of military affairs, taxation, and the recruitment of officials. First, he criticized Zhu Di's 朱棣 (1360–1424) relocation of the capital to the foot of the Great Wall and his ineffective defensive strategy against the attacks of the northern nomads, which left the capital vulnerable to capture. He noted that the Ming court did not place trust in the frontier generals and sought to control them from the imperial palace, crippling their ability to respond to rapidly changing military situations. He also noted the weakness of the Chinese infantry vis-à-vis the Mongolian and Manchu cavalries, lamenting the Chinese neglect of equine husbandry and training. While these observations and criticisms were valid, Wang ignored the problem of the hereditary imperial system, which did not ensure the competence of succeeding emperors to be fair-minded and able to select reliable, upright officials. For example, impatient for achievements, Emperor Chong Zhen changed his prime minister thirty-seven times,[1] reducing the court to chaos during his seventeen-year reign. As a result, the imperial court was torn by factionalism, national affairs were neglected, and the common people felt adrift (Wang 1996: 12:645–646). Although Wang Fuzhi

---

[1] The Ming had no position of prime minister, but used low-rank officials to serve in this function.

3 POLITICAL RECONSTRUCTION   39

observed that the Ming fell not for lack of talented officials but from impe-rial misrule (Wang 1996: 12:628), based on Chong Zhen's misrule, he did not go further to question the effectiveness of hereditary monarchy.

Wang Fuzhi diagnosed the widespread peasant uprisings of the late Ming to the court's mismanagement of field and taxation policy. Still, he did not criticize the imperial family for seizing large tracts of farmland from the peasants, but rather blamed the peasants for not appreciating the Ming emperor's leniency and humaneness in the form of lower agricul-tural taxes and expanded cultivated land (Wang 1996: 12:623). He did not approve of Zhang Juzheng's 張居正 (1525–1582) one whip law (*yi tiao bian fa* 一條鞭法), aimed at preventing local officials from manipulat-ing tax collection, but his own proposal was nearly the same: Wang advo-cated setting the amount of grain and corvée required of peasants, leaving no room for local officials to fudge the figures (Wang 1996: 12:452). He was unaware, however, that it was the local officials who set tax policy. Moreover, while the court set the tax amount, the collectors were permit-ted to add a small surcharge to obtain some profit for variety of reasons.

Wang Fuzhi showed insight and courage in criticizing the low salaries paid to officials by the Ming founder Zhu Yuanzhang, which led to official conspiracy and corruption. "A person's salary was not enough to support their life. In the beginning, officials embezzled government money for their personal ends. In the end, they became wolves and tigers, squeezing profits from the common people" (Wang 1996: 12:566). In his view, the strict Ming Code, which mandated that a custodian be beheaded for steal-ing, say, one thousand dollars, did not effectively prevent corruption; rather, it conduced to official conspiracy and cheating. The Code led imperial envoys, governors, and local officials to seek their fortunes, feel-ing immune from threat of punishment (Wang 1996: 12:520). Ironically, Wang's advice to those facing a despotic emperor was to await their pass-ing. He remarked, "When the Son of Heaven is impetuous, unruly, and cruel, such as King Jie 桀 of the Xia and King Zhou 紂 of the Shang, noth-ing can be done until he perishes, despoiling his ancestral temple with the stench of his misdeeds. No one would dare to overthrow him while he is alive" (Wang 1996: 6:1136). In this respect, Wang was not bold even though he deigned to discuss political affairs.

Given his bitter taste of factional strife at the Yongli court, Wang was highly critical of factional strife generally. He condemned both noble peo-ple and the petty minded who got embroiled in factional strife: "The so-called noble people start to argue with arch bravado while the petty-minded chime in with venom. How does their bravado differ from that venom" (Wang 1996: 11:103)? He thought the Donglin school's 東林黨 high-minded response to court eunuchs was counterproductive;[2] still, he avoided criticizing the Donglin school openly due to his close relationship with a Donglin leader.[3] In his view, a noble person should observe ritual propriety and exhibit dignity before the petty minded, thereby appealing to the latter's better nature and disinclining them from making trouble. He believed that such conduct would keep the situation in check; were the noble people to vie with the petty minded on their own terms, the situation would quickly get out of hand. However, Wang was neglecting the actual causes of the factional strife: the emperor's irresponsibility and the eunuchs' abuse of power. By failing to counsel the emperor and restrain the eunuchs, the noble people's aloof upright posture emboldened the petty minded and the eunuchs, leading to ever more problems at court and in society.

Like historian Ray Huang (1918–2000), who attributed the fall of the Ming to Emperor Wanli's neglect of national affairs and official misrule (Huang 1981: 90–94), Wang Fuzhi ventured to criticize Emperor Wanli for allowing wily ministers to conspire with eunuchs, encouraging official greed and corruption and stifling upright officials, and lamented that

[2] The Donglin party truly competed with the eunuchs with bravado rather than reason. A dialogue between Lou Jiang 婁江 and the Donglin Party leader Gu Xiancheng 顧憲成 (1550–1612) illustrated this:

> Recently, there was a strange matter, do you know about it?
> What is it?
> What the Cabinet of Government thinks is right, the external discussion will definitely regard as wrong. What the Cabinet thinks wrong, the external discussion will definitely regard as right.
> Mr. Gu said, 'There was a strange matter outside too.'
> What?
> What external discussion regards as right, the Cabinet will definitely think as wrong; what external discussion regards wrong, the Cabinet will definitely think as right. (Huang 2012: 17:150)

[3] In 1642, Gao Shitai, the nephew of a Donglin School leader, was Secretary Promoter of Education (*ti xue jian shi* 提學僉事) in Huguang Province 湖廣 and judged Wang Fuzhi's composition on *the Spring-Autumn Annals* as first class. Thanks to Gao's beneficence, Wang Fuzhi did not attack the Donglin Party publicly although he criticized factional struggle without sparing any energy.

Emperor Chongzhen had not employed upright scholar-officials. In Wang's view, the emperor should appoint officials according to ability, give them due respect, and regard the throne as an asset of the entire empire. Accordingly, the people would be confident and humane, the bold would vie to serve, and no barbarians would threaten the empire for generations (Wang 1996: 12:626–627). A modern historian, Ray Huang could see past the imperial system, but Wang still dreamed that a sage king or at least a competent emperor would appear on the scene. Such a sage emperor would serve as an exemplar and the people would emulate him and be humane and deferential. What Wang failed to realize was that emperors, too, were human beings, beset with human foibles and limitations and subject to the social trends and morays of their time.

3.2 Wang Fuzhi's Principles for Dealing with Nomads, Women, and the Petty Minded

Wang Fuzhi believed that to lead China well the emperor should observe three principles: oversee Chinese rule over China proper while confining the barbarians to frontier areas, appoint noble people while banning the petty minded from office, and encourage men to manage worldly matters and women family affairs (Wang 1996: 11:182). Wang observed that since the early Zhou kings realized the Kingly Way they could defend Zhou territory and keep the barbarians at bay. He also noted that during the Qin unification a clear division of labor between males and females was enforced. Also, the Han and Song dynasties were well governed because the majority of officials at court were noble people. In order to satisfy these three principles, an emperor would have to uphold righteousness and not covet profit.

3.2.1 The Chinese and the Barbarians

To prevent the northern nomads from seizing the capital and invading China, Wang Fuzhi proposed segregating them from the Chinese. His proposal was based on traditional geography: it was held that different places exuded different qualities of *qi* or vital force. The different *qi* or vital force of different places led to the differing habits and customs of the residents, such as the Chinese and the barbarians. With different habits and customs, the people gave rise to different modes of knowing and acting. Wang Fuzhi conceded that the barbarian tribes also distinguished superior and inferior among them (similar to Chinese rituals and ranks), but he insisted that they could not mix with the Chinese because of the geographical demarcation and climate difference. He feared that such ethnic mixing would lead to the breakdown of Chinese ethical human relationships and the assimilation of the Chinese into the barbarian tribes (Wang 1996: 10:502). Wang argued that these different peoples should stick to their own climates, geographies, customs, and cuisines. The Chinese and the barbarians alike should honor their respective leaders and serve their societies, and refrain from invading or infringing on each other's territory (Wang 1996: 11:174).

Wang Fuzhi defended his segregation policy from an ethno-cultural perspective. Like his Confucian forbearers, he regarded the Chinese as civilized and other peoples as barbaric. His standard for making this distinction was that the Chinese prioritized ritual propriety, by which to uphold humaneness and righteousness, over personal profit. In Wang's view, the northern nomads could not observe ritual propriety because they were raised in places where profit was prioritized and youth were taught to pursue their profit or benefit the tribe (Wang 1996: 10:503). Wang warned that even barbarians who were educated in the Confucian classics and rituals would easily discard propriety when presented with an opportunity for profit. Additionally, the nomads were unfilial because they allowed a son to marry his deceased father's concubines and to shave his forehead. He concluded, "Ritual propriety is what the human beings (Chinese) alone observe, the birds are blind to it, and the nomads do not understand it and would like to be rid of it" (Wang 1996: 5:146).

Since ritual propriety was the standard by which he distinguished the Chinese from the barbarians, Wang held that by upholding ritual propriety the Chinese could avoid improper interactions with them, resist their improper customs, and offer no chances for them to spy and plan to attack China. He noted that the Duke of the Zhou was praised for setting rituals that protected the Chinese from barbarian attacks for several centuries (Wang 1996: 6:978). Conversely, Wang criticized the Ming founder for not reestablishing and promoting ritual propriety at court and in society after driving out the Mongols, leaving the door open for the Manchu invasion (Wang 1996: 5:146).

However, Wang Fuzhi did not offer a compelling explanation as to why the nomads were ignorant of ritual propriety or apt cast it aside. While admitting that a nomad's humaneness and wisdom were superior to those

of a bird, he still charged that they "lacked righteousness and did not practice ritual propriety and thus were not really better than birds and limited
to the barbarian path" (Wang 1996: 5:145). In point of fact, righteousness and ritual propriety were attributes of humaneness, as Wang held
(Wang 1996: 2:315); since the nomads, like all human beings, bore the
sprouts of humaneness and could cultivate humaneness, they could also
establish righteousness and ritual propriety naturally. If this step was so
difficult, Wang had to explain how the Chinese became civilized. In fact,
in another place, Wang Fuzhi once claimed that before the legendary
emperor Xuan Yuan's 轩辕 time, the Chinese people were no different
than the barbarians; before the legendary emperor Tai Hao's 太昊 time,
the Chinese people were no different from birds and beasts (Wang 1996:
12:467). Obviously, these sentences severely weakened Wang's downplay-
ing the nomads.

Despite his efforts to distinguish between the Chinese and the barbarians, Wang Fuzhi supported the acculturation of the southern barbarians.
He praised Zhang Dun 章惇 (1035–1105) for expanding China's south-
western borders and assimilating the Miao 苗 minorities into Chinese culture and society. To avoid contradicting himself, Wang said that while the
barbarians residing outside of China should be kept out, those who resided
in China could be assimilated (Wang 1996: 11:174). The difference in
Wang Fuzhi's attitudes toward the northern and southern barbarians
reflected his hatred for the Manchus. He wanted to separate the Chinese
from the northern tribes because he deeply feared their threat of invasion
and conquest. In contrast, southern barbarians did not pose a military or
cultural threat. Since the Han Chinese could manage them, Wang supported their assimilation. In this respect, Wang's advocacy of separating
the Chinese from the northern tribes reflected his security concerns more
than any sense of righteousness. Gadamer said, "What should be done:
this is admittedly not just what is right, but also what is useful, purposeful
and in that sense 'right'. The interpenetration of these two senses of 'right'
in humankind's practical conduct is clearly what for Aristotle constitutes
the humanly good" (Gadamer 1999: 31). Wang's proposed segregation
policy between Chinese and barbarian could be regarded a combination of
right and useful in Gadamer's sense.

Wang Fuzhi's call for discrimination against the northern nomads was
reflected in his unease about their adoption of Chinese culture. For
instance, Wang charged that the Siberian ruler Tuoba Hong 拓跋宏
(467–499) had been insincere in his acceptance of Confucian rituals and

teachings and his tribe's adoption of Chinese culture, rudely comparing him to a monkey imitating a human being by wearing a hat. Wang acknowledged Tuoba Hong's putative Confucian activities, such as establishing a royal academy (*mingtang* 明堂) and ancestral temples, making a pilgrimage to Confucius' home, encouraging a three-year mourning for one's diseased parents, and so on; but, he offered the surprising criticism that these sorts of activities were not mentioned in Confucian classics or by Confucius or Mencius. He regarded Tuoba Hong's activities as publicity stunts or political theater, unsupported by virtue or sincerity (Wang 1996: 10:616–617). Wang's criticisms of Tuoba Hong were intended as slights of the Manchu emperor's practice of Confucian rites in the name of Tuoba Hong. At the time, the Manchu emperors were learning the Confucian classics and observing ritual propriety to legitimize their rule and be accepted by the Chinese. Wang dared not criticize them openly, and had to resort to criticize non-Chinese rulers of old to express his dismay.

3.2.2   Males and Females

Wang Fuzhi reflected traditional gender values in his calls to uphold the Confucian principle that males were family leaders, responsible for outside, worldly affairs while females were family followers, responsive for inside, household matters. He held that with a proper division of male and female roles, families would be harmonious and prosper. He classified females as yin and driven by desires that had to be checked. Females had to be submissive and accept the family order. Observing that the fecund intercourse between yin and yang gave rise to Heaven, Earth, and the myriad things, Wang dared not suggest restraining females, but ventured that, defining a proper role, females would contribute to family harmony. He declared, "For a sage king, the basic concern of governance lay in rectifying customs, distinguishing male and female and outside affairs and inside affairs" (Wang 1996: 10:195).

Since Wang Fuzhi put females and desire into one category, he inferred that woman, like desire and passion, would act unreasonably, so he held it was right for even a wise wife to heed a foolish husband, because even an average male would be more reasonable than a sage female (Wang 1996: 11:107). Hence, a woman's submission was crucial for the harmony and prosperity of a family. Indeed, a female family head would lead the family into decline; Wang attributed the fall of the Zhou dynasty to King Ping's

周平王 loss of power to his queen's family and the decline of the state of Lu to Duke Zhuang's 魯莊公 heeding his wife's counsel. Among the common people, Wang reported stories of families falling into disarray after the wife became dominant over the husband (Wang 1996: 5:140).

Well before Wang Fuzhi's time, Wang Bi 王弼 (226–249 CE) and Ouyang Xiu 歐陽修 (1007–1072) warned that the harmony and prosperity of a family depended on female chastity. Wang Bi advised that females be educated and corrected once they were betrothed (Lou 1980: 402). Ouyang Xiu cited the fall of the Liang dynasty (907–923) in addressing the potential harms wrought by unchaste females. He warned about the disasters wrought by women—fallen regimes, clans, husbands. Even if the husband escaped such a disaster, the lives of their descendants would be ruined. The moral was that the husband had to prevent his female (e.g., his wife, mother, and concubine) from interfering in outside affairs, whether local or national, and rectify them in the beginning. Ouyang concluded, "There would be no regret if the male could rectify his female early" (Ouyang 1974: 127). Wang Fuzhi followed Wang Bi and Ouyang Xiu in stressing the proper division of labor between males and females, as well as the appropriate education of females, especially wives. As to young girls, their parents should instruct them to be good and keep them on the straight and narrow. As to wives, their in-laws should guide them to act properly from the day they are married into the family. In this way, the clan leader would prevent her feminine wiles from influencing her husband's thought and action while softening her fury to preserve family harmony (Wang 1996: 1:313).

Wang Fuzhi offered cosmological justification for male dominance over female. In the *Book of Changes*, males, yang, and Heaven are presented as superior to females, yin, and Earth. The virtue of yin is manifested as the petty minded, female, and barbarian, and is associated with desire and profit-seeking (Wang 1996: 1:354). In contrast, the virtue of yang (Qian 乾) is manifested as noble people, and is associated with humaneness, righteousness, harmony, and firmness (Wang 1996: 1:51). Therefore, when interacting with a female, a male should be wary of her insatiable desire and respond to her with due measure. Otherwise, given a female's credulity and greed, a male would incur her complaints and infringements, and get ensnared in difficult situations if he could not satisfy her wishes and demands (Wang 1996: 1:880). To assuage a female and avoid being infringed upon by her, the male must assign her a role, so she has a proper role to play and can use her skills. In practical terms, this is to entrust her with household affairs, setting a limit on her range of activities. Wang likened this division of labor to using a female as a vehicle, or regulating her like a fish on a string. In this way, a female would be satisfied with her lot in life, and support her male's dominance. At the same time, Wang counsels to restrain and sublimate the female's emotions and desires by righteousness and ritual propriety (Wang 1996: 1:880).

3.2.3   Noble Persons and the Petty Minded

Wang Fuzhi followed Confucius and Mencius in distinguishing between noble people and the petty minded, hoping that noble people would be appointed to the court. In the *Analects*, noble people referred to scholars and officials, as well as to aristocrats, while the petty minded referred to either egoistic individuals or common people. For example, Fan Chi 樊遲 was considered petty minded by Confucius, not because he sought profit, but because he concentrated on farming but not on rituals and music (*Analects* 13.4). When Confucius asserted, "The noble person is conversant with righteousness while the petty minded is conversant with profit" (*Analects* 4.16, James Legge's translation), he was distinguishing righteousness from profit by a moral standard, and regarded the petty minded as amoral people.

Wang Fuzhi accepted Confucius' distinction yet used "petty minded" without always distinguishing its moral and social meanings. He held that noble people and the petty minded exerted different influences on customs due to their differing concerns and attitudes. Noble people were concerned about righteousness and for that reason would uphold humaneness and encourage people to cherish life and virtue. Unselfish, they always felt at peace and happy. By contrast, the petty minded sought their own profit and would corrupt social customs and incite people to be selfish, as well. Their selfish concerns caused them to be preoccupied with gain and loss. The situation would worsen when the petty minded formed cliques to pursue selfish ends and the social order would break down. Wang condemned the petty minded for the sorts of humiliation and misery he thought they wreaked upon society (Wang 1996: 5:461).

In order to prevent the petty minded from wreaking havoc on the social order, Wang counseled people to keep vigilant about lapsing into selfishness and partiality. He deemed it important to identify the petty minded based on the distinction between righteousness and profit. He held that whether one tended to seek righteousness or profit was related to whether they would pursue justice or evil, public welfare or personal profit. He recommended looking into one's motive for being monopolistic or frugal (Wang 1996: 7:300). After all, a person might be frugal to reduce the people's taxes or zealous in fighting for a worthy cause. Wang found it was only in the pursuit of public welfare that one's selfish or altruistic motives were revealed. This was the standard by which Confucius reckoned that Guan Zhong 管仲 was a man of humaneness despite his extravagance and monopolism (Analects 14.16).

After identifying the petty minded, Wang Fuzhi stressed more their difference from noble people than transforming them into the noble by cultivating righteousness and ritual propriety. Contrary to the popular view that by education, even base, coarse people could be purified, which was called the great way to transform the petty minded into the noble, Wang Fuzhi feared this method would give the petty minded the opportunity to abuse the nobles and to disarray the ranks. He argued:

> When the petty minded are introduced to the group of noble people, the consequence will be to degrade the noble people to the level of the petty minded. The petty minded mixed with the noble people, shared with them the same office and the same teacher, behaved the same way, married into the same clan. Then there would be no noble people under Heaven, and all of them would turn into the petty minded, the Chinese would become barbarians. No more deplorable than this! (Wang 1996: 10:566)

Wang deplored the collapse of the social rank system during the Spring-Autumn period when the petty minded could start to seek their wealth and glory by using their tongue or a brush and rise from the status of slave to governor. Consequently, the demarcation between the noble person and the petty minded became blurred and porous, and it became difficult to identify which people were truly noble. As this situation worsened, petty minded officials accepted barbarian chieftains, such as Jurchen or Mongol, as leaders, and undermined Chinese civilization. Wang concluded, "Alas, the noble person is to the petty minded as the Chinese is to the barbarian. These distinctions are natural, not artificial. If people do not observe these distinctions, then everything [of our civilized way of life] could be undermined" (Wang 1996: 10:566). Most likely, Wang Fuzhi spoke with deep emotions when he regarded the distinction as natural because this not only contradicted the fact that a wicked father could give birth to a noble son but also went against the vision of the sage's transformation of the petty minded to noble persons.

Wang Fuzhi advocated ritual propriety as the best bulwark for preserving the distinction between the noble person and the petty minded. The noble person ought to remain resolute and impartial, and deal with the petty minded with ritual propriety. He should always be just, reward the petty minded with what he deserves, but do not stir his dream of reputation and power. When the petty minded reveals his intentions, the noble person should endeavor to understand him well, purify his excessive dreams, and limit his potential harm. In this way, the petty minded would be transformed, and many disasters or conflicts would be averted. When the petty minded proves to be incorrigible, the noble person should stick to his principles and resist giving in or showing contempt. In this way, the petty minded could neither fathom the noble person's tactics nor act heedlessly or cause trouble. In particular, the noble person should express loyalty and trust in word, be upright and respectful in deed, remain solemn and upright, and convince the petty minded by his acts of magnanimity, good manners, ritual propriety, and righteousness. Shown respect, the petty minded would strive to emulate the noble person and work toward achieving propriety (Wang 1996: 1:200).

Wang Fuzhi discouraged noble people from directly vying with the petty minded for power or benefits, but he also opposed having the petty minded punished or exiled without investigation. Rather, he advocated dealing with them by righteousness and ritual propriety. When hosting them, receive them with dignity; when hearing their praises, stay alert to their wiles. When dealing with the petty minded, keep calm and alert to their intentions; seize chances to set limits to restrain them (Wang 1996: 1:881). In office and empowered to administer rewards and punishments, the noble person must settle on just punishments. Were he to decide unjust punishments, the petty minded would respond in kind, wracking the court in factional strife. The only option for the noble person would be to bide his time until the petty minded committed a crime or passed away. Wang thought such an approach would work better than directly vying with the petty minded, regardless of possible intermittent factional strife (Wang 1996: 11:101). Implicitly, Wang assumed this approach would reduce for the sort of factional strife that had persisted between the Donglin party and the eunuchs at the Ming court.

Wang Fuzhi based his approach of accommodation and non-competition with the petty minded on the system of hexagrams in the *Book of Changes*. Despite the basic distinction between the noble person and the petty minded, Wang saw that they were both natural types. He regarded the noble people and the petty minded as complements in society that reflected the interaction of yin and yang. The best way to adjust these complements would be by having the noble person cooperate with the petty minded such that "yin nourishes yang, that is, the petty minded support the noble people, the barbarians defend the Chinese." Yin (the petty minded) and yang (the noble person) would need to occupy their proper positions, and interact but not intermingle (Wang 1996: 1:368).

In practice, Wang Fuzhi suggested sincerely offering the petty minded a position and interacting with them. He did not recommend offering them a low salary, for it would not satisfy them; rather, he advocated paying them well to win their loyalty and support (Wang 1996: 1:969). Wang had noted the harm that the low salary system had caused during the Ming and proposed cultivating people's loyalty by first meeting their basic needs. He also sought to prevent the problems incurred by the factional strife in the Song and Ming dynasties by accommodating petty minded and working with them.

Notably, if a petty person were satisfied with his position and cooperated with the noble person, he would cease to be petty minded, for the essence of being petty minded was lack of principle and propriety. However, if the petty minded were not satisfied with his position, and did not face the threat of punishment or restriction, they would vie with the noble person for key posts and be disruptive. Therefore, Wang's strategy of generous pay, interaction, and cooperation would not reduce the potential harm of employing the petty minded. Seeing no alternative approaches, Wang advocated restraining the petty minded with reputation and titles (*ming* 名, social status). He suggested the noble person using reputation and titles as a lever to quash rebels and traitors in times of success, and showing his loyalty and uprightness in times of failure (Wang 1996: 5:575). However, Wang exaggerated the totem power of reputation and titles, forgetting that they must be backed up with real benefits and power. Without such backing, simply conducting rituals and sticking to reputation and titles would not ensure a stable regime. This was why King Xuan of the Zhou 周宣王 could not control the dukes and Emperor Zhao of the Tang 唐昭宗 was killed despite their titles and social status.

3.2.4   Righteousness and Profit

Wang Fuzhi regarded the distinction between righteousness and profit as crucial to maintaining the distinctions between Chinese and barbarian, male and female, and noble person and petty minded. He advocated that people should strive to prioritize righteousness over profit. Ontologically, he associated righteousness with yang and profit with yin, with yang dominant over yin. If people were to approach profit in the spirit of righteousness, moderate their desires by ritual propriety, and prevent laziness with reverence (*jing* 敬), they would be able to cope with any yin phenomena (barbarian, petty person, or female) (Wang 1996: 1:363). He cited Confucius in making this claim, for Confucius established the distinctions between righteousness and profit, public and private, leader and minister, and Chinese and barbarian, thereby focusing the virtues of humaneness and righteousness (Wang 1996: 8:520–521).

Drawing on the sayings of Confucius, Wang Fuzhi used the distinction between righteousness and profit as a standard for setting moral, social, and cultural virtues. As to moral realization, a person should strive to uphold righteousness to be morally worthy and exemplary, as people's differing prioritizations of righteousness and profit led them to the outcomes of being worthy or wicked. One who had upheld to righteousness over profit be considered exemplary (Wang 1996: 7:894). Again, Wang's point was not that people should avoid seeking profit *per se*. Rather, when considering a chance to gain profit, one has to be sure it would be done with righteousness, that is, consistent with morality; the noble person pursues profit only in a manner consistent with propriety and righteousness.

As to society, in making policy and setting laws, leaders need to weigh righteousness over profit to develop humane, healthy customs and educate the people. After all, righteousness is the root of honor while profit is the fount of shame. A leader who realizes the vital distinction between righteousness and profit would be able to stir the conscience of the people in even chaotic times. In practice, a person's preference for righteousness or profit would affect the truthfulness of his filial behaviors. If he prioritized profit over filial love, he would eventually neglect his parents and betray them in word and action (Wang 1996: 7:755). Therefore, a fundamental tenet of Confucianism is that no person should ever lose their sense of righteousness and conscience.

As to culture, it is in their preference for righteousness over profit that the Chinese differ from the barbarians, the civilized from the uncivilized; it is the barbarians' quest for profit that renders them less cultivated than the Chinese. Wang observed that barbarians grew up and lived in settings where profit was valued and pursued. The thirst for profit filled their minds and they devoted themselves solely to gaining profit. Although they were human beings like the Chinese, they were despoiled by their environment, culture, and education (Wang 1996: 10:503).

Consistent with these distinctions, Wang Fuzhi admired Dong Zhongshu's 董仲舒 (179–104 BC) call to "Rectify righteousness without scheming for profit; enlighten the Way without calculating effectiveness." He added, "Righteousness and profit cannot be combined. Dedicated to righteousness, a person would forget profit; pursuing profit, one would remain far from righteousness" (Wang 1996: 7:658). For his part, Wang Fuzhi did not deny the necessity of seeking profit, but counseled that profit should be pursued in light of righteousness. Although righteousness and profit set different orientations, Wang argued that they could be harnessed under heavenly principle, which is about improving public welfare. Heavenly principle signified a broad path. By taking this path, "Once everything is done properly, it can be extended to the world, without any loss of profit at all" (Wang 1996: 7:382).

Elsewhere, Wang alluded to Dong Zhongshu's avowal that, if one acted righteously, harm would be forestalled; if the Way were carried out, merits/achievements would not fail (Wang 1996: 5:177). In this, Wang found a way to bring righteousness and profit into harness: Righteous action and policy would produce sustained public welfare rather than short-term private profit. If a ruler were to act and govern by righteousness, he would realize a vast fortune for his realm and win the people's lasting support. Hence, Wang asserted, "If people were to use righteousness to direct their pursuit of profit and use principle to guide their desires, then heavenly principle would permeate their human desires. When heavenly principle prevails, one's pursuits, even if they be wine, women, and song, would be conducted in due measure" (Wang 1996: 1:355).

What, then, is righteousness? Mencius regarded it as a product of "the feeling of shame and dislike" (Mencius 6A.6). Wang Fuzhi interpreted it as "settled conscience (xin zhi an 心之安)," remarking, "Righteousness does not depend on external things or situations, but rather on one's conscience" (Wang 1996: 8:249). He instructed people to introspect on their intentions, and sweep away the evil ones. In this way, "They would understand righteousness clearly and not be confused [or led astray] by unrighteousness" (Wang 1996: 12:88–89). Still, Wang realized that basing righteousness on conscience alone could run the danger of making morality subjective and lack objective standards. For this reason, he advocated striking a balance between the inner mental and outer situational conditions. "To locate righteousness, it is better to examine it in one's conscience than in the order and disorder of the world; and, it is better to weigh it by people's expectations than one's own likes or dislikes" (Wang 1996: 7:402). That is, righteousness involved balancing self and other, large and small, constancy and change, and arriving at the condition of feeling no regret about one's actions and no unease in one's conscience (Wang 1996: 7:382). Hence, righteousness allows people to strike a balance between their inner conscience and the outer situation. It requires that people review their interpersonal relationships to ensure they are upright and weigh them with heart and conscience. If a person tried to assuage his conscience while being indifferent to the suffering of others, his assuaged conscience would be irresponsible rather than righteous in character.

For Wang Fuzhi, one's inner conscience operates in a dialectical relationship with outer situations through one's exercise of righteousness and propriety. On the one hand, conscience was the ultimate voice of righteousness. Yet, it required ritual propriety and external situations to guide and rectify its subjective ground. In this way, Wang avoided the misjudgments and practical errors of Wang Yangming's followers who accepted his teaching to "extend the inborn knowledge of the good." On the other hand, even though ritual propriety allowed for the realization of righteousness through following rules in concrete situations, righteousness also guided people in adjusting rituals to suit new situations and avoid being morally rigid. In this way, Wang sought a way to avoid the blind practice of ritual propriety that he attributed to followers of Zhu Xi's teachings.

3.3   Wang Fuzhi's Enlightened Empire

In addition to the aforesaid three guiding principles, Wang Fuzhi's reflections on the fall of the Ming led him to refine the concept and practice of imperial rule. He sought a solution to the misrule of the Ming by redefining the roles of the emperor, high ministers, scholar-officials, and common people. His suggestions ranged from limiting the emperor's power, empowering high ministers, and disciplining officials, to nurturing and educating the people. He displayed some insight in his discussions on the relations between popular opinion and truth (heavenly principle), satisfying the people's basic needs, and improving their social morality.

Despite noting the limited time, knowledge, and resources at the disposal of an imperial court for its operations, Wang held that the emperor was responsible to keep society orderly and peaceful. While assigning such responsibility to the emperor, Wang rejected Mencius' right of revolution, the idea of the popular overthrow of a despot. While this might seem to be overly conservative, this rejection sheds light on the present Chinese government's claim of legitimacy on the basis of its maintaining order and peace.

3.3.1 Encouraging an Emperor's Sense of Public Service

Like his Confucian predecessors, Wang Fuzhi regarded the position of emperor as a natural and necessary outcome of human history. He viewed its emergence as both determined by Heaven (i.e., natural and social factors) and a matter of human will. "In early times, the people chose a leader based on whether his virtues nurtured the people and his achievements brought benefits to them. As the population and territory expanded, the chosen leader was called the Son of Heaven" (Wang 1996: 10:67). In his comments on rulership, Wang stressed the emperor's duty to serve the people, and regarded this as the basic Way of the emperor. "The Way of the emperor is simply humaneness and righteousness. What makes the emperor noble is that his humane acts nurture the people and his righteousness conduct rectifies them" (Wang 1996: 8:243). For Wang, like other Confucian thinkers, such an emperor would be co-equal with Heaven and Earth. "Heaven gives form to all life on Earth. Earth assists Heaven in completing this process ... The emperor balances the functions of Heaven and Earth: he moderates what Heaven ordains so that yin and yang may be balanced and operate in harmony; he assists what Earth provides, whether soft or firm. He instructs the people by virtue, nurtures them by offering necessities. He unites the functions of Heaven, Earth, and Humanity, and ratifies the ultimate principle for human beings" (Wang 1996: 1:143).

By presenting the people's choice of leader in antiquity as based on service, Wang Fuzhi reimagined the ruler-subject relationship in the Three Dynasties period. He offered the view that the early sage kings made every effort to benefit the people. They neither clung to power nor asked the people for anything in return. Moreover, the people knew their kings well and loved them unreservedly. He compared this relationship to that between dew and grass: "When dew forms, it does not distinguish between the grass and other things. It just forms on the grass by chance, but its benefits are real enough. As to the grass, it cares not whether the dew forms or not, but it is moistened once the dew forms" (Wang 1996: 3:396). This analogy depicted the ruler-subject relation as natural and symbiotic as that between the dew and anything on which it forms. Since the dew and the grass expect nothing of each other, they stay in perfect harmony. As Zhuangzi wrote, "The fish forget each other in the rivers and lakes, and men forget each other in the arts of the Way" (Watson 1968: 62). By the same token, the early rulers and their people enjoyed their lives naturally and loved each other spontaneously.

As to rectifying and sustaining the people, the early sage kings upheld the Three Regularities (*shou sanzheng* 守三正)—the regularities of Heaven, Earth, and Humanity. They set the calendar based on the observed movements of the sun, moon, and stars. They conducted sacrifices to Heaven, measured the wind, announced the dates for sowing and harvest, and chose auspicious times for meting out punishments and rewards (Wang 1996: 2:282). In these ways, they charted the path for people to follow the Three Rectitudes, secured the people's necessities, and maintained harmony in the realm. Second, the early sage kings set standards for people to utilize the myriad things, based on reverence for the Five Phases (*jing wuxing* 敬五行). The Five Phases included metal, wood, water, fire, and earth, which together gave rise to the myriad things in the universe. By adjusting the Five Phases in human affairs, they protected the people's lives from possible harm due to imbalances. They had canals dug to carry away soil, fires built to cultivate healthy *qi*, forests cut down to expand human vital force, weapons hidden to put people at ease, and the land cleared to calm the public need. They ensured the supply of necessities so the people were provisioned. In particular, they did not allow there to be imbalances or excesses, which would disturb public sentiment (Wang 1996: 2:282). In these ways, the early kings set rules and standards in view of the Five Phases so that the public sentiment would be moderate and harmonious. Consider the Duke of Zhao 召公 (Zhou): "In leading the construction of the city of Xie 謝, he had the ground cleared for housing and canals dug for fresh water and sewage … The scholars felt at ease, the weak felt relieved of distress and failure, and people felt safe in their dwellings. For these reasons, the people served their rulers willingly but were unwilling to leave" (Wang 1996: 3:434).

Contrasting the emperors of the Ming dynasty to the kings of the Three Dynasties, Wang Fuzhi criticized their selfishness, denying their claim that the empire belonged to the imperial clan. He argued, "It is nothing but the Qin 秦 ruler's selfishness that the rulers of later generations criticized the Qin regime. While condemning the Qin ruler's selfishness, they expect their own progeny to hold the throne forever. Isn't that being just as selfish?" (Wang 1996: 10:68). Wang held that the emperor should regard the throne as public property, and fulfill his duty to nurture and educate the people and hand the throne to a competent successor. He admonished the emperor not to regard the throne as his private property. This would be a safeguard from usurpation, since usurpation would then be futile. The Qin protected the throne from Hun invasion but lost it to peasant rebels. The Song protected the throne from powerful ministers, but lost it to the Jurchens and later the Mongols. Now that the rulers regard the people as "others" and potential enemies, they cannot know who might neutralize them and seize the throne (Wang 1996: 3:365).

However, Wang Fuzhi had to temper his ideals with the reality that under the current system the throne did belong to one imperial clan and that emperors were selfish and always had been since the Qin dynasty. While advocating that the emperor's duty was to nurture and educate the people, he regarded maintaining social order as the emperor's basic function. For Wang, it was to the emperors' credit that the people lived well, secured in their dwellings, and farmed their plots in peace. Still, he blamed the people's ingratitude, selfishness, and disloyalty for the fall of the Ming while paying scant attention to the reason they felt that way: the emperors' heavy taxes and misrule. Wang said, "When the emperor's policies affect the interests of the people, they regard losses in their savings and commodities as cause for serious complaints, curse the emperor to a short life, and back robbers or traitors as their rulers. They bark and buzz like dogs and flies and complain unceasingly, forgetting the emperor's overall generosity" (Wang 1996: 10:1048). Wang concluded that the chaos during the transition period between the Ming and the Qing dynasties was aroused by the people. Wang thus sought to defend the Ming imperial court, ignoring the heavy taxes and rampant corruption of the late Ming court and forgetting his advocacy that the duty of the emperor was to serve the people.

Wang Fuzhi even sought to shift the Ming emperors' responsibility to their ministers and officials, for failing to rectify the emperor's misconduct or enact humane policies. He criticized the Donglin scholars for mistaking rebuke and censure for frankness, indulging in folk songs and satire, and leading people to complain and curse their emperor, which bred widespread disorder and conflict, including rebellion and chaos (Wang 1996: 10:1048). Wang overstated the influence that a minister could exert in counseling an emperor or saving the empire. Ever since the Qin, the emperor held absolute power over the ministers and people; if a minister who was not an intimate of the emperor ventured to point out that the emperor had erred, he could face execution without having improved the situation. During the Latter Han, when Liang Hong 梁鴻 passed the capital Luo Yang and satirized the splendid imperial palace in verse, he was hunted by Liu Xiu 劉秀, the founder of the dynasty, and forced to live in hiding on the coast (Fan 1965: 2766–2767). How could Wang expect that an emperor would change his behavior at a minister's remonstrance?

Facing this impasse, Wang Fuzhi turned to his dream that a great man (*da ren* 大人), that is, a sage, would arrive. Such a great man would know that the emperor's imprudent official appointments and general misrule had resulted from his confusion of right and wrong. He would admonish the emperor about joy and anger, introduce him to propriety in word and dress, purify his mind of popular and mercantile news, and uproot his desire to indulge in music and sexual relations. He would set rules to prevent the emperor from going astray, preventing any appearance of wicked or biased impulses. Once the emperor's wicked thoughts had been cleansed away, his sense of humaneness and righteousness would sprout and bloom (Wang 1996: 8:469). One might wonder how even a great man could have such leverage over the emperor. And, could a great man accompany the emperor day and night and counsel him on every affair? Even Confucius could not dissuade Duke Ai of Lu from indulging in women and music, yet had no way to resign. How could anyone less than Confucius to pursue this sort of mission?

Wang Fuzhi actually dreamed of the arrival of a great minister like Yi Yin 伊尹 of the Shang dynasty to serve as regent, dethrone an incompetent emperor, and expel the wicked ministers. According to the *Book of Documents*, after King Tai Jia 太甲 of the Shang continued to misbehave after Yi Yin admonished him several times, Yi Yin dethroned him and forced him to rectify himself. After Tai Jia had improved several years later, Yi Yin restored him to the throne. Wang Fuzhi commented, Yi Yin could do this because he was unselfish and did not covet the throne. His only concern was to reduce troubles and serve the empire. Yet, he was unique in the annals of Chinese history. It would require great self-discipline on the part of a great minister to prevent the dethronement of the emperor from devolving into usurpation. Wang criticized Huo Guang's 霍光 (?–68 BC) replacement of Liu He 劉賀 with Emperor Xuan 漢宣帝 during the Han as ill-advised and reckless. His reason was that, ever since the Qin, administration in the prefecture-county system differed from administration in the Zhou feudal system. Dethroning an emperor in the later period thus could lead to general chaos or usurpation, and should be avoided (Wang 1996: 6:1049).

Wang Fuzhi was willing to waive all moral principles and official responsibilities as long as the emperor maintained a stable social order. Any emperor who maintained the social order should be accepted regardless of despotism or incompetence. Wang said, "When the Son of Heaven behaves unjustly and cruelly, such as Jie 桀 of the Xia and Zhou 紂 of the Shang, there is nothing to be done. Just let him live out his days, despoiling his ancestral temple. No one would dare to dethrone him" (Wang 1996: 6:1136). With this sentiment, Wang began to support despotism and abandoned his ideal of humaneness. He neglected that a ruthless, heartless ruler would harm the people materially and morally, and incline them to be narrow self-seekers. For this, Wang could be labeled a village Confucian teacher who only understood a minister's obedience to the emperor, regardless of righteousness and humaneness.

3.3.2   Appointing Competent Prime Ministers

Wang Fuzhi realized that the absence of a competent prime minister was the main cause of the chaotic Ming rule. (The Ming emperors had entrusted the First Grand Secretary to act as the prime minister.) Wang ascribed this lack of a capable prime minister to the Ming founder Zhu Yuanzhang's suspicion that a strong prime minister would have ambitions of usurping the throne. However, the lack of a prime minister had left the emperors in a lonely and defenseless position, set apart from the other officials charged with managing national affairs. Also, the high officials at court shirked responsibility, since they did not have clearly assigned duties. Moreover, the door was left open for the eunuchs to fuel the corruption and factional strife at court that led to peasant rebellions and the Manchu conquest. To prevent such problems from recurring, Wang advocated restoring the post of prime minister. The emperor should identify several qualified candidates, and appoint one to oversee the performance of the high officials, take note of the people's needs, and oversee imperial affairs. With a clear division of labor and cooperation among the high ministers, the emperor could recruit worthy scholars from remote places, expel corrupt officials, reveal false accusations, and maintain the people's trust and loyalty (Wang 1996: 11:29–31). Nonetheless, the emperor's ability to appoint a prime minister was predicated on his humaneness, wisdom, and unselfishness. If the emperor was selfish and feared overthrow, he would choose a weak prime minister and make him a mere figurehead. In this way, proper governance would be supplanted by concern to protect imperial authority. Under such circumstances, how could Wang hope that an emperor would grant authority to a strong prime minister?

How should the emperor choose a prime minister? Wang Fuzhi did not give a clear answer. He suggested that the emperor observe the performance of the top candidates, and choose among them. He disagreed with Dou Yan 竇儼 (919–960), who advocated that the new prime minister should be recommended by the previous one, but have a trial term. He thought Dou Yan's proposal would undermine the emperor's power and encourage ministerial intrigue. But if the emperor chose prime ministers directly, he would need to know their abilities, on the one hand, and have the knowledge of society or the experience of administration, on the other. Regrettably, few emperors could know the candidate sufficiently well, since they tended to be brought up in isolation in the imperial palaces, cut off from social and political life.

Among the qualities of a capable prime minister, Wang stressed calmness and generosity, as well as alertness to the intentions and loyalties of others. Wang praised Guo Ziyi's 郭子儀 (697–781) calmness and detachment in holding high position and power and facing failure and success. Displaying a disquieting calm, Guo persuaded Tibetan and Turkish military officers to withdraw from Chang'an 長安 without a show of force (Wang 1996: 10:866). Wang eulogized Li Hang's 李沆 (947–1004) firmness and composure in presiding over discussions among high officials and maintaining an orderly court. In Wang's estimate, Li Hang succeeded because he had practiced the Confucian Way with magnanimity and foresight (Wang 1996: 11:85). Wang described the Way of a great prime minister as characterized by "carefully weighing the feasibility of measures, calmly awaiting unanimity among the people, and always displaying a leisurely composure whether in action or at rest. In this manner, he could grasp the principle and pattern of affairs and devise sound plans. If he were to rashly promote good policies and cancel harmful ones, he might leave the door open for treacherous ministers to pursue their own agendas" (Wang 1996: 11:69).

Next to generosity was discretion. Being discreet meant one could keep a secret; by respecting people's confidences, they would let others feel at ease. A prime minister who was generous and discreet would benefit the people and not precipitate disasters in the empire when out of office (Wang 1996: 3:336). Discretion for Wang did not refer just to respecting confidences or keeping secrets. It also included deliberation before taking action. Exercising discretion involved weighing the risks and leaving extra space and materials to deal with the unexpected. For example, the prime minister should be prepared to assess officials' reports in depth, so as to grasp their real intentions and loyalties, as well as to analyze the lessons of history to foresee the fate of a dynasty. He should stay calm and pursue his plans to the point of death. In this way, he would be equally at ease and discreet and act resolutely (Wang 1996: 11:89). Wang used the term "penetrating knowledge" (*tong shi* 通識), to express the foresight gained by being generous and discreet. With penetrating knowledge, one does things with nonchalance that most people would not dare to do and promotes what works and discards the useless.

Wang Fuzhi also stressed uprightness [lit. purity] (*qing* 清) as a necessary attribute of a great minister. He praised three prime ministers of the Tang dynasty who led officials to feel shame and honor, paving the way for the prosperity of the Kaiyuan era (*kai yuan shengshi* 開元盛世) (713–741). These exemplars were Song Jing 宋璟 (663–737), Lu Huaishen 盧懷慎 (?–716), and Zhang Jiuling 張九齡 (678–740). Song Jing was upright and resolute in taking on responsibilities, Lu Huaishen was upright and discreet in managing affairs, and Zhang Jiuling was upright and amiable in dealing with others. All three were generous and self-disciplined; they never contended with others for power or renown. Consequently, they worked well with talented ministers in running the court and thus differed from officials who were overly direct, short-sighted, and reckless (Wang 1996: 10:830–831). Wang described these three as exemplars who inspired others to engage in public service over personal renown and factional strife, implicitly criticizing the negligence of the Ming officials.

3.3.3   Disciplining Officials

Dismayed by the rampant corruption among the Ming officials, Wang Fuzhi proposed strictly regulating officials but being lenient on the common people. He cautioned against being harsh on the common people but lenient toward officials. He rejected *The Book of Rites* assertion that "The ritual rules do not go down to the common people. The penal statutes do not go up to great officers" (Wang 1996: 4:70), insisting that strict legal penalties be applied to officers and ritual propriety be extended to the common people. His rationale was that it was the nobility who controlled the wealth and power, and their misdeeds could disrupt society. According to history, whenever popular customs were corrupted, it was always due to the nobility and not the common people. "The nobles are those who govern peasants. If the nobles were morally transformed, the peasants could be transformed without effort" (Wang 1996: 7:944). Thus, a ruler should give priority to educating and disciplining the scholar-officials, for it is by their exemplary conduct that the people are awakened to humaneness (Wang 1996: 8:315). When the emperor is too lenient and exercises weak control over the conduct of officials, they begin to mistreat the common people with increasing impunity. Eventually, the common people would consider such a situation intolerable and rise up. Hence, Wang asserted, "A sage ruler would not make demands only on the common people and ignore the nobility's responsibility to provide upright governance" (Wang 1996: 5:349).

As to educating scholar-officials, Wang Fuzhi advocated starting with ritual propriety and deference to nurture their moderate qi, followed by having them instructed in righteousness and moral principle to arouse their moral conscience. If a scholar-officials were to study the Confucian classics from childhood, living by them year in and year out, he would be immersed in the spirit of ritual propriety, proper in what he sees and hears, and free of bad habits and ill-temper. In this way, "the worthy would advance to the vast sphere of the Way and generously accommodate the people within the four seas. The unworthy would, at the least, restrain their disruptive impulses and predatory habits, and refrain from seizing on the shortcomings and secrets of others to stir trouble and harm the people" (Wang 1996: 11:133).

Wang Fuzhi did not agree that legalist measures of examination and penalty be adopted to discipline officials although he maintained they should be penalized. He stressed nurturing the officials' sense of shame and honor over deterring them with threats of punishment. He argued that if a ruler despised corrupt scholars for their malfeasance and sought to rectify their conduct by penalty, he would never succeed. If he were to threaten them, they would play along for a time but later resume their evil ways. To prevent such recurrences, the ruler should adopt Confucian teachings to morally transform corrupt scholar-officials, not just punish them (Wang 1996: 11:25). Wang warned that coercion and threats of punishment would drive officials to cheat and even lose their inborn affection and respect. In the Liang dynasty (502–558), Emperor Xiao

Yan 蕭衍 promoted filial piety and would criticize officials severely and dismiss them from office if they did not disfigure their face or body during ritual mourning. As a result, some officials fasted to display their malnourished body and disfigured face, while others feigned weeping by putting mustard powder in their eyes. In the end, this enforcement of custom led to widespread hypocrisy and the collapse of the Liang (Wang 1996: 2:249).

Besides educating scholar-officials by ritual propriety, Wang Fuzhi suggested that rulers give corrupt officials sufficient time and space to feel shame and guilt and repent. In this way, the wrong doers would not be stimulated to commit more evil deeds (Wang 1996: 11:285). However, Wang overstated the transformative power of leniency on the common people, especially the wicked. It was common for wicked people to take advantage of such leniency to accumulate wealth and power. Just as Han Fei 韓非 (280–233 BCE) argued, a mother who treats her wicked son with love and advice could not forestall his evil; but a police officer could imprison him and change him with shackles and laws (Han 2000: 1099).

Realizing that ritual propriety and leniency were not sufficiently transformative, Wang proposed the two handles of leniency and penalties for disciplining officials. In the North Wei dynasty, Li Biao 李彪 (444–501) had suggested, "When a father or elder brother commits a crime, their sons and younger brothers should be made to expose their shoulders to express repentance at the imperial palace; when sons and younger brothers are found guilty, their father and elder brothers should publicly take the blame and resign their positions" (Wang 1996: 10:609). Wang praised this measure as an effective way to restore people's original human nature, and relationships. Although he was unsure whether the fathers and sons would feel compassion and mercy while repenting, he felt certain that their conduct would remind others of their own conscience and love, and keep them on the upright path (Wang 1996: 10:609). Wang did not realize, however, that Li Biao's approach of bundling family members to accept joint responsibility—in effect, requiring them to spy on and restrain each other—stripped away the people's mutual trust and individual freedom. While this measure may have served the interests of the officials and the family, it served to weaken the independence and morale of the scholar-officials and made them protective of their families above all else when remonstrating on the emperors.

Wang Fuzhi realized it would be difficult to discipline officials without securing their sustenance first. So, he advocated paying a high salary to nurture the officials' sense of shame and uprightness. He praised the Song emperors who had set up a rule not to kill scholars and officials but to secure their sustenance, observing that many worthy officials appeared during this period, as a result. He also believed that the emperor's commendations could stir and strengthen the officials' sense of integrity. In 62 BCE, Yin Wonggui 尹翁歸 (?–62 BCE), a governor of the Chang'an area, passed away. Owing to his integrity and lack of corruption, he left no money or property to cover his funeral expenses. Hearing about this, Emperor Xuan of the Han 漢宣帝 granted his son one hundred pounds of gold for his ancestral sacrifice. The emperor issued the same grant after the passing of another upright minister, Zhu Yi 朱邑 (?–58 BCE). Wang noted that what was desirable here was not just the money, but the honor of imperial recognition. These rewards were not issued in recognition of loyalty but for purity and uprightness. Without such incentives, demanding that officials be pure and upright while ignoring the maintenance of their family and ancestral sacrifices would not incline them to be upright. Also, when the ruler chanced upon pure and upright scholar-officials, they sometimes proved to be overly strict and merciless, hurting the social morality and fostering cruelty in that way. Happily, this sort of scholar-official was scarce. Most scholar-officials would accept a low salary as an excuse to be corrupt and procure wealth by hook or crook (Wang 1996: 10:164).

Wang Fuzhi criticized the Ming emperors for reducing officials' salaries, which drove them to be shameless and hypocritical. The Ming founder Zhu Yuanzhang did not pay his officials a full-year's salary, nor did he grant any reward over 100 taels of silver (Wang 1996: 10:164). Regardless of official rank, every Ming official was paid a monthly salary of 300 pounds of rice. This amount was not sufficient to support one official's family, let alone cover other activities, such as wedding ceremonies, the children's tuition, funerals, or ancestral sacrifices. As a result, officials resorted to appropriating public funds and increasing taxes and fees for personal expenditures. In the end, they turned to obtaining money and goods in whatever way they could. Wang concluded that the Ming emperors were not qualified to rule the people (Wang 1996: 12:565). He urged future rulers to remove unnecessary positions and offer high salaries to cover the officials' expenses and cultivate their integrity and dignity.

3.3.4   Securing the People's Livelihood

Wang Fuzhi felt bitter that the common people had abandoned their Ming rulers and embraced the Manchu regime—a feeling bolstered by the general apathy about resisting the Manchu invaders. He ascribed the people's attitude to the Ming emperor's neglect of the people and the officials' corruption and betrayals of the people. If a future ruler wished to win over the people, Wang suggested that he be a moral exemplar to the people and moreover that he understand the people's likes and aversions. Most importantly, he should secure the people's livelihood. Although Wang's view could be termed elitist, it can also serve as a reference for understanding China's current policy of securing the people's livelihood without respecting their human rights and dignity.

Wang Fuzhi believed that the people's primary concern was their livelihood. Any ruler who ensured the people's livelihood would win them over. "What the people desire is nothing but their sustenance and safety. To ensure these, the ruler should care for all of his people and allow them to realize themselves. What the people resented most were the sufferings of hunger, cold, and homelessness. To prevent such ills, the ruler should acknowledge the people's sufferings and make every effort to avert or ameliorate them" (Wang 1996: 8:440). As to practical measures, Wang stressed that the ruler must prioritize agriculture, reduce taxes and corvée, and regulate agricultural production and consumption by season and due measure. In these ways, the ruler could ensure there was ample grain to the people. With ample surpluses of beans and millets, the people would consider them cheap commodities and donate them readily. Nor would they compete or struggle for their selfish interests at the sacrifice of family affection and righteousness (Wang 1996: 8:865). Wang saw the possibility of transforming selfishness into altruism by the practical measure of providing sufficient food stuffs, and endorsed Guan Zhong's maxim, "When the barn is full, the people will observe ritual propriety and deference; when clothes and food are adequate, the people will have a sense of shame and honor" (Li 2004: 2).

Wang held that, with a guaranteed livelihood, the people would be secure and the ruler would have their loyalty and respect. He even advanced the view that "When the people have a certain livelihood, they will not envy each other but be stable. They will be immune to the seduction of outlandish fashions and music and treat them as dross to be cast aside" (Wang 1996: 3:351). At the same time, Wang did not think the ruler should simply follow the people's likes and aversions or popular opinion, but suggested that he distinguish the people's universal likes and aversions (*gongyu gongwu* 公欲公惡) from the merely partial ones. By distinguishing the universal ones, the ruler could fulfill the people's true likes, remove the causes of their dislikes, and achieve a mutual understanding with the people. The people would regard him as a father figure and remain loyal and at his service (Wang 1996: 7:89).

As to identifying the people's universal likes and aversions and balancing Heavenly principle with popular opinion, Wang Fuzhi proposed "to verify Heaven according to popular opinion, and employ popular opinion according to Heaven (*zheng tian yu min, yong min yi tian* 徵天於民, 用民以天)" (Wang 1996: 2:237). "Heaven" referred to truth or Heavenly principle. Although Wang dared not challenge the precept in the *Book of Documents*, "Heaven sees the same as the people see; Heaven hears the same as the people hear" (Qu 2014: 320), he insisted that this precept described the relationship between Heaven and the people during the Three Dynasties, when the people were simple, honest, and pure, and acted in accord with Heaven. He argued that ever since the Han dynasty the people had been lured by narrow self-interest, and fallen prey to the bribes of politicians and ensnared by their frenzied schemes to earn higher profits and ranks. What they saw and heard had departed from Heavenly principle; how could it now stand for what Heaven sees and hears (Wang 1996: 10:809)? Hence, a ruler should distinguish the people's true and universal needs from their popular opinion, and find the true and proper way to govern. For example, when Zi Chan 子產 (?–522 BC) reformed the well-field system and disciplined the people with ritual propriety, at first they were angry and expected him to be assassinated. After enjoying the fruits of his reform for several years, however, the people began to praise him and feared losing him. Similarly, when Li Gang 李綱 (1083–1140) rejected moving the Song capital to the south and swore to defend it with his life, the people in the capital acclaimed and supported him. But, how many of them were willing to defend the capital with their lives? The people were only concerned about losing their own property and estates if the capital was moved. Wang Fuzhi condemned this sort of situation:

> In later dynasties, the whims of the common people were the origin of widespread chaos. If you give them food in the morning, they praise you at once; if you strip off their clothes in the evening, they curse you without hesita-

tion. Small kindnesses or grudges can stir them to excitement and seduce them from their old ways. They can choose to pursue the profits at hand heedless of any risk lurking behind it. They would pursue their desires at the sacrifice of their own security, rebelling when a ruler openly restrains their desires while quietly planning their welfare. (Wang 1996: 10:810)

Indeed, Wang Fuzhi had discovered some facts about the common people. They were short-sighted, ignorant, and gullible. Nonetheless, these facts did not support the contention that public opinion was the source of chaos. These facts only showed that common people were simple and easily manipulated. Moreover, because the people were short-sighted, ignorant, and gullible, they were not in a position to cause serious damage to society; only if they were led astray by politicians or rebel leaders.

Why and how was a ruler to "verify Heaven from the popular opinion"? Wang indicated that if a ruler did not care about the people, the ministers needed to show him that Heaven manifested itself through the people's likes and aversions, and nothing was more fearful than the people (Wang 1996: 2:327). A recurrent phenomenon in China history was that whenever heavy taxes exceeded the people's tolerance, Heaven was said to utter its warning through their protests and rebellions. If the ruler did not rectify his tax policy, he could be overthrown. In this way, Heaven thus acted as a principle of upright governance, sensitive to the tolerance of the people. Hence, by carefully heeding the people's complaints and rebellions, a ruler could discern heavenly principle and rectify his policies and improve his governance.

Wang Fuzhi also recommended "employing popular opinion according to Heaven," to rulers who patronized the people, to remind them to seek the truth in popular opinion and heed it carefully (Wang 1996: 2:327). Li Gang had been misled by popular opinion, resulting in the fall of the Song capital and the capture of the Song emperors. In contrast, Zi Chan saw the short-sightedness of the people's whims and instituted reasonable reforms, achieving long-term stability and public welfare. "Heaven" here referred to the historical trend and real situation. The lesson was that the ruler had to balance Heaven (principle) and the desires of the common people (popular opinion) if he hoped to avoid being misled by unfiltered popular opinion and govern the state well. By striking this sort of balance, a ruler could discern whether people's complaints and praises were justified and respond to them effectively. He should distinguish when people have ulterior motive from when they express affection or present complaints. He should execute or exile serious wrongdoers to prevent the spread of criminal practices, and rectify the people with heavenly principle (through ritual propriety) to improve social harmony (Wang 1996: 12:71). In short, Wang deemed it necessary for rulers to identify their people's actual needs in seeking to secure their livelihood and maintain social order. He regarded such actual needs as the index of public welfare and the foundation of social ethics.

Wang Fuzhi accepted Confucius' saying that the people could be educated only after their basic needs had been met. They could conduct rituals expressing respect for the Son of Heaven and their ancestors and grasp filial piety and fraternity only after their they could support their parents (Wang 1996: 10:254). Wang also viewed righteousness and ritual propriety as social measures for moderating people's pursuit of profit and satisfaction of desires. Understanding that human greed could be insatiable, he advocated values and measures to moderate greedy impulses. First, he advocated providing for common prosperity or equal distribution of wealth to avoid jealousy and competition. Second, he advocated moderating the people's desires with righteousness and ritual propriety while securing their basic needs. He argued that after the ancient sage kings had provided for the people's basic needs, they educated them to understand shame and honor. If the people felt no shame or honor and only sought to satisfy their desires, their desires would become limitless and they would want even more after reaping profits that equaled Heaven and Earth. For this reason, Wang rejected taking the people's poverty as an excuse to postpone their education as a misreading of Guan Zhong's words, "When the barn is full, people will know ritual propriety and deference; when clothes and food are enough, people will have a sense of shame and honor." Wang contended:

> After the people's basic needs are met, their sense of shame and honor arise; after their material necessities are provided, they practice rituals and music. Does this mean that before their material necessities are provided, they will not feel shame and honor or practice rituals and music? Lacking a sense of shame and honor, not practicing rituals and music or setting them aside, the people would start to gain profits by any means they could. Shame and honor would be discarded as empty words and the spirit of rituals and music (humaneness) would vanish. After the people's minds became obsessed with property ownership and selfish interests, they would become excessive, arro-

gant, wicked, and evil, and it would be impossible to return them to the upright path, just as it would be impossible to navigate a large rudderless ship with just an oar in the Three Gorges pass of the Yangtze River. (Wang 1996: 3:394)

As to practical measures, Wang Fuzhi advocated that the nobility should educate the common people with rituals and the proper conduct of drinking, archery, and reading, to help them understand rules, orient them toward filial piety, fraternity, and husbandry, and lead them to shed bad habits and customs and pursue *bona fide* aspirations (Wang 1996: 7:136). At the same time, Wang thought that education was not a panacea. He knew it was difficult to rectify people's behavior and that some people were incorrigible. He did not believe that farmers would uphold ritual and behave perfectly after just studying the teachings of the sages. He assumed that, at best, people could be encouraged to be honest and women simple. He argued, "The sage Yao had a mischievous son; the sage Shun had a disrespectful younger brother; the Duke of the Zhou had a rebellious elder brother; Confucius had an incorrigible student. Regarding the untutored people in the countryside, is it safe to assume that they would maintain polite manners while on a journey?" (Wang 1996: 10:170). The sages' instructions are not a panacea; they can encourage the people to be simple and honest, but they cannot ensure the people will be as civil and elegant as the sage and noble person.

Wang Fuzhi identified a condition for initiating moral transformation: arousing people's sense of shame and humaneness. People would arrive at the right path only if they felt stirrings of humaneness and shame. Wang cited the example of a filial son, Chen Yuan 陳元, of the Han. At first, Chen Yuan was considered unfilial to his mother. However, when magistrate Qiu Xiang 仇香visited the Chen family, he found that Chen Yuan did things quite well and was considered outstanding in his neighbors, so he concluded that Chen Yuan had a sense of shame and could be reformed, and Chen indeed soon became filial. In contrast, a person who had behaved shamelessly would tend to be incorrigible. The only solution would be to execute him (Wang 1996: 10:316–317).

Moreover, while Wang conceded that ritual propriety was the general way to rectify a person's will, he insisted that laws were needed to punish those who repeatedly violated ritual propriety. For example, in commenting on the traitorous ministers of the Jin dynasty, Wang advocated punishing the traitors and unfilial sons so that loyalty and filial piety would be upheld. He considered that, facing harsh penalties, a disloyal person would not dare to become a traitor and an unfilial son would not dare to become a rebel. The function of harsh penalties was the converse of rituals. Penalties were not just to threaten transgressors with death but with stripping away their sense of honor and glory. The wrong doers would fear losing their honor and glory more than death (Wang 1996: 10:531).

The goal of educating the people was to lay the ground for an ethical society, at least to prevent the decline public morality. Wang suggested three ways to reach this goal. First, moderate the ruler's likes and dislikes by observances of ritual propriety. Wang reasoned that the ruler not only controlled the people's life and death and conditions of life; cosmologically, the ruler shared the same cosmic cycle of yin and yang with the people, which formed the medium in which they interacted (Wang 1996: 13:205). Wang held that an upright society was crucial for maintaining the harmony of the universe; hence, the ruler, the ministers, and the people should moderate their emotions and express them in due measure.

Second, show the people how to live properly, supported by the threat of rewards and punishments. In Wang's view, since even the wicked did not want to be called criminals but to be considered meritorious, if the ruler were to praise the people of good reputation and condemn wrong-doers, the people would choose the course of good reputation and avoid the road to notoriety (Wang 1996: 10:389). Appealing to the people's desire for honor and reputation, Wang suggested that they cultivate civility (*wen* 文) to refine their emotions and restrain them from excess. Moreover, in this way, excellent customs would be sustained.

Third, discourage the people from accepting heterodox teachings and poor habits. As noted, Wang favored righteousness over self-interest, and urged the noble people to lead the people with righteousness and good faith. In his view, Mencius was wise to dissuade the kings of Chu and Qin from going to war by an appeal to humaneness and righteousness rather than self-interest, because making self-interest a primary concern would encourage the people to value self-interest above even loyalty and filial piety (Wang 1996: 8:769). Since merchants were wont to pursue self-interest regardless of righteousness or humaneness, Wang advocated limiting their activities to the most basic necessities, stressing agriculture over commerce. In this way, however, Wang overlooked the positive function of commerce, for example, the movement of goods from one place to another, increasing the flow of goods and enhancing people's lives.

3.4   Wang Fuzhi's Ideal Politics: The Kingly Way

The Kingly Way (*wangdao* 王道) was Wang Fuzhi's ideal form of governance, which he hoped would be observed by subsequent rulers. The Kingly Way referred to the humane style of governance and institutions established by the sage kings of the Xia, Shang, and Zhou dynasties, as discussed in the *Mencius*. Wang asserted, "When kings Wen and Wu of the Zhou were alive, the Kingly Way prevailed in the world" (Wang 1996: 7:172). The heart of the Kingly Way is the virtue of humaneness, manifested in the ruler's loving and educating the people. "The Way is nothing but humaneness, if the ruler aims to protect the people and govern the world" (Wang 1996: 8:67).

Wang Fuzhi regarded the ideal of the Kingly Way as relevant to the conduct of all forms of governance, regardless of time or place. In his view, all forms of governance could draw upon the ideal of the Kingly Way. In particular, such measures as official recruitment, tax collection, military maneuvers, penalties, and ceremonies all depend on the ideal of the Kingly Way to be conducted appropriately (Wang 1996: 10:1180). To put it into practice, what was crucial was the monarch's state of mind: Was he attentive or heedless? He must keep on guard against being lazy, negligent, cruel, procrastinating, and hasty; he must recruit the worthy and promote educating the people; he must love the people and set up reasonable norms of conduct (Wang 1996: 10:1179).

Wang Fuzhi did not expect later rulers and dynasties to rigidly apply the ideal of the King Way. He understood that the established teachings and forms of governance were suitable for their times and places; but, a present ruler would need to adapt them to his situation by grasping their spirit, not insisting on the details of their policies and institutions. Their spirit was to retain the throne with humaneness and to govern the world with righteousness, while their fixed institutions were their methods of classifying officials and their duties (Wang 1996: 2:396). Humaneness and righteousness as an essence would last forever while institutions must change according to the time and situation.

Without grasping the spirit of the King Way, it would be difficult to realize it in practice. Even though the deeds of kings Wen and Wu were well documented, their own grandsons did not inherit it and could not carry it out (Wang 1996: 7:172), because their grandsons could not grasp the spirit of the Kingly Way. This fact reminds us of Zhuangzi's story of Wheelwright Bian 輪扁 in which it is said that, "When a sage dies his experience vanishes with him; the teachings in his book are no better than dirt" (Guo 1961: 490–491). While not denying the value of written records altogether, Wang allowed that words and texts had preserved and transmitted the "essential meaning (*jingyi* 精義)" of the sage kings—humaneness and righteousness: if a ruler could grasp this essential meaning, he would be able to restore the Kingly Way.

Wang Fuzhi believed that the spirit of the Kingly Way, that is, humaneness and righteousness, was to be expressed in the ruler's compassion and in his leadership. Once the ruler felt compassion arising, and preserved and expressed it, his inner humaneness and righteousness would suffice to sustain the four seas and benefit the myriad things (Wang 1996: 8:76). He described this manifesting the sprout of commiseration in kingly rule as fulfilling "the Way of inner sageliness and outer kingliness (*neishang waiwang zhi dao* 內聖外王之道)." That is, if a ruler were to cultivate himself fully and be brimming with humaneness, he would love the people and make efforts to protect them. The Zhou kings did this and became role models for their officials. They thus transformed the world without using rewards or punishments (Wang 1996: 7:239).

However, Wang Fuzhi did not think that every ruler could carry out the Kingly Way simply by extending their humaneness. Besides rectifying their mind, a person needed a seat of power, that is, rulership of a state or a dukedom and control over the rituals and institutions. He noted that the first Zhou king had moved the capital to Bin 豳 and secured suitable land for founding the Zhou kingdom, thus enabling his descendants to practice the Kingly Way (Wang 1996: 6:899). In his commentary on the *Mencius*, Wang supported the decision of King Xuan 齊宣王 of Qi to expand his state, insisting that a strong, large country was a prerequisite of practicing kingly governance. If a country was small, it would be difficult to defend its borders, not to mention governing it according to the ideal of the Kingly Way.

3.4.1   Inner Sageliness (neisheng 內聖)

In striving to realize the Kingly Way, the ruler must rectify his conduct by ritual propriety and concentrate on cultivating his virtue, especially humaneness and righteousness. Yao and Shun practiced proper governance and realized the Kingly Way by expressing their inner virtue, that is, their inner sageliness (Wang 1996: 11:153). With this precedent, later rulers didn't need to worry about reforming degenerate customs. They could focus on propagating virtues like humaneness and righteousness as the heart of good education, cultivation, and governance. Moreover, they would be role models for the people to emulate such that the people would care about each other and carry out the virtues of filial piety, fraternity, and interpersonal harmony. Indeed, they would become humane and righteous (Wang 1996: 8:495).

How could a ruler cultivate his humaneness? Wang Fuzhi first urged that he look within to pique his conscience and feel commiseration, keeping attentive to his moral sensitivity at all times (Wang 1996: 8:821). He should express his conscience and sense of commiseration not only when witnessing the suffering of others, but even when serving his parents and elder brothers. By nurturing his conscience and sense of commiseration, the ruler would be sincere, free of selfish desires, and regard the throne and empire as public assets. By putting these virtues into practice, he would act with utmost propriety and due measure, without excess or deficiency (Wang 1996: 7:104). Notably, Wang regarded being "free of selfish desire" as a condition for fulfilling humaneness. In fact, he sometimes asserted that a ruler who was "free of desire (*wuyu* 無欲)" could "discover the Kingly Way" (Wang 1996: 7:551). To be precise, "free of desire" meant being free of selfish desires, not Zhu Xi's and the Buddhists' more radical call to cut off all desires. By "free of desire," Wang was thinking of a sage king who would heed the Mandate of Heaven and attend to the people's needs, and not just strive to hold power. "Although his humaneness sustained the people in the world, he did not do it for the throne; although his achievements benefited the whole world, he did not do it to win the people's support. He just strove to carry out his duty to properly govern the people and affairs on behalf of Heaven" (Wang 1996: 7:551).

While being "free of desire" let the king to put public welfare before his own interests, it did not exclude his "desire to benefit the people." Instead, this latter sort of ethical desire should be regarded as consistent with heavenly principle and the virtue of humaneness. For instance, Wang Fuzhi argued that "The Kingly Way is based on having a pure mind and few desires, but this does not mean that living a simple life, being free of desires, and 'forgetting' external things would be sufficient to ensure that the king will extend his humaneness to all the people in the four seas" (Wang 1996: 8:118). On this point, Wang criticized the Song Emperor Gaozong 宋高宗 (1107–1187) for weakening the people's vitality and ceding the empire to the Jurchen with his weak, desireless personality. He cautioned that "A person with few desires will likely avoid taking on heavy responsibilities; hence, a robust Confucian scholar should be careful not to brag about having 'few desires' " (Wang 1996: 11:255–256).

Wang Fuzhi further advocated that rulers nurture their humaneness and righteousness by observing ritual propriety. By observing ritual propriety, the ruler would add luster to his humaneness and righteousness, and respond appropriately with humaneness in his seeing, hearing, words, and deeds (Wang 1996: 2:315). The reason is that ritual propriety is the due measures and manners established to express humaneness, and so the practice of it in turn becomes the method to cultivate humaneness. Hence observing ritual propriety became a method of cultivating humaneness. In particular, the practice of ritual propriety encouraged moderation, so one would avoid excess and impropriety, for example in the practice of filial piety, and realize humaneness (Wang 1996: 2:315). In this light, Wang reinterpreted Confucius' statement, "to overcome the self and return to ritual propriety is what is called humaneness" (*Analects* 12.1). Unlike the Song Confucians who separated the two tasks of overcoming the self and practicing ritual propriety, Wang insisted that practicing ritual propriety itself was overcoming the self. He held that by practicing ritual propriety one overcame selfishness and expressed interpersonal regard. One who did not observe propriety would still harbor selfish desires. However, even if one has overcome the self, one still must master ritual propriety. Thus, to cultivate humaneness, one must strictly abide by the rules of hearing, seeing, and thinking as endowed by Heaven and carry them out sincerely; in this way, one's mind will be illuminated with heavenly principle and one can deal properly with the myriad affairs of the world (Wang 1996: 6:765).

3.4.2   Outer Kingliness (waiwang 外王)

Wang Fuzhi believed that the ideal of the Kingly Way involved the ruler's inner sageliness giving rise to his outer kingliness. Like Confucius, Wang assumed that the conduct of the nobility was emulated by the common people and played a critical role in shaping social morality. He observed that a noble person's rise would lead others to be noble in the world, while a petty person's emergence would incline people to be petty minded, as well (Wang 1996: 7:709). To make the world more just and harmonious, the ruler should cultivate himself and be a moral exemplar for the people. If a ruler could realize utmost modesty and impartiality and encourage the people to better themselves every day, he would lead them to uphold the five cardinal ethical relationships by example; they would perform good deeds without persuasion, and a pure and simple society would be formed without resort to punishments or rewards (Wang 1996: 8:228–229).

Wang Fuzhi associated this proposal with a stress on filial piety and mercy. In order to incline the people to filial piety, the ruler must display it himself. In order to incline others to be merciful, the ruler must show mercy. By leading the people by example, the ruler could transform the social morality and reform the world (Wang 1996: 6:596). Wang argued that the ruler's behavior could have such positive effects, not just because it was a spectacle on high, but through the ruler's moral *qi* interacting with and influencing the people's *qi*. Their *qi* endowments would feed off and share the same cosmic *qi* and spirit (*shen* 神). They thus were thought to move each other unconsciously, whether to be sagely or heedless (*kuang* 狂), shrewd or stupid (Wang 1996: 12:43).

Wang Fuzhi further advocated ritual propriety as a means to rectify people's conduct, "For self-cultivation, one won't feel at ease unless observing ritual propriety; for governance, one won't win the people's respect without observing ritual propriety" (Wang 1996: 7:818). Ever since ancient times, the emperors and kings of China governed and instructed the people by ritual propriety; moreover, later generations followed this precedent as the Way of the early sage kings, they also established the standard of humaneness for ritual propriety (Wang 1996: 7:329). Wang held that the practice of ritual propriety was conducive to harmony and peace and instilled the people with integrity and moderation. Applied to the empire, it could induce a peaceful transformation; applied to a region, it could banish vulgar, harmful customs. A person who practiced ritual propriety would embellish his personality; if the people were to adopt such conduct, as well, they would distance themselves from evil and wickedness even if they did not understand it thoroughly (Wang 1996: 7:904).

Due to his respect for the early sage kings, Wang Fuzhi sometimes viewed the Kingly Way as the key to a magic transformation. In his comments on Mencius' account of such kingly transformations, Wang imagined that when the sage king traveled around the state, or visited a suburb of the capital, his subjects would be transformed simply by coming into his positive aura. Were the ruler to fret that the people were not deferential, a noble person would arise who grasped ruler's concern and lead people to be deferential; were the king to fear that Heaven was not easily moved, Heaven would respond, favor his plan, and vitalize the people. All such happenings would occur at a deeper level than positive social institutions and education (Wang 1996: 8:843).

In more realistic moments, Wang admitted that inner sageliness had limited effect. For example, whether inner sageliness could give rise to the Kingly Way depended, not only on the ruler's inner virtue, but also on the time and situation. In his comments on Confucius' failures in politics, Wang conceded that while Confucius had sagely virtue, he still was not appointed to office; hence, he could not propagate the Kingly Way from the state of Lu 魯, despite his wish to establish another Zhou house in the east (Wang 1996: 8:954). Next, Wang denied that the Kingly Way could induce a sort of magic transformation in his notes on Zhu Xi's commentary on the *Mencius*. Wang argued that even the ancient sage kings needed proper institutions and measures to govern the state, and could not lead by whim or fancy. "If, when the sage kings ruled the world, they did things on impulse, such as just taking a quick glance before deciding that a thing was square or circular, just briefly hearing some music before deciding how well it expressed the harmony of the five notes, or just considering the issue briefly before deciding that humaneness should prevail in the world ... This would not have been the conduct of Confucian sages but that of Buddhist patriarchs, spouting exaggerations and inauspicious chants" (Wang 1996: 6:987). Unlike Zhu Xi and other earlier Neo-Confucians, Wang did not believe that a ruler of perfect virtue would necessarily provide good and sagely governance. Being virtuous could only lay the foundation and chart the course for realizing sagely governance. However, achieving sagely governance would require much more, such as regulating the great clans, governing the realm, and putting the world in order. How could being enlightened about virtue be sufficient for effectively putting the world in order? Moreover, self, family, state, and the empire each has its own properties and principles, and they should not be confused or conflated with each other, even though humaneness runs through them all (Wang 1996: 6:440–441). In short, even though the harmony in each of these realms is rooted in humaneness or the principle of life, the measures for managing them differ. Therefore, one should not expect the people to be transformed or the Kingly Way to be realized if the ruler simply rectifies himself and experiences self-realization.

In effect, Wang shed the sort of pure talk in which previous Neo-Confucians engaged, and expected Confucians to turn their positive good will into real life practice. In his view, it was not enough to claim one affecting his kin, it was necessary for him to demonstrate his affection in filial conduct and extend it to others, including providing for their liveli-hood and security. Citing the Duke of Zhao's construction of the city of Xie, Wang pointed out that a ruler should devise a calendar for farming, have channels be dug to let field water flow into rivers and out to sea, have the weeds and forests removed for cropland, and have the land cleared for fields and houses, and so on. Hence, unlike previous Neo-Confucians who had tended to see an opposition between utilitarian merit and virtue, Wang insisted that utilitarian merit was the natural product of sagely virtue and should not be disregarded. Without utilitarian merit, the sage kings could not benefit the people and the people's assets and standard of living would wane (Wang 1996: 1:960).

In summary, Wang advocated that the Kingly Way was the Way of humaneness, to be realized by practicing and propagating ritual propriety. A ruler who at the same time cultivated humaneness within would realize his virtue as inner sageliness. When he manifested his virtue in conducting affairs, it would result in kingly governance. In order to cultivate virtue, the ruler must stay sincere and reverent in observing ritual propriety; in relation to governance, he must respect and feel affection for the people and be reverent in conducting affairs and practicing ritual propriety. In this fashion, his inner sageliness would conduce to outer kingliness.

Despite Wang Fuzhi's practical reformulation, the Kingly Way remained a utopian ideal in the history of China. Wang held that the Kingly Way arose in primitive society when exemplary tribal chiefs were humane and unselfish, and sincerely served the tribe. But, this ideal was not directly applicable to the bureaucratic regimes of imperial China since the Han dynasty. As Wang noted, society in imperial China was complicated and vast. To govern, a ruler had to adapt various methods from regulating his family to coordinating different people and states; simple extensions of humaneness and righteousness would not be enough. Also, people became increasingly cunning and opportunistic as society became ever more com-petitive. A ruler must rein in utilitarian uses of humaneness and righteous-ness, lest certain unintended consequences arise, as suggested by Zhuangzi: "Adapt humaneness and righteousness to reform the people, and thieves will steal by means of humaneness and righteousness" (Watson 1968: 110). The result would not be putting the empire in good order, but reducing it to chaos. Therefore, while the ideal of the Kingly Way can be used to remind the ruler to be humane and righteous in leading the peo-ple, for example as a humane condition on rule by law, it cannot be con-sidered an appropriate or practical way to govern in the modern world.

3.5   CONCLUSION

Wang Fuzhi's ruminations on the Manchu overthrow of the Ming led him to emphasize the distinctions between Chinese and barbarian, man and woman, and noble people and the petty minded. He hoped that people of each of type would keep to their "natural" category without undue intermingling or mixing. This separation policy reflected not only his fear and hatred of the northern nomads, but also his ineptness at dealing with the petty minded. Nevertheless, he believed that if a ruler was to govern the state properly by education and ritual propriety, society could be harmonious, and acrimony and conflict would be prevented.

In practice, Wang Fuzhi advocated enlightened rule, with clear roles set forth for the emperor and the prime minister, strict propriety and discipline for the officials, and moral education of the common people. He criticized the Ming founder's selfishness and suspiciousness, which led to the low salary system for officials that bred official corruption. He also stressed the importance of ensuring the sustenance of the common people, for which they would support the emperor, and he lamented the Ming emperor's irresponsibility and neglect of the people's welfare. He also advocated educating the people by ritual propriety. However, he betrayed his ideals when he advised against overthrowing a tyrant at the expense of the people's welfare. Evidently, he was a prisoner of his time, unable to come up with a new kind of remedy for the inherent evils of the imperial rule.

He continued to hope a sage king would appear to save the empire, and did not imagine establishing new official institutions to avoid the evils of empire. He firmly held that if a ruler were to practice the Kingly Way, on condition that he adapted it to the current situation, he would govern the empire well. Again, he regarded the virtues of humaneness and righteousness as the spirit of the Kingly Way, to be manifested in practical governmental measures and institutions, from rectifying oneself, regulating one's clan, governing the state, to putting the empire in order. Although he remained at the level of theory and did not offer practical measures, he consciously distinguished himself from his idealistic Neo-Confucian predecessors who had dreamt that a sage king would naturally transform the people by virtue of his charisma.

As to moral learning, Wang Fuzhi still accepted Confucius' precept that a truly noble person would morally transform people around him, just like the wind bends the grass. He further insisted that universal Confucian moral education would refine the people and make the world harmonious. In his words, a noble person's rise would conduce to the proliferation of noble people in the world; while a petty person's emergence would incline others to be petty minded. Given the uncertainty of human affairs, only if all people were to commit themselves to cultivating their virtue could the empire remain harmonious. These considerations lead us to the formation of Wang Fuzhi's moral thought.

BIBLIOGRAPHY

EARLY CHINESE TEXTS

Fan, Ye 范曄, *Hou Han Shu* 后漢書 (*The History of the Later Han*), Beijing: Zhonghua Shuju 北京: 中華書局, 1965

Guo, Qingfan 郭慶藩, *Zhuangzi Jishi* 莊子集釋 (*Collected Commentaries on the Zhuangzi*), Beijing: Zhonghua Shuju 北京:中華書局, 1961

Han, Fei 韓非, *Han Fei Zi Xin Jiaozhu* 韓非子新校注 (*A New Proofreading and Annotation to the Hang Fei Zi*), Chen Qiyou陳奇猷 Annotated. Shanghai: Shanghai Guji Chubanshe, 2000

Huang, Zongxi 黃宗羲, *Huang Zongxi Quanji* 黃宗羲全集 (1–22 冊) (*The Complete Works of Huang Zongxi*), Volume 1–22, Hangzhou: Zhejiang Guji Chubanshe 杭州:浙江古籍出版社, 2012

Li, Xiangfeng 黎翔鳳, *Guanzi Jiaozhu* 管子校注 (*A Correction and Annotation of the Guanzi*), Beijing: Zhonghua Shuju, 2004

Lou, Yulie 樓宇烈, *Wang Bi Ji Jiaoshi* 王弼集校釋 (*An Exegesis of Wang Bi's Works*), Beijing: Zhonghua Shuju 北京: 中華書局, 1980

Ouyang, Xiu 歐陽修, *Xin Wudai Shi* 新五代史 (*New Version of the History of the Five Dynasties*), Beijing: Zhonghua Shuju 北京: 中華書局, 1974

Qu, Wanli 屈萬里, Shangshu Jishi 尚書集釋 (Collected Notes on the Book of Documents), Shanghai: Zhongxi Shuju 上海: 中西書局, 2014

Wang, Fuzhi 王夫之 *Chuanshan Quanshu* 船山全書 (1–16 冊) (*Complete Works of Wang Chuanshan*, Volume 1–16), Changsha: Yuelu Shushe 长沙: 岳麓書社, 1996

Wang, Yu 王敔, *Daxing Fujun Xingshu* 大行府君行述 (*A Brief Biographical Sketch of my Diseased Father*), in *Chuanshan Quanshu* 船山全書16 (*The Complete Works of Chuanshan*), Volume 16, Changsha: Yuelu Shushe 長沙: 岳麓書社, 1996

SECONDARY SOURCES

Gadamer, Hans Georg, *Hermeneutics, Religion and Ethics*, trans. Joel Weinsheimer, New Haven: Yale University Press 1999

Huang, Ray, *1587: A Year of No Significance*, New Haven and London: Yale University Press, 1981

Wang, Fansen 王汎森, *Ten Essays on the Scholar's Thought at the Late Ming and Early Qing* (*Wanming Qing Chu Sixiang ShiLun* 晚明清初思想十論), Shanghai: Fudan University Press, 2004

Watson, Burton, *The Complete Works of Chuang Tzu*, New York: Columbia University Press, 1968

CHAPTER 4

Moral Reconstruction

Besides Wang Fuzhi's criticisms of official misrule during the Ming dynasty, he argued that the teachings of Wang Yangming had led to the moral degeneration of Ming society and institutions. In particular, he argued that the teachings of Wang Yangming and his followers had caused people to shed their sense of shame and honor, which opened the door for bandits and thieves to thrive and the Manchus to invade (Wang 1996: 12:371). In Wang's view, by the Ming dynasty, mainstream Neo-Confucians of both the Cheng-Zhu and the Wang Yangming schools alike had incorporated Buddhist elements and did not prioritize the ethical teachings of the early sage kings, thus undermining not only their students' cultivation efforts, but the social ethics in society. Wang therefore dedicated himself to removing the Buddhist elements from Confucianism by offering fresh interpretations of the Confucian classics. His aim was to rectify the Cheng-Zhu School readings of the classics and purge the Chan Buddhist elements from the teachings of the Wang Yangming School.

Beyond restoring social ethics during the late Ming, Wang Fuzhi also advocated a sort of moral heroism. In support of moral heroism, he cited Guan Ning (管寧 158–241 CE; Three Kingdoms), who upheld humaneness (*ren* 仁) and preserved the distinction between human beings and the birds and beasts by promoting the Way of Confucianism in anarchic times (Wang 1996: 10:346). Wang held that if even in such dark times noble people could manifest humaneness and righteousness within, they would spread the seeds of those virtues to others and assist in maintaining an

M. Tan, *Wang Fuzhi's Reconstruction of Confucianism*, https://doi.org/10.1007/978-3-030-80263-9_4

ethical society. He pinned this hope on the possibility of awakening and preserving the sprouts of humaneness and moral conscience latent in the mind of every person. He regarded individual conscience as a potent personal resource for resisting the degeneration of social ethics and maintaining positive ethical customs. Consequently, he focused his moral reconstruction efforts on the project of Confucian self-cultivation.

Like Mencius before him, Wang Fuzhi held that every human being was endowed with the sprout of humaneness at birth and could nurture and realize it through learning and reflection, while feeling contemptuous of obtuse people in society who only concerned themselves about food and sex. He insisted it was the responsibility of noble people to preserve their humaneness within so as to stir the moral conscience latent in other people's minds. He admitted that food and sex were essential to human life but denied they were the be all and end all. He further urged that dignity and righteousness were more precious than official rank, food, or sex. For this reason, he expressed dismay at the opportunism of officials like Feng Dao 馮道 (882–954), notorious for supporting usurpers to preserve his favor at court and high rank. Feng had justified his conduct with the platitude, "Whatever one does should be practical." In his comments, Wang replied, "What was Feng Dao's practical concern? It was merely the concerns of the birds and beasts: how to seize food from a brother or to have sex with a neighbor's daughter. His behavior was just like pigs and dogs feeding on dirt, and deer and moose producing offspring through random sexual intercourse" (Wang 1996: 10:1127). In short, Wang criticized Feng Dao for pursuing selfish interest without regard for righteousness or ritual propriety.

Wang Fuzhi distinguished human beings from the birds and beasts on the basis of knowledge of the principle of life: humaneness. Although human beings shared perception and movement with animals, what distinguished them from animals was their knowledge of human nature—the principle of life. Wang argued that this principle of life also embraced the principles of perception and movement and the appetites of food and sex; however, crucially, it grounded the humaneness and righteousness inherent in the mind. Consequently, by fully grasping the principle of life a person would be well on the way to becoming a realized human being (Wang 1996: 8:675).

At the cosmic level, Wang Fuzhi defined the principle of life as the productive power of the Great Harmony. It was to be realized in the human mind as humaneness and human nature, and manifested in human conduct as righteousness and ritual propriety. Consequently, the mind, human nature, and humaneness together formed the nucleus of the Way of humaneness, in Wang's view. To cultivate and practice humaneness, a person would need to preserve the nature, nurture compassion, and practice ritual propriety.

With this cosmological grounds for conducting moral cultivation, Wang distinguished him from contemporaries who stressed only the sociopolitical virtues of Neo-Confucianism. For example, while Gu Yanwu and Yan Yuan emphasized practicality and achievement, Wang stressed rectifying the mind and embracing righteousness as a requirement for the ethical pursuit of profit and achievement. Unlike Chen Que 陳確 who simply denounced the Cheng-Zhu School, Wang reconstructed Neo-Confucianism based on his in-depth critiques of both the Cheng-Zhu and Wang Yangming schools. To a certain extent, Huang Zongxi was close to Wang in examining the Ming Confucians in his compilation. *Biographies of the Ming Confucian Scholars* (*Mingru Xuean* 明儒學案), but Huang did not establish a system of his own, nor did he elevate self-cultivation to the sphere of "assisting in the transforming and nourishing process of Heaven and Earth." Wang justified each person's contribution to the Great Harmony by preserving and nourishing their harmonious *qi*, thereby offering a meaningful life goal for people as a positive alternative to Buddhist Nirvana.

Wang Fuzhi, however, tended to exaggerate each person's independence and integrity in facing social situations. Mencius had said, "A great man will not be dissipated by the power of riches or honors, swayed from principle by poverty or mean conditions, or bent by power or force" (Mencius 2A.2). Wang had the discipline to uphold Mencius' maxim and was praised as a "superman" and "maverick" for enduring bitter hardship and poverty without complaint (Hu 1996; Zhang 1996). But, how could he expect others to follow his example? After witnessing how easily the people had switched their loyalty to the Manchu conquerors, Wang began to appreciate the importance of sustenance and livelihood in people's lives, and how the life necessities provided ballast for their nascent moral sense. Although he ultimately gave up his hope that gifted mavericks would appear among the people, Wang still placed hope in the scholar-officials, which was why he condemned Feng Dao so harshly. However, to his dismay, Wang found that many scholar-officials were like Feng Dao, and responded to situations pragmatically and did not uphold principle during chaotic times, except when if it was profitable or they were compelled to do so. Indeed, the majority of people could not uphold principle or act as a great person in life and death situations, so Wang's teaching and example of moral heroism did not gain a wide following. Nonetheless, Wang did identify what was crucial for maintaining a healthy, harmonious society; the virtue and practice of humaneness.

4.1   Humaneness

Wang Fuzhi based his account of humaneness on Heaven. Heaven was the foundation of traditional Chinese beliefs, owing to its constancy and eternity. Confucius appealed to Heaven to assuage his fears when Huan Tui 桓 魋 threatened to kill him (Analects 7.23). Dong Zhongshu 董仲舒 based his thought on Heaven, asserting, "The great source of the Way or *Dao* is Heaven. Since Heaven does not change, the Way will not change, either" (Ban 1962: 2518–2519). Wang affirmed that Heaven was the origin of humaneness, stressing, "Heaven is the whole of humaneness, and humaneness is the mind of Heaven. They are identical" (Wang 1996: 12:66). Thus, humaneness existed originally and naturally as endowed by Heaven and was not just an acquired human attribute that was read back into Heaven.

As to the affirmation that "Heaven is the whole of humaneness," Wang Fuzhi explained that while Heaven was the origin of all creatures, humaneness was the impulse of life. Heaven endowed the impulse of life in every creature. "Humaneness is what all living creatures must have. But life is the natural impulse of the humaneness of Heaven above" (Wang 1996: 10:1122). "Humaneness is the principle of the production of the myriad things. For this reason, once a thing has been produced and its nature is formed, it will follow its nature long as it lives" (Wang 1996: 12:157). In short, humaneness is the productive and sustaining function of Heaven. Without Heaven, there would be no humaneness, ultimately, no human life.

As to the significance of "Humaneness is the mind of Heaven," Wang Fuzhi interpreted humaneness as the intention of Heaven to produce and sustain every living being. Although Heaven and Earth were not conscious *per se*, their operation of producing all living creatures was fixed and unceasing. Wang likened this ceaseless operation to human will (Wang 1996: 1:227–228). In other words, he took the mind of Heaven as a metaphor for Heaven's ceaseless production and sustenance of the myriad things. Once a creature was conceived, its process of maturation and growth would continue until it reached maturity. The process could be likened to the human will to produce a result. In short, humaneness as the mind of Heaven referred to the ceaseless operation of Heaven's productivity.

Wang Fuzhi also affirmed that, as the basic impulse of human nature, humaneness expressed the principle of life and was inherent in the mind. While a person's humaneness would be stirred whenever they responded to and interacted with other people or things, it was prior to and independent of any such response or interaction (Wang 1996: 12:203). In other words, as the principle of life present in the mind as the nature, humaneness was latent, but it would be aroused once one's compassion was stirred. For example, anyone would feel unease and concern when seeing an infant crawl near a well. With this explanation, Wang presented humaneness as something detached, like a mirror, reflecting but not pursuing, a Daoist description of the mind. His reason for this was that he took humaneness to be an altruistic impulse, unaffected by one's inclinations or preferences, nor swayed by their desires (Wang 1996: 12:157).

Wang Fuzhi also characterized humaneness as the principle of love; for the act of sustaining the life of a person or other creature would be an act of love. People first generally manifest the principle of love as filial piety, that is, in their childhood love for their parents, an impulse shared by all human beings (Wang 1996: 8:483). Wang elaborated, "Only because a person does not neglect this principle of life but manifests it as humaneness, do they love their parents as their first manifestation of humaneness in knowledge and actions" (Wang 1996: 13:676). Wang regarded a person's love for their parents as an instinctive expression of the principle of life. He held that all human beings initially express humaneness as filial piety and thus manifest the principle of life. In this way, Wang justified his account of filial piety as a primary virtue in moral cultivation.

4.1.1   Humaneness as Commiserating Mind

Corresponding to the productive impulse of Heaven, Wang Fuzhi believed that human beings manifested humaneness through their commiserating mind, the source of filial piety. With this commiserating mind, a person would feel unease when witnessing the suffering or death of another. Thus moved, they would go on to restrain their desires, cherish the lives of others, and act thoughtfully. Wang regarded the commiserating mind as the "mind that cannot bear" (to witness the suffering of others) (*Mencius*

2A6), which he called the inner voice of Heaven. He commented, "Once humaneness has been stirred by Heaven [as compassion], it is deeply rooted in the human mind. It will be manifested as one's natural love of one's parents. Consequently, one will extend love to other people and creatures in the world and establish the Way of humanity" (Wang 1996: 10:1122).

Wang Fuzhi supported his understanding of the commiserating mind by reference to Confucius' term "peace of mind (*xin an* 心安)" (*Analects* 17.21). "As [the root of] the commiserating mind, humaneness is the moral compass of what one ought and ought not to do. A person who heeds this inner voice of humaneness will have peace of mind. This inner voice is prior to the moral norms or even the Way because it is their source" (Wang 1996: 8:920). For example, when a filial son sincerely serves his parents, he serves them with his commiserating mind. It is this commiserating mind that moves him to carry out the duties of a filial son without fail. It is also this commiserating mind that impels him to make adjustments in serving his parents (Wang 1996: 8:476). Anyone would feel distressed to witness the suffering or death of a close family member; anyone would strive to save them without thought of personal risk. Anyone who failed to save them would feel regret for the rest of their days. As Wang observed, "A person may set a limit on their love for others; however, they will stand ready to sacrifice their own life to save a close family member" (Wang 1996: 10:1123).

Although Wang regarded the commiserating mind as the source of filial piety and the origin of the rules of propriety in deportment, sight, speech, and movement (Wang 1996: 12:66), he did not deem it a sufficient ground for cultivating humaneness, and also stressed the study and practice of norms and rituals, to avoid falling into moral subjectivism. In Wang Fuzhi's view, Wang Yangming's subjectivist teaching that each person's inborn knowledge of the good was their ultimate standard of moral conduct had led to the widespread breakdown of people's ethics during the Ming, when the weak-will identified inborn knowledge of the good with their selfish desires.[1]

---

[1] Wang Fuzhi criticized Wang Yangming because he believed that the latter had proposed that inborn knowledge of the good was, in itself, neither good nor evil (Wang 1996: 13:677). Wang Fuzhi was on the mark because Wang Yangming had identified inborn knowledge of the good with the void and subtle perception (*xu ling ming jue* 虛靈明覺): "The mind is the master of human body. Yet, the void and subtle perception of this mind is the so-called natu-

To avoid the trap of moral subjectivism, Wang Fuzhi sought a way to balance peace of mind with observing norms and rituals: "A person whose mind is not at peace when he receives a title should not accept the title. A person whose mind is satisfied with a title should not heed his mind when the title is not good enough" (Wang 1996: 2:319). "Title" here refers to an official position and involves norms, rituals, responsibilities, and renown. Thus, in Wang's view, realizing humaneness included striking the right balance between peace of mind and observance of norms and rituals.

Wang Fuzhi explained this as a matter of balancing humaneness, righteousness, and ritual propriety. While humaneness was first to be manifested as the commiserating mind, one had to cultivate ritual propriety to guide the commiserating mind and grasp righteousness to distinguish right and wrong in making moral choices. On the one hand, ritual propriety and righteousness were grounded in humaneness: Righteousness took root once a person heeded their commiserating mind and achieved peace of mind, while ritual propriety would commence when they assigned a thing to its proper place or an action to its kind. On the other hand, the humane mind had to embrace righteousness in its expressions, to fully realize humaneness. Humaneness and righteousness both required ritual propriety to express and confirm them in action. That was why Confucius recommended that one cultivate humaneness by mastering the self and practicing ritual propriety (Wang 1996: 2:315). With this mutual support, Wang Fuzhi tried to guide the love arising from one's commiserating mind with righteousness and ritual propriety, and prevent it from excess. For example, guided by righteousness and ritual propriety, a funeral mourner would refrain from considering self-mutilation as a way to mourn the passing of a parent. They would be guided to satisfy humaneness and express their sorrow, never to the extent of self-harm, in violation of filial piety. In sum, righteousness and ritual propriety served to guide one's expressions of love to achieve humaneness and harmony.

Wang Fuzhi also distinguished between humaneness and love to avoid moral subjectivism, such as Wang Yangming's inborn knowledge of the good. He held that, while love was an emotion and involved vital force or *qi*, humaneness was the nature and rooted in principle (*li* 理). "Love is not yet humaneness; it is the principle of love that is humaneness … Love is an emotion, while the principle of love is the nature" (Wang 1996: 6:1060).

ral inborn knowledge of the good" (Wang 2012: 104). Although the void and subtle perception can discern good and evil, it itself is beyond good and evil.

Wang offered this analysis because he knew that a person's love could be excessive, obsessive, lacking, or null. He thus explained humaneness as the meeting of love with principle, or reasonable love. He viewed the reasonable love as the expression and function of the principle of love. He asserted, "To make manifest the content of humaneness, we call it the principle of love (*ai zhi li* 愛之理). To distinguish the nature from the emotions and humaneness from non-humaneness, we could say that humaneness is reasonable love (*li zhi ai* 理之愛)" (Wang 1996: 6:1061).

Wang Fuzhi used an example to elucidate how humaneness was the meeting of love with principle. He noted that a person's fraternal love of his younger brother would not manifest humaneness if he did not express his emotion of love with probity and propriety. To manifest humaneness in his fraternal love, his manifestation of that love would need to resemble those of the sage emperor Shun: Shun's younger brother Xiang 象 often schemed to kill him, but Shun still loved him and openly discussed his joys and cares with him. "For most people, their love for their younger brother would still just be love; to Shun, however, his love of Xiang was the meeting of love with the principle that they inherited from their parents" (Wang 1996: 6:1061). In other words, only fraternal love that was expressed *like* Shun's could be called humaneness. The fraternal love of most people was based on the natural affection of their shared *qi*, but they did not know principle or why they should be fraternal. Shun's fraternal love manifested humaneness because he knew he shared not only *qi* but the principle of life with Xiang; in this respect, his love was not influenced by personal interest or emotion. Humaneness among family members should transcend personal concerns, even life and death, and manifest the meeting of the *qi* and principle of life shared among siblings.

By regarding humaneness as the commiserating mind, Wang Fuzhi, like Confucius before him, registered its physical-psychological basis and justified it as a universal and inalienable feature of human beings. Moreover, to avoid falling into moral subjectivism, Wang characterized it as reasonable love to be distinguished from most people's emotional love, cautioning, "Scholars must avoid identifying the commiserating mind directly with love … The commiserating mind is humaneness, while love is only love. The former belongs to the nature while the latter belongs to the emotions" (Wang 1996: 6:1066). In this way, Wang sought to rectify the popular view that the emotions and even the selfish desires were the human mind. As Li Zhi (1527–1602) proclaimed, "It is normal for the human mind to be selfish. A person must be selfish before their mind is exposed [to phenomena]. Without selfish desires, there would be no human mind" (Li 2010: 526). Moreover, to ensure the proper expression of the commiserating mind, Wang insisted that it be guided by righteousness and ritual propriety, thus correcting Wang Gen's and Li Zhi's neglect of norms and rules.

4.1.2 Humaneness as Filial Piety to Serve Parents and Heaven

Wang Fuzhi regarded filial piety as an instinctive love arising from the principle of life as well as each person's earliest expression of humaneness. Again, he defined humaneness as a reasonable love or love that meets principle. Was filial piety also a form of love that meets with principle? Wang replied in the affirmative, observing that all natural things and creatures manifest principle. He wrote, "Principle comes from Heaven. Whatever exists naturally manifests principle" (Wang 1996: 12:438). Hence, because filial piety is an instinctive form of love, it is a matter of love meeting principle.

Wang Fuzhi did not think, however, that an instinctive love like filial piety would ensure that one would cultivate humaneness. He viewed filial piety as a stirring of humaneness, and urged students to earnestly practice filial piety and observe the ritual rules. He noted that when a bird hatched, it would soon have the instinctive knowledge and ability needed to live out its days. In contrast, a human baby would need to learn and think, which birds lacked. By learning and thinking, a human being can develop its sensitivity, knowledge, and conduct (Wang 1996: 13:675). In this respect, Wang's filial piety was similar to Mencius' four beginnings: basically good, but requiring a positive environment and cultivation.

Wang Fuzhi also advocated that human life became meaningful in the way people manifested humaneness, commencing with their manifestations of filial piety. One who failed to manifest filial piety and humaneness would be a walking corpse, a moral zombie. Wang affirmed:

> The glory of my life lies in glorifying those who gave me life. The extension of my life lies in the extension of my commiserating mind. If I did not glorify those who gave me life, but just glorified my own life, what greater shame could there be than this? If I did not extend my commiserating mind, but just extended my own life, then the days of my life would just be days of death. (Wang 1996: 3:496–497)

"Glorify those who gave me life" expressed Wang's filial spirit. "To extend my commiserating mind" referred to his humaneness. Thus, the meaning of life lay in one's dedicated filial and humane practice, not in one's longevity or physical health. Longevity and physical health, without humaneness, are the life of a bird or beast.

From the cosmic perspective, Wang Fuzhi regarded filial piety as the proper way to serve Heaven and Earth. At this level, one's filial duty is to love every creature in the world, expanding the Confucian sphere of care to "assist in the transforming and nourishing processes of Heaven and Earth." The *Book of Changes* and *Zhuangzi* both teach that all creatures are formed by yin-yang intercourse. They depict Heaven and Earth as cosmic manifestations of yang and yin, while Qian 乾 and Kun 坤 epitomize their virtues, respectively. As to the remote origins of human life, Heaven and Earth, Qian and Kun, yang and yin, are all our origins, our ancestors. As to causation, however, Heaven and Earth produce human beings indirectly through human parents. Hence, by serving their parents with filial piety, children are serving Heaven and Earth: "There is no Qian anywhere else, my father is the Qian that gave life to me; there is no Kun anywhere else, my mother is the Kun that completed me" (Wang 1996: 12:353). "Serving one's father with respect is serving Heaven. Serving one's mother with love is serving Earth" (Wang 1996: 12:352). People ought to serve their parents before thinking of widely serving Heaven and Earth; for it was our parents who gave life to us and raised us. A person who forsook their parents and sought to love Heaven and Earth, even if they were to love their parents later, would lack compassion and the heart of being unable to witness the suffering of others (Wang 1996: 12:352).

Wang Fuzhi thus both defended the Confucian tenet that a person can serve Heaven only by practicing filial piety and justified Mencius' teaching of graded love. That is, Wang underscored that even though other creatures share the same origin as human beings, Heaven and Earth, people should prioritize love for their kind, because their parents are of the same species. Moreover, although one shares the same genes and ancestry as other people, a person should prioritize their filial and fraternal love, for they are directed at kin with common *qi* and nature. Wang criticized the Mohists and Catholics for failing to understand properly graded love. In his view, by stressing the duty to love Heaven or the Lord over filial piety for one's parents, and regarding all people as brothers and sisters, they had denied the natural love that people feel intensely toward their close family members (Wang 1996: 6:974–975, 1:1015–1016). Wang held that it would be hypocritical to accept such unnatural heterodox teachings, which undermine authentic love and humaneness.

Wang Fuzhi's teaching of graded love, however, had problems of its own. When explaining why a person's parents were a microcosm of Heaven and Earth, Wang asserted that man and Heaven were the same in principle (*li* 理) and vital force (*qi* 氣). And, when parents had a baby, their offspring bore the same principle and vital force they had received from Heaven. At this level, Wang acknowledged no gap between one's parents and Heaven, which supported the notion that serving one's parents would be serving Heaven (Wang 1996: 12:352). However, Wang also regarded parents as the interface between Heaven and their child, and justified the notion of graded love with the notion that one served one's parents first and only later served Heaven. But, if Heaven and man are the same in principle and *qi*, why shouldn't a person be able to serve their parents and Heaven simultaneously, and live at one with Heaven by following the nature? Wouldn't it be redundant for a person to serve and achieve oneness with Heaven and Earth only after they had served their parents? The Daoist teaching of following nature and the Mohist teaching of impartial regard both propose directly serving and being one with Heaven and are more theoretically consistent than Wang in this regard.

4.1.3   Why Does Humaneness Need to Be Cultivated?

Since humaneness is endowed in human nature and activated as the commiserating mind or filial piety in life situations, why does it need to be cultivated? Wang Fuzhi, like Mencius, blamed human desires for causing one's humaneness to be obstructed and atrophy.[2] Citing the *Mencius*, Wang said that, without exception, a person's original pure *qi*, which was restored by the night vapor (*yeqi* 夜氣; Mencius' term for a person's revived sense of conscience or humaneness), would be tainted by the desires that are aroused during the day. To make their humaneness resilient, a person had to continuously cultivate it and reduce the obstruction of the desires (Wang 1996: 1:712). For example, when seeing others in

[2] In the beginning of 3.1, Wang Fuzhi affirmed that as the correct course of human life and nature, humaneness would arise spontaneously, and be immune from the influence of preference and desires. That view emphasized the spontaneously arising of humaneness. In the present context, Wang focused on one's expansion of humaneness when competing with desires in daily life conduct.

misery, people would feel pity or compassion. However, most people would soon disregard those feelings, for they did not grasp humaneness and were driven by selfish concerns. Thus, a person had to nurture and extend the commiserating mind to preserve their humaneness.

Wang Fuzhi considered the commiserating mind to be instinctive (*tian-neng* 天能) while holding that nurturing and extending commiseration took effort (*renmou* 人謀). Instinct alone could not make a person be consistently humane, so Wang insisted that people make efforts to nurture and extend the commiserating mind. He characterized the commiserating mind as the innocent child-mind (*chizi zhi xin* 赤子之心) and urged that people nurture and extend it by nurturing their feelings of shame and honor, respect and deference, and so on. Wang thought of the preserved innocent child-mind as the body (*ti* 體) and its extension as the function (*yong* 用) in one's cultivation of humaneness. If one only nurtured the innocent child-mind but did not to extend it, as by supporting one's parents and being kind to others, the child-mind would atrophy and turn insensitive (Wang 1996: 1:203).

As to cultivating humaneness, Wang Fuzhi compared the mind to a vessel and humaneness to its contents. To make the mind replete with humaneness, one had to act humanely by observing ritual propriety. Wang also likened the mind and humaneness to a seed and the germ. To sprout and grow, a seed does not rely solely on the germ, but it depends on external factors, as well. Growth begins with the coming of spring and April showers, and continues under gentle breezes and warm sunlight. The seed absorbs water and nutrients and vital *qi*; finally, its outer shell breaks and sprouts appear. Similarly, a noble person cultivates humaneness by learning to accumulate it, by introspecting to penetrate it, by thinking to grasp it, and by practicing ritual propriety to embellish it. They accumulate righteous deeds to propagate righteous *elan*, practice reverence to nurture reverential regard, and investigate events and things to comprehend their principles. Finally, grasping that every creature under Heaven is animated by humaneness, their minds become replete with humaneness (Wang 1996: 3:501).

Wang Fuzhi held the extension of humaneness lay in learning and ritual propriety. By nurturing reverence and practicing ritual propriety, one would realize that humaneness runs through all things in the world. The love and humaneness of a person who had achieved this realization would not only fill their mind but extend to the cosmos. This is the sphere at which the mind unites with Heaven in humaneness. In Wang's words,

4 MORAL RECONSTRUCTION 91

"The substance of my mind will be identical with the inexhaustible principle of life in Heaven and Earth, and the function of my mind will be operating in harmony with the myriad things fulfilling their nature" (Wang 1996: 7:538). At this level, one would form a unity with everything in the world, participate in the processes of Heaven, and sustain the growth of all things.

4.2   THE MIND (XIN 心)

The definition of humaneness was closely related to the mind. On the one hand, humaneness was to be manifested as peace of mind; on the other hand, humaneness was identified with the nature, the essential content of the mind. Hence, Wang Fuzhi held that it was incumbent on people to explore the origin and structure of the mind and the virtues to elucidate the role of the mind in the cultivation of humaneness.

4.2.1   The Origin and Structure of the Mind

Wang Fuzhi offered a naturalistic explanation of the origin of the mind. Based on his *qi*-monism, he assumed that the mind was formed of the finer strains of yin and yang and their derivatives—the Five Elements (*wuxing* 五行). Mind had natural inborn abilities; it was the abode of human nature, and in charge of processing and displaying perceptions (Wang 1996: 6:1111). He characterized the mind as the operation through wave motions of the fermenting *qi* emerging from the Great Void (Heaven). Through these motions, the sun emitted light and thunder rumbled. In the mind, these motions induced the formation of spiritual awareness and the processing and display of perceptions, such as seeing and hearing (Wang 1996: 12:147).

As *qi* had its inherent principle, Wang Fuzhi insisted that the mind took shape through the principle of *qi*, and in turn bore principle. He said, "From the perspective of origin, through transformations, Heaven creates the mind according to the principle of *qi*. From the perspective of outcome, each person receives what Heaven endows, and bears principle in mind" (Wang 1996: 6:1112). However, Wang did not affirm whether "the principle of *qi*" involved in producing the mind was identical with "the principle borne" in the mind. Wang's following remarks indicated that he regarded "the principle born within" as the nature and distinguished it from "the principle of *qi*" involved in producing the mind. He asserted, "The mind contains a principle, so it cannot be said that the mind is same as the principle. When the mind does not bear principle, it can still operate just by using the ears, eyes, mouth and body" (Wang 1996: 6:1112). Hence, for Wang, the mind possessed both "principle" and perception. Without "principle," the mind could continue to exist through its powers of perception. Wang viewed the mind and "the principle it bore" on the model of a vessel and its contents. Consequently, he did not hold that "the principle born in mind" was identical with "the principle forming the mind," because the latter could not be separated from the mind just as the principle of eyesight could not be separated from eyes.

Notably, Wang Fuzhi discussed "principle" from two points of view: (1) the physical principle forming the mind, which was inseparable from the mind, and (2) the "contained principle," which was separable from the mind and was identical with "the nature." We may compare the former to the coronary artery, which creates the heart's function, and the latter to the aorta, which is supported by the heart. In many remarks, Wang used "principle" in the second sense, viewing it as related to the mind as the contents to a box. He said, "The function of the mind is to be open, intelligent, and discriminating. It contains principles, yet it is not itself a principle. It responds to all things, yet its response may not be on the mark" (Wang 1996: 6:1077). Following this logic, Wang admitted that the mind and principle were two things; the mind bore principle within, but it still had to make efforts to grasp them.

To justify this bifurcation of the mind, Wang Fuzhi quoted Zhang Zai's words, "The unity of the nature (principle) and perception is called the mind," and called perception the human mind (*renxin* 人心), and the nature the Way mind (*daoxin* 道心) (Wang 1996: 6:1112). He here affirmed that the human mind referred to the mind of perception and movement, the abode of the nature, and has its body even without the nature. The Way mind appeared when the nature was manifested, but the human mind was dominant when the nature was obstructed or ignored (Wang 1996: 6:1086). This account differs a little from the previous one. That is, Wang Fuzhi here regarded the unity of the human mind and the nature as the Way mind. However, he usually upheld the previous bifurcation: the nature was the Way mind and perception was the human mind. The last quotation, however, presented the human mind and the Way mind as two different things, and indicated that the human mind could awaken or not, to the nature as its content. In light of such uncertainty

Wang urged his students to seek and reflect on the nature and maintain the unity of the two minds. What he did not realize was that the process of seeking and reflecting on "the nature" would disclose that "the nature" was not inborn, but rather something acquired; for a truly natural endowment would not need to be disclosed by effort.

Wang Fuzhi proposed this bifurcated model of the mind to avoid confusing the nature with the desires, and to guide the desires with the nature. On his view, the nature as the Way mind was purely good, so it could be a proper guide for human effort. The human mind, as the origin of the emotions and the desires, should not be confused with the nature, but needs to be guided by the nature. In this way, Wang sought to avoid the subjectivist consequences of Wang Yangming's inborn knowledge of the good, namely, the lack of a distinction between the human mind and the Way mind and between desire and the nature. Indeed, if the human mind and the Way mind were regarded as the same thing, people could easily mistake the human mind for the Way mind, and conclude that human desires and emotions were the nature.

Regrettably, Wang Fuzhi was using Wang Yangming's own idea to criticize Wang Yangming! Wang Yangming also drew a distinction between the Way mind and the human mind. He said, "The mind is one. It is called the Way mind before being contaminated by hypocrisy (*wei* 偽); it is called the human mind after being contaminated. If the human mind were to follow the right course, it would become the Way mind. If the Way mind were to lose the right course, it would become the human mind. There are not two minds, indeed" (Wang 2012: 17). We cannot make out any difference between these words and the previous quotation from Wang Fuzhi.

Based on these quotations, we can clarify some of Wang Fuzhi's misunderstandings of Wang Yangming's teaching, "The mind is principle (*xin ji li* 心即理)." When Wang Yangming uttered this proposition, he meant the content or essence of the mind was principle. When a student asked how evil could arise, since all human minds bore the same principle, Wang Yangming replied, "The mind of an evil person has lost its essence (*benti* 本體)" (Wang 2012: 34). "This essence of the mind is the nature, while the nature is principle" (Wang 2012: 56). This shows that Wang Yangming did not simply identify the heart-mind with principle. Therefore, Wang Fuzhi made a false criticism when he took "The heart-mind is principle" to mean, "There is no principle outside of the mind, nor any mind beyond the principle" (Wang 1996: 6:1112), for Wang Yangming accepted that the mind was more than principle.

Wang Fuzhi's misunderstanding was the product of Wang Yangming's ambiguity in defining the mind as principle. Despite defining inborn knowledge of the good as the essence of the mind, he also compared the mind to a mirror (Wang 2012: 26, 48), and regarded inborn knowledge as the void and subtle perception (*xu ling ming jue* 虛靈明覺) (Wang 2012: 104). "The inborn knowledge of human beings ... is the marvelous intelligence of the mind" (Wang 2012: 230). These descriptions gave readers the impression that Wang Yangming regarded the mind as perceptive mind.

Wang Fuzhi supported this bifurcated structure of the mind by distinguishing its substance and function. He saw the Way mind as the humaneness and righteousness born within the mind, and the human mind as the operation of the mind. "Humaneness and righteousness are the substance of the mind, just as Heaven has yin and yang; perception and movement are operations of the mind, just as Heaven is the transformations of yin and yang. If one forsakes the substance but only discusses the operations, one only grasps this intelligent organ of perception and movement. It will turn out to be dissolute and immoral when set loose. Yet, it can only perform its proper functions of attacking and obtaining and liking and disliking, when it is preserved" (Wang 1996: 6:893). Again, the Way mind (principle, humaneness, and righteousness) was the substance and guide of the perceiving mind. Without it, the perceiving mind would be nothing but a tool, liable to do good or bad. What a person should do in cultivating their mind was not just to make their perception more acute, but to make their mind replete with humaneness and righteousness. In this way, Wang shifted the focus of discussion from the mind in general to the cultivation of the Way mind. The aim of preserving and realizing the mind, and seeking the lost mind, lay in making the human mind replete with the Way mind, that is, with humaneness and righteousness.

4.2.2   How to Realize and Preserve the Mind

The bifurcated structure of the mind required one to fulfill the Way mind and unify it with the human mind. This was also Mencius' aim: "If a person realizes the mind (*jin qi xin zhe* 盡其心者), they will know the nature" (Mencius 7A.1). However, this did not mean that a person needn't do anything about the human mind. In fact, Wang also asked students to sharpen their perceptual acuity to better understand the nature. For instance, he expressed wonder at the intelligence and adeptness of the mind, and asked students to make use of these capabilities, but not be blind to principle (Wang 1996: 8:823). But, as to how to make use of these capabilities, Wang advocated using the nature (principle) as a guide. He noted that, "The mind (spiritual awareness) changes without cease, and only functions well under the guidance of a constant nature. With the guidance of a constant nature, one's spiritual awareness would be focused on knowing the nature; and one would come to grasp all the principles within and be able to deal with all things and affairs with propriety" (Wang 1996: 6:1106).

Notably, in Wang Fuzhi's discussions, the nature mostly had to do with the principles of human relationships. Its essence was humaneness, conscience, and the principle of life, and its concrete forms were ritual propriety and the norms aimed at achieving harmony in human relations. His advocacy that human mind be guided by the nature meant following conscience and practicing ritual propriety. When he advocated exerting spiritual awareness to grasp the nature, he meant heeding the voice of conscience with propriety in practice. He regarded the nature as the source of the principles of human affairs, so grasping the nature would ensure that the mind had grasped all principles and could deal with things with propriety. For this reason, Wang denied that fulfilling the Way mind included letting the imagination roam freely, but insisted that it involved grasping the nature as a guide in applying principles to deal with events.

Related to fulfilling the Way mind was preserving the mind (*cunxin* 存心). What was to be preserved in the mind was the ethical nature, not the spiritual awareness. This was to prevent the spiritual awareness from going astray and ensure that it embraced the principle of life in its responses and interactions with things. To preserve the mind, one was to embrace the nature within to master the mind and maintain equanimity in the face of rising emotions and desires (Wang 1996: 8:823). Since the nature was the root and composite of the principles of human affairs, Wang further asserted, "To preserve the mind is to preserve principle—the principles one has grasped by learning, questioning, thinking, and diligence"(Wang 1996: 6:882). On the surface, the principles preserved by mind appear to be the principles grasped by learning and thinking. If one remembers that the nature was the principle on which, as Wang insisted, one should deeply reflect, one will know that the principles grasped by learning and thinking can be crystalized through the nature. It was always the nature that Wang, first and foremost, asked students to preserve in the mind.

Wang Fuzhi clarified that preserving the mind was also preserving humaneness, as the essence of the nature. "What one preserves is humaneness. One preserves what is manifested through humaneness in events and patterns and what one has obtained by learning, dedicating, questioning, and thinking about humaneness" (Wang 1996: 6:883). He supported this view by interpreting Confucius' words, "It will be there if you grasp it" in terms of grasping the humaneness and righteousness in the mind. As to Confucius' next words, "it will disappear when you give it up," Wang interpreted it as referring to the loss of one's sense of humaneness and righteousness when straying from the commiserating mind (Wang 1996: 6:1077).

Once a person preserved the mind, they would realize the nature was the manifestation of heavenly principle and the source of social norms, human relationships, and the patterns of things. Such realization would prevent them from falling into the snares of self-interest and desire. It would make their mind replete with the principles of things and guide their dealings with events. As a result, "they would not strive to preserve an empty and luminous mind, to be grasped and maintained: to act as vigilant as a crane, as clever as a parrot, or as indifferent as a fed ox or pig" (Wang 1996: 6:1023). Wang here was warning students to avoid two extremes—indulging in one's desires and interests and mistaking the perceptive mind for the Way mind. Identifying Zhen Dexiu 真德秀 (1178–1235) as an example of the second extreme, Wang criticized Zhen's failure to grasp that the nature and the emotions formed the substance and function of the mind, respectively, that they were the root and branch of human goodness. Zhen reduced the mind to a luminous, perceptive awareness, and saw preserving the mind a matter of staying alert without dozing (Wang 1996: 6:1022). Wang Fuzhi viewed the nature as the essence of mind and considered spiritual awareness as an epiphenomenon or a tool of the nature. For him, preserving the mind was preserving the Way mind or the nature; it was not preserving spiritual awareness. Therefore, when Wang said to bring spiritual awareness into play by following the nature, it was not about sharpening one's intelligence, but rather directing it to grasp and follow the nature. He held that only by grasping and following the nature could sharpening one's intelligence have positive value.

The opposite of preserving the mind is losing the mind (*fangxin* 放心). As the nature or humaneness is the essence of the mind to be preserved, losing the mind refers to losing sight of the nature or humaneness. Wang declared, " 'The mind is not present,' this is what Mencius called 'losing one's mind.' Does 'losing one's mind' refer to losing one's empty, luminous mind? No, it refers to losing one's humaneness and righteousness" (Wang 1996: 6:422). Again, "What is lost is called the lost mind, and what is lost is humaneness" (Wang 1996: 6:1083). However, since Wang believed that human beings were endowed with humaneness by Heaven, how could a person lose their humaneness or the nature? In response to this question, Wang interpreted "lose" to mean "be overwhelmed by one's desires and self-interest." This happened when one could not rein in the desires and greed when brooding and interacting with things (Wang 1996: 8:713). To prevent the desires from overwhelming the mind, Zhu Xi had proposed "preserving heavenly principle by extinguishing human desires." Since Wang did not accept that principle and the desires were antagonistic, he recommended that students pursue the nature (principle) and make the mind replete with it, and not just make the mind vacuous by extinguishing the desires. In Wang's opinion, Cheng Yi and Zhu Xi both had confused the human mind with the Way mind, and lost sight of how to recover the lost mind (*qiu fangxin* 求放心). For example, Master Cheng had said, "Once a person becomes sleepy or faint, they have already lost their mind."[3] Master Zhu had said, "Restrain the mind and not allow it to accommodate things" (Li 1994: 371, 373). In Wang's opinion, both of these statements were faulty. "To recover the lost mind was to recover one's humaneness." "'Losing one's mind' was losing one's humaneness, when heavenly principle was eclipsed by the obstruction of selfish desires and intentions. Once a person had recovered heavenly principle, however, the mind would be luminous and replete with all principles; it could then accommodate all things … While Mencius had urged people to seek humaneness, Cheng Yi and Zhu Xi had recommended entering a dark, vacuous mental realm, lying there, indifferent. A strange teaching. I dare not follow them there" (Wang 1996: 6:1082).

In Wang's view, neither Cheng Yi nor Zhu Xi had realized that the lost mind referred to one's lost humaneness or the nature. They understood the lost heart-mind as a perceptive mind that strayed from the right path, and were preoccupied with purging desires. Accordingly, they asked students to focus the perceptive mind on principle or free it of the desires or

---

[3] This sentence cannot be found in *The Extant Book of the Two Chengs* (Er Cheng Yi Shu 二程遺書), but a similar sentence is found in Volume 59, *Zhu Zi Yu Lei* 朱子語類 (Li 1994: 1406). "If one becomes sleepy, it is called having lost one's heart-mind too."

intentions. Once a student had focused the perceptive mind on what they were doing and was not tempted by desires, it would be declared that they had "recovered the lost mind." In this way, Cheng and Zhu had focused on resisting the temptations of the desires, not knowing there was a master in the mind, which was also why they stressed expunging the desires. Wang's criticism of Zhu's explanation of the quoted sentence was well taken. Zhu had said, "When the mind is concentrated on one matter and undistracted by other things, it is said the mind does not accommodate anything" (Li 1994: 373). Clearly, Zhu regarded the mind as the perceptive mind. In contrast, Wang asked students to guide their emotions and desires by humaneness or the nature, and taught that seeking the lost mind involved recovering humaneness or recalling conscience; he was unconcerned about the ebb and flow of the emotions and the desires, or the recovery of a vacuous, luminous state of awareness.

Wang Fuzhi further explored the reason why Zhu Xi interpreted losing the mind as loss of the perceptive mind, and confused humaneness with the perceptive mind. In Wang's view, Zhu feared that the distinction between the human mind (perception) and the Way mind (the nature or humaneness) would lead students to think there were two opposed minds in each person. For example, Zhu said, "The recovery of the lost mind is not a matter of using one mind to seek another, for the seeker (spiritual awareness) is itself the lost mind" (Li 1994: 1408). Focusing on Zhu's considering the perceptive mind as the lost mind, Wang criticized him for mixing Confucianism with Buddhism and undermining the core project of Confucianism: to pursue humaneness and promote the Way of humaneness. Zhu Xi resembled Buddhists and Daoists, for fearing the eclipse of the perceptive mind by selfish desires and interests, and advocating purging selfish desires and interests to purify the mind. In Wang's view, the dilemma was that once the selfish desires and interests had been purged, the perceptive mind would be vacant—and open to new desires. Consequently, Zhu Xi's students tended to be anxiety-ridden and felt they were walking on thin ice or at the edge of a precipice, alienated from human affairs. To avoid Zhu Xi's errors and distinguish Confucianism from Buddhism, Wang suggested stabilizing the perceptive mind by focusing on humaneness or the nature. He wrote:

> Humaneness is at one with one's spiritual awareness. Once a person has lost their mind, they have lost humaneness but kept their spiritual awareness. So, to recover the lost mind, they need to use their spiritual awareness to seek

humaneness. As to substance, the mind cannot be differentiated into the Way mind and the human mind; however, as to function, these two minds cannot easily be conceived of as one. (Wang 1996: 6:1082)

4.2.3   Rectifying the Mind and Making One's Intentions Sincere

Losing one's mind results from being led astray by the desires and interests. On Wang's analysis, in such cases, a person's spiritual awareness was distracted from principle and lacked humaneness or principle as its content. To return the mind to its proper stance, Wang advocated rectifying the mind (zhengxin 正心) and making the intentions sincere (chengyi 誠意), especially in commentaries on the Great Learning.

What made the mind susceptible to the temptations of desires? The answer went back to its bifurcated structure. The human mind gave rise to the emotions and the desires (desires viewed as extensions of the emotions) (Wang 1996: 6:473; 12:41). Once the emotions and the desires no longer expressed or complied with the nature (principle or the Way mind), the human mind could be led astray and possibly turn evil (Wang 1996: 8:698). Moreover, as spiritual awareness, the human mind was unpredictable and drawn to good or evil. To avoid this uncertainty, Wang identified a touchstone for preserving the moral mind and managing the emotions (Wang 1996: 13:633). This touchstone was the nature or the Way mind. The rectification of the mind referred to transformation of the human mind by the Way mind, or guidance of the spiritual intelligence by the nature. Wang deemed this to be the only way because if the mind were not rectified, it would not bear principle as its master (Wang 1996: 7:70). As to how the mind could adopt principle or the nature as its master, Wang advocated "maintaining the will (chi zhi 持志)." In a word, "Rectifying the mind lies in maintaining the will" (Wang 1996: 6:415).

Wang Fuzhi regarded the will as a person's determination to uphold the nature or humaneness as their aspiration. It was the means by which the rectified mind was to monitor and guide a person's seeing, hearing, speech, and action (Wang 1996: 6:401). As the nature was to be manifested as righteousness and the Way, preserving the will meant preserving righteousness and the Way within the mind (Wang 1996: 6:421). In summary, Wang's aim was to discipline the spiritual awareness to heed the nature or principle. Once a person established righteousness and the Way as their will, they would embrace the Way mind to moderate their intentions and ideas and prevent them from going astray. Having established the nature as their inner master, they could begin to manage their intentions and ideas with propriety and express their emotions in due degree (Wang 1996: 13:634). This would be the function and operation of their rectified mind.

Having criticized Zhu Xi for not knowing how to recover the lost mind, Wang Fuxhi doubted whether Zhu knew how to rectify the mind, either. He accused Zhu of reducing rectifying the mind to making the perceptive mind lucid and vacuous. Indeed, Zhu had instructed making the mind tranquil, vacuous, lucid, and luminous like a bright mirror. Moreover, Zhu said, "Before an event arises, do not expect anything; after it passes, do not hold onto anything. When engaging with an event, do not be attached to it."[4] Wang argued that rectifying the mind in the *Great Learning* was bringing mind into compliance with the nature or principle, not making it vacuous, lucid, and luminous, for the spiritual intelligence was naturally vacuous and lucid anyway. To bring the mind into compliance with the nature, one had to have expectations, be committed to principle, and stay focused. Such dedication and focus were the basic requirements of rectifying the human mind. Otherwise, if a person kept a vacuous perceptive mind without expectation or attachment, they would do no better than keeping a still or inactive mind. Then they did not need to further rectify the mind (Wang 1996: 6:420).

Zhu Xi's mirror analogy was a borrowing from Zhuangzi and Chan Buddhism. The latter, for example, compared the mind to a bright mirror and sought to maintain its purity and brightness by dusting off expectation and attachment. Their purpose was to concentrate on the task at hand, since expectations and attachments were distractions from the task at hand. Zhu applied this method to learning and mastering principles, on the premise that the mind must be vacuous to be receptive to principle. This indicated that Zhu thought the mind did not originally bear principle, and thus the rectification of the mind for him was just to make it vacuous, not to adopt principle as its guide. Hence, Wang accused Zhu of not understanding the meaning of "mind (*xin* 心)," by reducing mind to the perceptive mind and ignoring its substance—the nature. This was why, in Wang's view, Zhu did not know how to rectify the mind (Wang 1996: 6:422).

---

[4] This sentence is not found in *Zhu Zi Yu Lei* 朱子語類.

Wang Fuzhi recommended reflection (*si* 思) as a way to discern principle or the nature and rectify the mind. Reflection referred to introspection to understand the nature bequeathed by Heaven and born in mind; it did not concern perceptual phenomena. Wang followed Zhang Zai in regarding the knowledge obtained by reflection as knowledge of virtue and the nature (*dexing suozhi* 德性所知), which could not be acquired by perception. He requested that students reflect on principle prior to perception, unlike most people who based their thoughts on what they had seen or heard (Wang 1996: 6:1093). Interestingly, Wang further suggested that focusing on perceptual knowledge would limit one's thinking to concrete affairs, hampering one's capacity to grasp the nature. He argued, "As to depending on the senses to realize the function and capacity of thinking, not only in cases where one sees what one has seen and hears what one has heard, but also in cases where one sees what one has never seen and hears what one has never heard, what one knows will still be limited or obstructed by that one concrete thing. In this way, how could one grasp the realm of the myriad things, the principles of which are already contained in the mind" (Wang 1996: 6:1094)? Wang was here suggesting the deeper purpose of thinking was to reflect on the nature and employ the nature to weigh one's perceptions. If one could understand the nature—the heavenly and universal principle bequeathed by Heaven—one would understand the principles of all things and accommodate them luminously in the mind.

In summary, to rectify the mind, a person should first apply their spiritual awareness to seek and understand the nature in a process of introspection independent of perceptual knowledge. They could then use the nature to moderate their perceptions and immunize their minds to the temptations of improper ideas, desires, or things. They would be forearmed to distinguish chastity from adultery, good from evil, and screen their perceptions with the rectified mind, such that the emotions and the desires would never overpower the mind or lure it to stray from the nature. People who rectified the mind would set up rules and measures by which to be a great person while dealing with the myriad temptations in the world with propriety (Wang 1996: 8:739–740).

The rectification of the mind leads us to Wang Fuzhi's discussions on making the intentions sincere (*chengyi* 誠意). While the *Great Learning* made the process of rectifying the mind contingent on making the intentions sincere, Wang insisted that rectifying the mind came before making the intentions sincere, regarding the latter as a supplement to the former.

He argued that a person who did not first rectify the mind could not make the intentions sincere; lacking a rectified mind, they could not distinguish good from evil, the first step in making the intentions sincere (Wang 1996: 6:580). In sum, rectifying the mind was a fundamental goal, while making the intentions sincere supported that goal.

To ensure the legitimacy of making the intentions sincere, Wang Fuzhi appealed to the distinction between the mind and the intentions, and counseled making the intentions sincere by making them compliant with the rectified mind. At the same time, he regarded the mind as the (public) will while the intentions included hidden, private, and unpredictable thoughts. If a person did not heed their will, they could be overwhelmed easily by unsettled hidden thoughts, especially when they could not distinguish good from evil. A person who was weak willed or easily strayed from principle could one day detest what they originally loved and love what they originally detested; their mind would be out of joint (Wang 1996: 13:633–634). Wang called this phenomenon self-deception (*ziqi* 自欺): "What one's mind originally bears is good, not evil. However, evil appears together with the emergence of the intentions. When the intentions sway the mind, one falls into self-deception" (Wang 1996: 6:415). "What the mind originally bears" was the nature, which was always good. But, the intentions arose from the human mind and may become excessive. Excessive intentions could become desires and turn evil, swaying the mind and stymieing principle.

Since the intentions arose randomly through one's interactions in the world, Wang Fuzhi counseled embracing the rectified mind as one's inner master, keeping tranquil, and moderating the intentions, to avoid falling into self-deception. When one monitored the intentions with the rectified mind, no excessive intentions would arise to sway the mind (Wang 1996: 6:995). By deploying the rectified mind as a monitor, one could trace the intentions and make sure they kept compliant with virtue and principle.

Wang Fuzhi regarded rectifying the mind and making the intentions sincere as dialectically related. On the one hand, a person ought to rectify the mind to make the intentions sincere. Rectifying the mind itself involved grasping the nature—the inner principle by which to distinguish good from evil. The capacity to distinguish good from evil made possible monitoring and directing the intentions (Wang 1996: 7:48). On the other hand, Wang realized that a surge of intentions could sway the mind, so he asked students to trace the source and development of their intentions. One who could uphold goodness while pursuing their intentions would be able to preserve the original mind and not let it be swayed by bad intentions. On this score, he suggested cultivating sincere intentions to support the rectified mind: "Once the intentions are sincere, one's intentions and actions will be in compliance with the will and purely good; one will not be subject to evil influences and one's mind will not stray" (Wang 1996: 7:49).

In conclusion, Wang Fuzhi advocated reflecting on the nature to rectify the perceptive mind and enlisting the rectified mind and the nature to moderate one's intentions and conduct. At root, this would involve embracing the nature to regulate the human mind. Still, while the nature was static and constant, one had to embrace the nature while monitoring the intentions and various ideas as they arise. In this way, one could ensure that their intentions and ideas are sincere and in compliance with the nature and principle. Otherwise, the overflowing ideas will destroy the rectified heart-mind and cause the rise of evil. In this way, making and keeping the intentions sincere supports the rectification of the mind.

4.2.4   Righteousness: Source of Moral Decision Making

In his account of making the intentions sincere, Wang Fuzhi stressed embracing the nature as a condition to make moral decisions. He asserted that the source of the mind's moral decision making was "righteousness (*yi* 義)" and advocated dealing with things and affairs with righteousness. In his view, a person who upheld righteousness would first consider a new situation from their inner measure; they then would consider the perspective of others. The maxim went: a person who could resist the temptations of things would be able to deal with them by righteousness. Wang declared, "Righteousness is internal, and external things have no decisive power over it. Therefore, one who realizes righteousness within the mind should make efforts to keep the mind in compliance with righteousness" (Wang 1996: 5:111).

How did righteousness arise in the mind? Wang Fuzhi once declared that righteousness arose from the decisiveness of the heart-mind (*xin zhi zhi* 心之制) (Wang 1996: 5:130). Elsewhere, he asserted that one would realize righteousness when one heeded their rectified mind in conduct, and felt at ease (Wang 1996: 2:315). Clearly, Wang regarded righteousness as the decisiveness of the commiserating mind and the judgment of humaneness in real situations. As to practicing righteousness, a person ought to exercise their favors, authority, rewards, and punishments in compliance with the commiserating mind, and not adulterate their conduct with selfish concerns (Wang 1996: 10:84). In this respect, Wang's analysis recalled Lu Jiuyuan's (1139–1192) teaching of the original mind. Lu strongly recommended that his students heed their conscience alone in conduct. Lu once said, "Your ears are naturally sharp in hearing; your eyes are naturally bright in seeing. When you serve your father, it is certain you are filial; when you serve your elder brothers, it is certain that you are fraternal. All of these virtues are originally present in your mind; you do not need to seek them without. What is necessary is to behave according to your inner self" (Lu 1980: 399). To Lu, objective norms and rules were but footnotes to the original mind and conscience. The common view that Wang Fuzhi was critical of Lu Jiuyuan and Wang Yangming, but supportive of Zhu Xi, should be reconsidered (Ji 1962: 109; Chen 2004: 7).

Wang Fuzhi further advocated that a hero or a great person would value the intuitions of the commiserating mind when making decisions, and not be easily swayed by the views of others. At a critical juncture, in particular, the great person should heed their inner counsel and avoid the distractions of debates and discussions. Wang called this approach "drawing on one's unique insight (*yongdu* 用獨)." He elaborated on this idea when praising Li Longji's 李隆基 (685–762) resoluteness in deciding to kill Empress Wei of the Tang. He justified Li Longji's action on the consideration of moral expediency (*quan* 權). He regarded following the orders of one's father or master as the standard way while heeding one's conscience in special situations as moral expediency. He cautioned that only a hero could draw on their unique insight in making crucial decisions while ordinary people had better follow the established rules and norms. Moreover, he held that those who strived to become a noble person needed first to uphold righteousness and learn to make fitting determinations in situations where the standard norms and rules did not apply. After all, norms and rules were just footnotes to the rectified mind.

Wang Fuzhi did not deny the function of norms and rituals *tout court*. In his view, rituals originated from the due measure or pattern of the mind (*xin zhi jie* 心之節) (Wang 1996: 5:130–131), and were set by righteous judgments, by which things were assigned their proper places according to category and function (Wang 1996: 2:315). In this way, rituals served to expand people's minds and regulate their manifest conduct. Moreover, Wang held that, by practicing ritual conduct, most people could awaken to their inborn knowledge of the good and restrain their evil impulses, intentions, and conduct, while noble people could manifest humaneness and righteousness properly. With the exception of sages, no one can act righteously all the time just by heeding the mind. To keep the mind in compliance with righteousness, a person must rectify their mind by practicing ritual propriety. Only after having informed their mind with principles and cultivated their heavenly endowed virtue would they be set to rely on the mind in responding to situations, anomalous situations, in particular.

Wang Fuzhi drew on the dialectical relation between the mind and ritual propriety in responding to the negative impact of Wang Yangming's inborn knowledge of the good. As noted, the popularization of Wang Yangming's teaching had caused people, including scholars, not just to disregard norms and rituals, but to justify all sorts of conduct with the claim that they were following their conscience. Wang Fuzhi offered a remedy for this trend in a comment on Du Yu's 杜預 (222–285) remark, "As to ritual propriety, it is enough that a noble person bear it in mind" (Wang 1996: 10:422). Wang responded by observing that if a person were to claim they had not forgotten filial respect while just sitting by and not attending to their old father, or that they still felt fraternal love for their elder brother while breaking his arm in rage, was it really sufficient just to bear ritual propriety in mind? (Wang 1996: 10:422). Wang's observation revealed the lies of "loving" kin who had appropriated one's property while feeling familial love. Wang recommended unifying the inner (mind) with the outer (ritual propriety) and making them mutually supportive. A filial-minded person still must observe the norms and rituals; one who observes the norms and rituals equally should be motivated by filial love and respect.

4.3   The Nature, the Emotions, and Habit

Wang Fuzhi held that humaneness was the principle of life, which man shared with the myriad things (Wang 1996: 12:202). It was contained in the mind and manifested whenever a person interacted with things; however, it did not depend on things for its existence. It was the essence of the nature (Wang 1996: 12:203), so the nature was the humaneness in the mind. Expanding one's humaneness was tantamount to realize the nature. This fulfillment had to be undertaken by the mind because the nature and humaneness were not volitional or active in themselves. Hence, Wang accepted Zhang Zai's teaching that the mind could realize the nature; the nature could not examine the mind (Wang 1996: 12:124). Once the nature was endowed at birth, it was a person's mission to strive to grasp and realize the nature, opening the path to sagehood. At the same time, the mind would produce emotions and desires in response to external influences; hence, one had to moderate the emotions and desires and keep them in compliance with the nature and principle. This involved rectifying the mind, making the intentions sincere, and realizing the nature. In this perspective, these three efforts were three aspects of a single process of self-realization.

4.3.1   The Origin of the Nature

Wang Fuzhi followed the *Doctrine of the Mean* in accepting that Heaven endowed the nature in human beings. He regarded the nature as the Way of humanity, part and parcel of the Way of Heaven. The Way of Heaven was the fundamental principle by which yin, yang, and the Five Elements were to produce the myriad things (Wang 1996: 7:105). He used spirit (*shen* 神) to unite nature and the Way of Heaven, and affirmed that "Spirit has its principle which is the Way in Heaven, and is nature when gathering in human beings" (Wang 1996: 12:42). It is through the spiritual trans-formation that the Way of Heaven gathers in human beings and becomes nature. Wang also identified spirit as the principle of yin and yang, saying, "The Great Harmony consists of both *qi* and spirit. Spirit is precisely the pure and penetrating principle of yin and yang" (Wang 1996: 12:16). For this reason, Wang sometimes went on to identify the nature and the Way of Heaven as spirit (Wang 1996: 12:95).

Wang Fuzhi also endorsed the dualism of body and spirit maintained in the traditional Chinese worldview. He assumed that, as spirit, the nature transcended a person's perceptions and movements, and existed forever. He argued:

> A living person has perception and movement, and their vitality disperses when their life ends. The nature is the heavenly principle. When *qi* gathers, it gathers to form a person; when *qi* disperses, it returns to the Great Void. Just as Heaven carries on without interruption despite the cycle of day and night, there is no real life or death for the nature. (Wang 1996: 12:126)

Wang argued for the eternity of the nature by reference to the continu-ity of heavenly principle versus the changeability of the human body. However, in this argument, he confused both the nature with heavenly principle and the spirit with Heaven. First, according to the *Doctrine of the Mean*, it was only after heavenly principle was endowed in a human being that it would be called the nature. Before this instantiation, heavenly principle would be a universal principle governing all things, and not reduceable to the nature of the human species. Hence, the eternity of heavenly principle should not be attributed to the nature. Second, if Wang were to identify the nature with spirit and deem it eternal, he would contradict his other discussions on the relationship between spirit and Heaven. For example, in the *Annotation of the Zhuangzi*, he wrote:

> A person is born when spirit enters a formed body. However, when the body decomposes and cannot hold the spirit, it will be abandoned. The liberated spirit will no longer be called spirit, but Heaven. It is called spirit when it is in a body, but will be called Heaven when it is not there. Is there any difference between its being in a body or not? (Wang 1996: 13:124–125)

Here, Wang Fuzhi attempted to deny the difference between the spirit when in a body and when not instantiated, but these two states were truly different reflecting a basic difference between spirit and Heaven. It would have been more accurate for Wang to assert that the nature and spirit were the concrete forms of the Way of Heaven, qualified by instantiation in a body. In this respect, they could not be considered to be eternal in the same sense as Heaven.

By elevating the nature and spirit to the eternity of heavenly principle, Wang Fuzhi sought to encourage students to realize the nature, unite with Heaven, and achieve immortal renown by moral heroism. By distinguishing bodily perception and movement from the nature, Wang aimed to mark a key distinction between human beings and animals, that is, while the latter understood perception, movement, and food, the former also grasped the principle of life. As a human being, it was incumbent to grasp and fulfill the principle of life, not just aim to satisfy their bodily needs and desires. Those who viewed perception and movement as the nature limited themselves to the level of birds and beasts (Wang 1996: 8:676).

In order to justify his prioritization of the nature over perception and movement, Wang Fuzhi argued that they were based on different qualities of *qi*. The nature was the principle of life instantiated in a *qi* formation while perception and movement arose directly from the mechanism of *qi*. He admitted that perception and movement were also basic parts of human life, but he expressed concern that human beings would degrade themselves to the level of birds and beasts if they regarded the nature as just the result of mechanism of *qi*, forgetting it was the instantiation of the principle of life (Wang 1996: 8:682). For this reason, he accused Gao Zi 告子 of mixing man with beast in his discussions on the nature.

Wang's distinction between the principle of life and the mechanism of *qi* implied that he tacitly held that human nature had two aspects—the moral nature (the principle of life) and the biological and physical nature (the mechanism of *qi*), which corresponded to Zhang Zai's distinction between "the nature of Heaven and earth (*tiandi zhi xing* 天地之性)" and "the nature of physical temperament (*qizhi zhi xing* 氣質之性)." However, this distinction not only posited the existence of transcendent principle (beyond *qi*), recalling Zhu Xi's dualism of principle and *qi*, but also landed Wang in paradox, because he had also insisted that the nature of physical temperament referred to the nature in physical embodiment and was not different from the original nature (nature of Heaven and Earth) in kind (Wang 1996: 6:857–858). That was to say, he also held that the principle of life did not exist beyond the mechanism of *qi*, in line with his *qi*-monism.

As to the content of the nature, besides humaneness and the principle of life, Wang Fuzhi regarded it as "the principles of harmony and transformation in the Great Void (*taixu he tong er hua zhi li* 太虛和同而化之理)" (Wang 1996: 12:116). This was a reasonable view because the harmony and transformation in the Great Void was the result of yin-yang intercourse, which gave rise to the myriad things. In essence, the principles of harmony and transformation were the principles of life, which gave rise to the humaneness and righteousness in the mind.

Wang Fuzhi called the principles of harmony and transformation "harmony-deference (*heshun* 和順)." In his view, in the process of heavenly transformation, what Heaven and Earth endowed in human beings was harmony and deference, and what the myriad things received was similar. "Harmony and deference are the nature and endowment which, in turn, give rise to the Way and its virtue" (Wang 1996: 1:1074). With such observations, Wang completed his argument that human nature was innately good and everyone could become a sage through moral cultivation.

4.3.2 The Nature to Be Renewed and Completed Daily

Wang Fuzhi endorsed the idea that "What Heaven endows in us is called the nature," but regarded this endowment as an active and ceaseless process between Heaven and human beings. In this way, he avoided the notion that the nature was endowed already complete from birth. He was afraid that the belief that the nature was fully endowed at birth[5] would incline people to believe that human good and evil were predestined and that it would be futile to engage in self-cultivation. He reasoned, "If people believed not only that birth marked the beginning of a person's life when they received human form, but also that the moral nature would remain constant their entire life, then they would not feel moved to cultivate virtue beyond nourishing their bodily form" (Wang 1996: 6:751). By arguing that the nature was renewable, Wang wanted to convince people that the nature could be enhanced by personal effort, such as moral cultivation.

Despite his distinction between the principle of life and the mechanism of life (qi), Wang Fuzhi appealed to qi-monism when defending the view that the nature could be renewed as a renewal of heavenly endowment on a daily basis. He affirmed that:

> The nature is principle. The principle modulates qi and is the principle of qi. How could it be that principle transcends qi but runs through qi? … The qi that Heaven endows in human beings is never interrupted, so the principle (*li* 理), thus endowed will never be interrupted either. Consequently, Heaven continues its endowment, and the nature is daily renewed. (Wang 1996: 6:1076)

Wang here insisted that human beings received the principle ceaselessly together with their reception of qi from Heaven. As qi and principle were one, so the nature would also be renewed along with the renewal of a person's qi.

If the nature was the principle of qi, since qi could not be said to be good or bad ontologically, the heavenly endowment and the nature could not be regarded as good or evil either. But, as we just discussed, Wang did hold that what Heaven and Earth endowed the myriad things with was harmony and deference (*he shun* 和順), and harmony and deference were good. Thus, the heavenly endowment and the nature were basically good, and the nature could be renewed by Heaven every day.

---

[5] The *Zhuangzi* claims that inborn nature cannot be changed, fate cannot be altered (Watson 1968: 166).

Wang Fuzhi also described the renewed endowment and the nature as the Way that made Heaven as it was and the Way to sustain all things. He considered that, at birth, these two Ways were instantiated in the human body and gathered there as virtue (*de* 德). From birth, they would go on operating in the human body, never ceasing their function (Wang 1996: 13:663). Virtue here referred to the moral efficacy of the nature and humaneness, the instantiation of the two Ways in human body. It was these two Ways that formed the nature and that would continue to shape and renew it after a person was born.

Still, Wang had to answer two questions. First, can something be regarded as human nature if it keeps changing from birth to death? Is there an essential difference between the nature formed at birth and the nature that was subsequently transformed? If the nature were to keep changing during a person's life, wouldn't it possible for a male nature to change into a female nature? Wang did not venture to give clear answers. Instead, he ambiguously distinguished the nature at birth from the nature after birth in terms of "measure (*liang* 量) and realization (*zhen* 真)."

> The heavenly mandate is what is endowed; the nature is what is received. The nature is the principle of life, so a person's period of life is the time they are first endowed with the mandate and afterwards realize the nature. At birth, one receives the measure of the nature (*xing zhi liang* 性之量); after birth, one achieves the realization of the nature (*xing zhi zhen* 性之真). (Wang 1996: 12:413)

Wang did not specify what he meant by the measure and realization of the nature. To venture a guess, perhaps he understood the measure to be the substance or type of nature while realization referred to realizing the significance of the nature. Metaphorically, the measure determined whether the nature in question was, say, either human nature or swine nature, while realization would dictate the scope and changeability of the (human) nature from goodness to evil. If this reading is accurate, the scope that Wang allowed for renewing the nature would appear to be quite limited, and weaken the usefulness of his suggestion that "the nature renews itself along with one's endowment each day" as a replacement for the Neo-Confucian notion of a static nature at birth.

Taking into account Wang Fuzhi's notion of "transforming the physical embodiment (*bianhua qizhi* 變化氣質)," we can justify our assumption. Wang discussed the different functions of *qi* 氣 and materiality (*zhi* 質) in transforming a person's physical embodiment. Materiality would determine whether a body was a human body or a pig's body, while the *qi* would allow the body to change within the limits of the material formation. Under normal conditions, *qi*'s coming and going would not significantly influence one's bodily embodiment unless one made conscious efforts to regulate it. Since the nature was the principle of bodily embodiment the heavenly renewal of the nature would be unable to modify a person's nature as a human being. If a person intended to renew their nature, they had to regulate their bodily endowment by cultivating good habits and making prudent choices. Even under ideal conditions, the extent to which a person could change the nature would be limited by their materiality. That is, while a person could make efforts to be a noble person or sage, they could not change their male physical embodiment into that of a female, or their human nature into that of a swine.

Another question for Wang Fuzhi concerned the relationship between personal effort and heavenly endowment in the process of renewing the nature. That is, provided that the nature would naturally be renewed in step with the heavenly endowment, how could personal effort contribute to the renewal process to any significant extent? Wang held that human beings received their heavenly endowment in two ways—breath and food and drink (desires and the emotions were considered to be drivers to obtain them). Since nobody could alter the air they breathed, the purity and turbidity of the *qi* they imbibed was beyond their control. Fortunately, since people could choose what food and drink they consumed, they could purify their bodily *qi* and enhance the nature by their intake of food and drink. Nonetheless, the outcome always remained uncertain, for people could not alter the air they breathed and could not always control their food or drink intake. Consequently, the renewal and enhancement of the nature was not guaranteed cosmologically, either.

One may wonder why Wang Fuzhi did not leave the nature to run itself but contended that personal effort was necessary. Wang might have responded that the nature would be obstructed by the emotions and the desires if a person did not make efforts to preserve it. He observed that obtuse, unfilial people could neglect or erode their nature and conscience by giving in to their desires and emotions. Nonetheless, their conscience could always be stirred, like the appearance of pure, bright *qi* at dawn, due to the renewing influence of the ceaseless heavenly endowment. Their renewed nature, like the pure, bright *qi* at dawn, would remain weak and easily swept away by the emotions and the desires of the daytime, so they would have to make efforts to preserve the nature, and not just depend on the renewing influence of the heavenly endowment. Wang could have added that, even if the emotions and the desires were kept under control, they would still need to make efforts to preserve the nature and not simply accept the uncertain ebb and flow of the *qi*. This situation arose with the advent of human beings. That is, people were born with intelligence and could not automatically follow the Way of Heaven. It was incumbent on man to assist Heaven and carry out what Heaven could not. If men did not assist in the process of Heaven and left the nature in its nascent state, they would hand their destiny and responsibility back to Heaven and Earth.

4.3.3   *The Nature and Habit*

Since the renewal of the nature depended on not only Heaven's endowment but also personal effort, human choice played a key role in the process of enhancing the nature. Wang Fuzhi viewed this as crucial for the maturation of the moral nature. Wang defined human choice as habit or practice (*xi* 習), conditioned by likes and dislikes. Wang believed that "Habit participates in the formation of the nature. That is, the nature is formed together with the formation of habit" (Wang 1996: 2:299).

In explaining the role of habit in the formation of the nature, Wang Fuzhi exculpated Heaven from the formation of the evil nature. He held that the heavenly endowment in human beings was entirely good. When the nature was renewed in step with the process of heavenly endowment, it would remain good, as long as it did not succumb to poor human choices. He argued, "After birth, the heavenly endowment and human choice work together to form human nature. Human choice depends on one's ingrained habits, and a person makes choices based on the likes and aversions of the emotions, hence the nature could easily be tainted or corrupted" (Wang 1996: 2:300). In this way, Wang ascribed the formation of an evil nature to the vicissitudes of human habit and choice.

Since everything that was endowed by Heaven was good, and human choices and actions were originally from Heaven, how did human impurity and corruption arise? Wang surmised that human impurity and corruption resulted from heedlessness or carelessness, as when people were tempted into making poor choices. Just as overeating would cause obesity and fasting would lead to malnutrition, people's excesses and obsessions would affect not just their judgment, but their nature, as well. In general, whenever a person obtained something, they would become healthier if the thing was in plentiful supply and used properly. They would become better if the thing was pure and used for good ends, and they would become worse if the thing was impure and used for mixed ends. Consequently, to become a noble person, they would need to be judicious and self-disciplined in making choices and their preservation efforts to enhance the nature (Wang 1996: 2:300).

Citing the moral transformation of Tai Jia 太甲, a Shang dynasty king, Wang Fuzhi explained that revival of the nature depended on both the heavenly endowment and personal choice. On the one hand, Heaven would sustain the endowment even though a person had developed bad habits and tainted their nature. Given the unending endowment process, the nature could be renewed whenever a person shed their bad habits, even if only temporarily. "The nature cannot be eclipsed entirely. Although it might be eclipsed in some cases, it still may reappear, despite their contrary intentions" (Wang 1996: 6:395). Wang cited the sprouts of the commiserating mind once one sees a baby crawl near a well, and inklings of a clear, bright mind at dawn after having set aside one's cares, calculations, and selfish plans during deep sleep. Wang asserted, "Because the heavenly endowment is ceaseless and free flowing, the nature can be altered and even transformed. Because heavenly principle is perfect and originally flawless, goodness can be recovered without difficulty" (Wang 1996: 2:300). Hence, Wang felt positive about the possibility of renewing the nature from the perspective of Heaven.

Still, Wang Fuzhi did not ignore the role of personal effort. Even though the heavenly endowment had played a role in Tai Jia's alteration, Tai Jia himself also shed his bad habits and disciplined himself with positive virtues. "During the time when he was wallowing in his transgressions, Tai Jia's nature was no longer the original nature endowed to him at birth. Later, when he nurtured good virtues in mind, Tai Jia's renewed original nature cast off his unrighteous habits ... Therefore, the nature can be realized even if it is not complete, and altered even if it is already complete. How could the nature not be malleable after it was received" (Wang 1996: 2:300)? Even though a person had bad habits and an obstructed nature, they still could begin to alter them by a careful examination of their likes and aversions and recover their good nature, just as Tai Jia's nature had changed from its original goodness to recalcitrance, and then from recalcitrance to renewed goodness. "Therefore, when a noble person cultivates their nature, they act spontaneously and do not let the nature go its own way. They carefully choose goodness, firmly grasp the mean (*zhong* 中), and dare not indulge in ease or idleness" (Wang 1996: 2:301). The critical point in personal effort was to set the mind firmly on goodness and be judicious in making choices.

Based on this argument, Wang Fuzhi distinguished the role of Heaven from the role of human beings in the renewal and development of the nature. As to endowing and developing the nature, this was the role of Heaven, including both the endowed substance at birth and the accumulation after birth. To choose things well and use them judiciously, and thus to form and enhance the nature, this was the role of personal effort. This factor was not present at birth, but grew in importance during a person's life, from childhood through adulthood (Wang 1996: 2:302). Because the heavenly endowment itself was always good and a given beyond human control, Wang assigned more importance to personal effort. He pointed out that once a person had succumbed to bad habits, it was difficult for them to renew the nature, even if they had newly awakened to it, let alone if they had never awakened to it (Wang 1996: 12:484). He compared the harm of bad habits to that of miasma infecting a person imperceptibly. Once a bad habit was ingrained, it was hard to overcome it, unless one were dedicated to a complete makeover. Wang lamented that habits were critical to upholding or undermining a person's virtue. Habits could shutter a person's eyes and muffle their ears, affecting the clarity of their vision and acuity of their hearing. It could shape their reception of opinions and relations with kin and neighbors, and impact their thinking. Once a person's seeing, hearing and thinking had been swayed and distorted, they would no longer be able to *see* the Great Mountain or hear the rolling thunder. Therefore, it was said, "habit joins in the formation of the nature" (Wang 1996: 10:375).

Wang Fuzhi recommended that people cultivate good habits from an early age through education to forestall the formation of bad habits, which were difficult to change. He accepted the precept, "To educate children with proper teachings is a sagely endeavor" from the *Book of Changes*, and believed that a child's developing good habits was necessary for their achieving sagehood. He esteemed and wrote a commentary on Zhang Zai's text *Rectifying the Ignorant Children* (*Zheng Meng* 正蒙). He also recommended that people associate with noble persons, as well as observe norms and ritual propriety, in order to form good habits. When associating with noble persons, one should emulate their likes and aversions (Wang 1996: 12:490). By such efforts, one will gradually shed bad habits and obtuseness and become dignified. Wang understood that family background and social environment impacted the formation of a person's personality and nature (character). He regarded these factors as so significant that he urged officials and educators to strive to refine the social ambiance. He remarked:

> A person's parents are their Qian and Kun who endow them with their nature. Teachers, classmates, and associates affect their attitudes, and influence their expressions of the emotions. Seeing, hearing and practice are matters of heavenly transformation, which alter a person's *qi* and body. (Wang 1996: 10:375)

Developing good habits and nature depended not only on the heavenly endowment but even more directly on a person's associations and environment. Growing up in a place with healthy customs and society, a person would be likely to develop good habits and a virtuous nature. A society with more individuals of good habits and virtuous nature would tend to be beautiful and harmonious. As Gadamer has said, "Family, society, and state determine the essential construction of the human being, in that its ethos replenishes itself with varying contexts" (Gadamer 1999: 35).

4.3.4   The Origin of Emotions

Clearly, habit played a role in shaping the nature, but what was habit? Habit could be called an abiding preference for, or aversion to, something. Based on preference and aversion, habit was connected to the emotions. To a certain extent, good habits referred to moderate emotions, while bad habits referred to excessive or unrestrained emotions. Therefore, as to the habits' impact on the nature, it was the emotions that provide motive force. This was why Wang Fuzhi paid close attention to the origin and regulation of the emotions and discussed them in detail, with finely drawn, even contradictory distinctions between his ontological and ontic definitions.

On the ontological level, the emotions were a mechanism of yin-yang intercourse, while the nature was the substance of such yin-yang intercourse (Wang 1996: 6:1066). The emotions originated from the nature and manifested and substantiated the nature in their expressions (Wang

1996: 6:473, 1:1023). The relation of the emotions to the nature was that of function to substance. The emotions and the nature were naturally unified, just as the function of the eyes (seeing) was unified with the eyes. But then, why did the emotions need to be regulated by the nature? In responding to this question, Wang likened the relationship between the nature and the emotions to that between father and son, observing that the nature could not manipulate the expressions of the emotions any more than a father could control his son (Wang 1996: 6:964). Using this analogy, Wang neglected that while the emotions were a function of the nature and the two were inseparable, the son was independent of the father. If the emotions could completely contravene the nature, the mechanism of yin-yang would be separable from their substance. This would be absurd in the context of Wang's *qi*-monism.

At the ontic level, Wang viewed the emotions in context of interactions between the mind and things. For example, in daily life, the mind would be alert and activate, and responsive to things. It would seek things. Attractive (and repulsive) things would stir the mind and the emotions would be aroused. In this respect, the emotions were neither purely external nor purely internal; they would be aroused in the interactions between the mind and any of the myriad things between Heaven and Earth (Wang 1996: 6:1067). That is to say, the emotions were manifested in a person's efforts to pursue or avoid certain things. Wang analyzed this interaction as a resonance between the mechanism of yin-yang in the aroused mind and the myriad things. Once the yin-yang mechanism was stirred in the mind, the things would respond. When things would appear without, the emotions would be aroused within (Wang 1996: 3:323). This correspondence between things and emotions reflected the fact that the emotions did not originate from the human nature alone. Wang affirmed, "The emotions do not originate from the human nature, they are a natural mechanism in the world that arises spontaneously" (Wang 1996: 6:1069). "The human nature runs through the emotions. It is not the case that the nature gives rise to emotions, nor is it the case that the nature directly interacts with things and converts itself into the emotions" (Wang 1996: 6:1066).

Why did Wang Fuzhi offer two apparently contradictory explanations for the origin of the emotions? The reason was that he initially held that the regulation of the emotions by the nature was inborn and spontaneous, since the nature was the substance and the emotions were the function. However, this view could not explain how the emotions (function) could and sometimes did contravene the nature (their substance and principle).

And, he must have realized that his father-son analogy for the rebellious emotions was unpersuasive. As a result, in accounting for the regulation of the emotions by the nature, he had to abandon the substance-function model and view the nature and the emotions as independent, but closely related matters.

> The nature comes into existence along with the birth of a human life. It continues to exist no matter whether it interacts with external things or not. When it interacts, there arise the discord of difference and identity, gain and loss for humanity. This discord stirs the mind and arouses the mechanism of joy, anger, sadness and happiness. This interaction is called the emotions. (Wang 1996: 8:698)

Here, Wang presented the nature as independent of the emotions, capable of existing apart from the emotions. Obviously, this construction of the relationship was a tacit denial of the previous substance-function model. Moreover, if the emotions were aroused when the nature interacted with things, they did not arise from the nature alone. The emotions existed at the interface between inner and outer, and could accord with or contravene the nature. Wang further remarked: "When the emotions are not in due measure and perverse, it is called 'the emotions going against the nature.' When the emotions are in due measure and not perverse, it is called 'the nature giving rise to the emotions'" (Wang 1996: 7:107–108). On this view, the nature was the principle with which the emotions ought to accord when aroused, but did not necessarily do so. When they accorded with the nature, it would be called "the nature giving rise to the emotions." Otherwise, it would be called an outburst of the emotions. Wang thus maintained the regulation of the emotions by nature but gave up his *qi*-monism and paradoxical definitions of the emotions.

Notably, Wang Fuzhi focused on the statement, "The emotions give rise to the nature" (Wang 1996: 10:132). In his comments on Zhufu Yan 主父偃 (?–126 BC) and other officials, Wang observed that while they offered good proposals as low-ranking officials, their principles changed when they reached high positions. Wang ascribed this sort of change to the situation that high-ranking officials at court were subject to the emperor's likes and aversions and lost their power of impartial judgment. "In most people, the emotions give rise to their nature, but the nature cannot regulate their emotions. What can change their emotions is their superior's opinions and the fashions of the time" (Wang 1996: 10:132). That is, the emperor's likes and aversions and popular fashions could change a person's emotions, and their changed emotions could alter the nature. This reminds us of the precept that "habit participates in the formation of the nature." In fact, the changed emotions were nothing but the new habits formed by popular fashions and the emperor's preferences; the nature that the emotions gave rise to was precisely the nature formed by habit.

4.3.5   Moderating the Emotions by the Nature

In an effort to further justify "the moderation of the emotions by the nature," Wang Fuzhi abandoned his substance-function model of the origin of emotions. He began to advocate that the nature was independent of the emotions, and that the emotions and nature were in a relationship like that between a river and the river bank. "Because a person cannot regulate the emotions by the nature, the emotions overflow at the temptations of things" (Wang 1996: 8:698). He viewed the emotions as the human mind (*renxin* 人心) and the nature as the Way mind (*daoxin* 道心), and insisted that the former should be at the service of the latter (Wang 1996: 6:473, 1066). He admitted that, in reality, the emotions often went out of the control of the nature, losing their moral/social service or function, and needed to be moderated by the nature.

As to unrestrained states of the emotions, Wang Fuzhi discussed two types: overflow of the emotions (*qing zhi liu* 情之流) and partiality of the emotions (*qing zhi pi* 情之毗). Partiality of the emotions could lead to their excess and overflow, and the cause of partiality was the seduction of the emotions by the temptations of things. Partiality of the emotions referred to cases in which one indulged one kind of emotion at the neglect of other kinds. Taking the emotion of joy as an example, Wang Fuzhi advised that one should not indulge in joy but forget anger, sorrow, and pleasure; nor should one lose joy in order to be impartial to joy and the other emotions; nor should one lose joy for the sake of other emotions (Wang 1996: 6:470–471). In other words, the partiality of joy includes two cases. The first is that one indulges in joy and forgets anger, sorrow, and pleasure. The second is that one loses joy in order to be fair to the other kinds of emotions. Wang described both cases as being partial to one emotion. In the first case, a person would not only forget the existence of other emotions, they would also ignore the fact that other people may have felt the same emotion. Therefore, partiality would blind a person to other possibilities of emotion. Such blindness reflected that one was overly self-absorbed and was unable to think or feel in another's shoes. In the second case, a person was inhibited from expressing their emotions properly, which caused them to be hypocritical. Wang tended to focus on the first type of case, as illustrated in his criticism of a low-ranking official's complaint about his mission, presented in the *Book of Odes*.

> What I think is urgent—who knows but that other people in the world would think it trivial? What I regard as trivial—who knows but that other people in the world would think it urgent? Thinking highly of the affairs of state and the ancestral temple while looking down on the tasks of runners and servants, thinking loftily of the relationships between ruler and minister, and elder and younger brother, while regarding the union of husband and wife as selfish, a person would not be satisfied even if the people in the world sacrificed their lives and death for the fulfillment of one of his/her sentiments. Clearly, this attitude is not permissible in the purview of reason. (Wang 1996: 3:384–385)

Wang Fuzhi here pointed out that people tended to consider things from their own point of view and ignore the feelings of others. Ignoring the standpoints and possibilities of others, one would exaggerate the importance of what one was doing and complain about not being appreciated by others. Worse were nobles and officials who demanded that the people sacrifice their lives for their preferences or emotions and wreaked disaster on them.

Partiality of emotions would inevitably lead to indulgence in one emotion and its overflow. Wang Fuzhi said, "If a person sets the emotions free and goes against the nature, at the peak of joy they would become indecent, and at the peak of sorrow they would become melancholic" (Wang 1996: 7:344). On his view, such incidences of indecent joy and melancholic sorrow manifested overflows of the emotions. To avoid such excesses, a person should moderate their emotions with the nature. Being joyful but in due measure, being sad but moderate; in this way, they would ensure that the nature ran through the emotions (Wang 1996: 7:344).

Wang Fuzhi also described the nature as "the heavenly rule" or "the principle of joy, anger, sorrow and pleasure," indicating that the emotions would overflow when they were not in accord with this principle (Wang 1996: 6:473). Such overflows of the emotions would open one to succumb to temptations. Once this occurred, it would be difficult to rein in the emotions and transform them by education and punishment. However, if one were to always express the emotions in due measure, they would be in accord with the nature. One's expressions of joy, anger, sorrow, and pleasure would be consistent with the entire body of rituals, music, penalties, and upright governance (Wang 1996: 8:698). What was crucial was to always express the emotions in accordance with principle, the nature.

As to how to regulate emotions by the nature, Wang Fuzhi prescribed several methods. First, one should choose the most appropriate emotion in context. As to different people's experiences of the same things and emotions, where a noble person tasted sweetness, the petty minded would taste bitterness; as to crossing a river, where a noble person crossed it, the petty minded would drown. The reason for the different results was their different choices (Wang 1996: 3:323–324). Their different choices reflected the fact that the noble person would cross the river at a shallow place or a proper time while the petty minded would attempt it without prudently considering the water's depth. To be prudent, a person should choose emotions and things according to principle, and not let themselves be subject to the temptations of things. They should not indulge one emotion at the expense of the other emotions, and they should grasp the reality and value of the object of the emotion. In this way, whether feeling sorrow or joy, they would not indulge in the emotion and respond to the situation in due measure. For example, a poem in the *Book of Odes* describes how the poet felt sad when leaving for the frontier, but sang "the willows are drifting beautifully," and how he felt happy when returning home, but sang "the snow is falling heavily." The poet did not indulge in one kind of his emotion at the expense of others, but opened his eyes wide to other nuances. He thus found things of joy when he felt sad, and things of deep sentiment when he felt happy, differing from shallow people who focused just on their personal sorrow or joy at some matter at hand. Hence, "A person who is adept at expressing their emotions will not simply use the flourishing or withering of things to express their personal joy or sorrow" (Wang 1996: 3:392).

Wang Fuzhi further indicated that the noble person would be prudent in making choices because they let the nature moderate the emotions. They did this by preserving their mind to stay tranquil; what they preserved was the nature (Wang 1996: 8:858). Wang urged that "a noble person's mind has no intention, except for the nature; a noble person's body has no business except for the nature" (Wang 1996: 8:860). As the nature was the inner source of Confucian moral principles, Wang hoped that people would cultivate and discipline themselves as well-rounded, reasonable, moral persons, who acted according to ritual propriety. Truly, people who achieved this state would be tranquil, but over-commitment to principle and purity could diminish the vitality of their emotions or *qi* and lead to a narrow, empty, senseless life.

Second, as to moderating the emotions, Wang Fuzhi requested that students express their likes and aversions in accord with the Way and not let their emotions go astray. Those who upheld the Way would not like "this" simply because they disliked "that," nor would they praise a bad person simply because they had the same dislikes (Wang 1996: 5:187). Since following the nature would be acting in accordance with the Way (Wang 1996: 12:182), expressing likes and aversions in accord with the Way would be also to express the emotions as moderated by the nature.

Because the Way and nature were originally heavenly principle, Wang Fuzhi concentrated on moderating the emotions by principle, too. He insisted that people "express their emotions in accordance with principle. Being in accordance with principle, they would express their emotions properly" (Wang 1996: 3:323–324). "A person who expresses their sorrow and joy according to principle does not ignore the principles in the world; a person who experiences happiness after feeling sorrow does not bear the residue of the previous emotion and will not ignore the range of emotions in the world" (Wang 1996: 3:385). Hence, it was by expressing worries and joys according to principle that the emotions would be aroused in due degree and with propriety. Conversely, it was through appropriate expressions of the emotions that principle was fully realized, for at such moments the emotions and principle would be mutually supportive.

Third, the nature, the Way, and principle were all to be expressed concretely in acts of ritual propriety and righteousness. Hence, the practical way to regulate the emotions would be by practicing ritual propriety and righteousness. Wang Fuzhi said:

> The purpose of ritual propriety is to keep human emotions in due measure. The emotions may or may not be fully expressed. Frank, direct expressions of the emotions will often result in regret. However, there is no a fixed method to regulate the emotions. If one masters ritual propriety, moderates the emotions, and expresses them in due degree, one will not be swayed

from propriety. A person who has not mastered ritual propriety will be unable to achieve due degree and achieve propriety. If they bend down and crouch in supplication, they will not meet the measure; and if they arise and stretch in reverence, they will not meet the measure. As a result, they are confused in their dealings, lacking the inner compass for expressing the emotions in due degree and never achieving propriety. (Wang 1996: 7:999)

Wang Fuzhi here stepped out of the realm of abstract discussions on moderating the emotions by the nature, the Way, and principle, and stressed the need to adopt concrete measures, such as ritual conduct. He advocated that people practice norms and ritual propriety to emulate the emotions and conduct of the sages. By mastering the rules of propriety, and their animating spirit, a person could learn to express the emotions in due degree and reach utmost propriety, the sphere of the sages.

4.3.6   Calming the Nature by Proper Expressions of the Emotions

Wang Fuzhi held that the nature and the emotions were mutually supportive; that is, while the emotions substantiated and manifested the nature, the nature moderated the emotions. "Heaven gives me eyes and ears, and entrusts me with these emotions to serve the nature. Heaven gives me my mind, and grants me the nature, to establish the control of the emotions" (Wang 1996: 8:740). The emotions were associated with the senses and represented the vitality of life. Without the emotions, there would be no intentional human life, not to mention realization of principle. Therefore, although the emotions could give rise to evil when a person felt excessive joy, anger, sorrow, and pleasure, and did not maintain the state of equilibrium before the emotions were aroused (*weifa zhi zhong* 未發之中) (Wang 1996: 8:698), Wang never considered extinguishing the emotions to prevent evil. He even drew a line separating his teaching from Buddhism, which instructed extinguishing the emotions to recover the Buddha Nature. He understood that the Buddhists advocated purging the emotions so as to cut off evil at its root. In his view, however, the Buddhists had failed to realize that while a person devoid of emotions would not do evil, they would not do good, either. Moreover, such a person would be unable to realize their talents or the original nature (Wang 1996: 6:1069–1070). The issue for Wang was not how to purge the emotions, but rather how to express them in due degree, that is, how to moderate the emotions to achieve utmost propriety. He recommended "calming the nature by expressing the emotions in due degree (*xun qing yi ding xing* 循情而可以定性)" (Wang 1996: 3:353).

Notably, the nature one was to calm was not the original nature; it was the second nature, a product of habit and the original nature. Most people were subject to their second nature almost from birth. Since habit was a lasting and repetitive preference or feeling, the second nature could be swayed by the emotions, as well. Therefore, to calm the nature, one had to grasp one's emotions. And, to assist in calming the nature of others, one had to grasp their emotions and carefully express one's own emotions in due degree in one's interactions with them. If a person failed to understand the other's emotions, yet wanted to influence them, the other would feel misunderstood and set his/her advice aside. To achieve sympathetic understanding of the other, one needed to think and feel in the other's shoes and to express oneself frankly to gain their trust. In this way, they could begin to understand each other and share their joys and sorrows. In *Cock Crows* (*jiming* 雞鳴) from the *Book of Odes*, a woman's husband wants to indulge in the pleasures of the bedroom and is reluctant to depart on an official mission. She tells him, "I too wish to enjoy this pleasure with you, yet I fear that others will blame me for this dalliance and negligence of your duty." By expressing her emotions frankly, she persuades her husband to depart for his official mission. Wang concluded, if a noble person wanted to transform a petty person, he would be unable to move him unless he enlisted his own emotions and understood the emotions of the other (Wang 1996: 3:353). "The emotions are pivots of safety and risk, and it is by pacifying the emotions that the nature is preserved" (Wang 1996: 2:366).

Wang Fuzhi discussed how the early sages had utilized honors and rewards to moderate the people's emotions. In his view, the people had differing likes and dislikes, especially concerning honor and shame. Even though they took joy in the pursuit of things, if they won no recognition for this pursuit, they would take little delight in the effort. In such a case, even a merciful father or a wise ruler could not persuade his son or force his subjects to perform a task. Consequently, in their efforts to improve the people, the early sage kings utilized honors to stir their emotions and used ritual propriety to preserve their honor and reliability, knowing it would be hard to govern well if their efforts did not appeal to the people's emotions. Hence, "The emotions are dependents of the nature. Disregarding the emotions would incline one to disregard the nature. The nature, however, is the endowment of Heaven. Disregarding the nature would mean disregarding Heaven" (Wang 1996: 10:389). If a person's nature were to be overwhelmed and eclipsed by the emotions, they should first strive to moderate the emotions. However, once the emotions had overwhelmed the nature, the emotions (and habit) would engulf the nature. Consequently, for Wang, a fundamental tenet was to moderate the emotions and keep them in check, to preserve the original nature.

Wang Fuzhi also held that, while the emotions provided the means by which to express and realize the nature, for this to happen one had to carefully preserve the original nature and not lose it. Were a person to lose or not know the original nature, they could not moderate the emotions or calm the original nature even though the original nature might occasionally appear with the emotions. For example, as to the concern and consternation that people would feel when seeing a baby crawl near a well, Wang regarded it as just a pang of conscience. Since most people had lost their Way mind or original nature, this feeling of concern would just be a glint of the diminished heavenly light (the original nature) in their perceptions and movements (Wang 1996: 6:1093). This feeling could be used as evidence for the prior existence of the original nature and a starting point for cultivation, but it would be insufficient for recovering it. To recover the original nature and achieve sagehood, one would have to reflect deeply on the original nature and discipline the self by practicing ritual propriety. One could not depend on the emotions alone, that is, on one's spontaneous reactions to phenomena. In particular, "when a person establishes their great body (the nature) and has the mind that cannot bear to witness the suffering of others (*Mencius* 2A.6), they will differ from ordinary people who would just feel concern and consternation upon seeing an infant crawl near a well" (Wang 1996: 6:1093). In short, the response one who had established their great body (the nature) would be to save the infant at once, as a spontaneous expression of their humaneness.

4.4   The Desires and Principle

In essence, the relationship between principle and the desires paralleled that between the Way mind and the human mind, as well as that between the nature and the emotions in Wang Fuzhi's works. However, Wang did have a reason for distinguishing them. Generally, he regarded the human mind as the aspect of cognitive awareness, and the Way mind as the principle that guided awareness, preventing it from going astray. Although one's ideas and intentions would include the emotions, they were also bound up with one's responses to situations. As to the emotions, they were the conative aspect of the mind, and more general and aesthetic than the desires. The desires reflected a person's biological needs, wants, and fulfillment (see below). Confucians tended to regard the desires as degraded or snarled emotions. One's primary concern with the emotions was to express them in due degree; with the desires, the concern was how to restrain them in an acceptable scope. As Zhu Xi said, "The desires emerge from the emotions...The emotions flow like water, but the desires drive like waves and wrinkles of water" (Li 1994: 93).

Wang Fuzhi sometimes distinguished between the emotions and the desires by saying, "Joy, anger, sorrow, and pleasure are just the human mind, not human desires" (Wang 1996: 6:473). Again, the emotions were the conative aspect of the mind. But, Wang also regarded the emotions as the source of the desires. In his comment on Zhang Zai's dictum, "The emotions of love and hate both arise from the Great Void, and finally become the desires," Wang remarked:

> When yin and yang are at odds, hatred assuredly arises. When yin embraces yang, and yang embraces yin, the offspring of their intercourse, love, assuredly arises. These are the workings of material qi in the Great Void. When interacting with things, they are manifested as desires. The desires are spontaneously produced by the emotions. (Wang 1996: 12:41)

Wang Fuzhi regarded the emotions and the desires both as mechanisms of qi in the Great Void; but, it was the emotions that gave rise to the desires. Given this causal relationship, Wang discussed them without sharply distinguishing between them. For example, he regarded the arousal of joy, anger, sorrow, and pleasure as the starting point of the emotions and the desires alike (Wang 1996: 6:640). He also considered them both normal manifestations of heavenly principle (Wang 1996: 1:421). In particular, he advanced the proposition that heavenly principle could not be realized beyond the human desires and rejected any teaching of purging the desires to realize heavenly principle, which he ascribed to Zhu Xi (Li 1994: 301).

What were the desires and how did they arise, in Wang Fuzhi's view? He tended to define the desires biologically as the satisfaction of bodily organs. "Desire is that the ears, eyes, mouth and body all have their likes and seek to satisfy them" (Wang 1996: 10:1149). In his view, it was natural for the ears, eyes, mouth, and body each to pursue its respective attractions, and he held that the desires were as much part of the noble person as the petty minded.

Wang Fuzhi offered an ontological account of the origin of the desires, drawing on the *Book of Changes*. According to the *Changes*, *qi* divided into yin and yang. Yang was correlated with the nature while yin was correlated with the body. Hence, principle arose from the nature while desire originated in the body (Wang 1996: 1:837). The virtue of yin was Kun, manifested as the petty minded, and gave rise to desire and profit-mindedness in human beings (Wang 1996: 1:354). The virtue of yang was Qian, manifested as the original nature and humaneness (Wang 1996: 1:51). Accordingly, Wang distinguished principle (the nature) from desire (body) based on the virtues of yang and yin, and established the dominance of principle over desire. However, Wang also recognized that yin and yang were complements that operate together, achieving unity and harmony. Consequently, there was ambiguity in his account of the relationship between yin and yang. Sometimes, he spoke of the co-establishment of Qian and Kun (*Qain Kun bing jian* 乾坤並建); that is, he presented yin and yang as the two basic elements that formed the universe (Wang 1996: 1:989); sometimes, he insisted that yin and yang were two aspects of the one *qi* (Wang 1996: 12:42). As to the relationship between body and the nature, the desires and principle, Wang proposed the unity of the desires and principle, body and the nature, on the one hand while insisting that the desires and principle shared the same human body but had different contents (*tianli renyu tongxing yiqing* 天理人欲同行異情) (Wang 1996: 1:837), on the other.

4.4.1   The Unity of the Desires and Principle

As the nature and the desires corresponded to and arose from yang and yin, respectively, and yin and yang were two phases of the undifferentiated *qi*, the nature and the desires were originally one, and represented different aspects of *qi*. As the nature manifested itself as humaneness and ritual propriety in social intercourse, Wang Fuzhi sometimes discussed the nature in terms of ritual propriety. He considered that "ritual propriety and humaneness arose from yang's initiation and interaction with yin. So, as pure *yang*, ritual propriety had to reside in *yin*. Consequently, ritual propriety as the pattern of heavenly principle had to be manifested through human desires" (Wang 1996: 6:911). Ritual propriety bodied forth principle to guide the desires and be manifested through the desires; it could not exist beyond the desires. In this way, Wang sought to justify the unity of principle and the desires ontologically in terms of their common origin—the intercourse of yin and yang.

Since principle could not exist beyond the desires, it was impossible to seek principle beyond the desires and impracticable to purge the desires. Rather, one had to seek principle in the desires and master how to express the desires properly. This in mind, Wang proposed several ideas concerning the unity of the desires and principle, which later scholars have found appealing. For instance:

> The sages have desires, yet their desires are heavenly principle… Scholars have both principle and desires. When they realize principle, it matches their desires. When they extend their desires properly, they encounter heavenly principle. So, it is evident that the fulfillment of human desires lies in the universal realization of heavenly principle; the universal realization of heavenly principle is no different than the fulfillment of human desires. (Wang 1996: 6:639)

Wang Fuzhi here made a distinction between the sages and scholars (ordinary people) based on how they managed principle and the desires. The sages could express their emotions and fulfill their desires naturally in due measure, thus their desires would match principle. Ordinary people could not satisfy their desires properly, so their desires did not match heavenly principle. To unify their desires with principle, ordinary people had to master principle and extend their desires to other people.

These quotations show that Wang Fuzhi did not think that the desires and principle were united in ordinary people. (This differed from his ontological view that the desires and principle had a common source.) To mark the distinction between ordinary people's desires and those of the sage, Wang coined the term "universal desire (*gongyu* 公欲)," insisting that only universal desire was identical with principle. In other words, the sage's desires were universal desires and thus matched principle. But, ordinary people's desires were not universal desires, and had to be extended before they could match principle. Hence, Wang said, "The universal aspect of human desires matches the perfect rightness of heavenly principle" (Wang 1996: 7:137). "The universal desire under Heaven is principle. It is called universal that everyone gets their desires fulfilled" (Wang 1996: 12:191). He further specified this universal desire as the basic need and satisfaction of human beings. "Among sound, color, smell, and taste, one broadly finds the universal desire of the people, and this universal desire is the common principle that people follow when exploring the myriad things" (Wang 1996: 6:911). Sound, color, smell, and taste are basic and universal sensory needs of the human body. Among them universal desire is manifested, so Wang regarded universal desire as a basic biological need to be satisfied, which corresponded to the human right for survival and the principle of life or humaneness.

Wang Fuzhi went on to identify this universal desire as the epitome of the mind of compassion, that is, the golden rule expressed as "wishing to establish oneself, one seeks to establish others; wishing to be eminent oneself, one helps others to be eminent" (Analects 6.28). Wang assumed that the mind of compassion was universally endowed in every human being, due to its origin in the Great Harmony. Given the mind of compassion, whatever one desired, other people would desire it, as well (Wang 1996: 12:157). In other words, Wang assumed that everyone shared the same mind of compassion. The desire arising from this mind would be universal, and it would underwrite love and humaneness. In this way, Wang tacitly characterized the content of universal desire as humaneness, and held that a ruler would be able to transform even the most perverse of people if he could realize the universal desire of the people and not deviate from the proper path of yin-yang intercourse.

Confusingly, however, Wang Fuzhi also expressed doubts about and arguments against the idea of universal desire. In *Instructions for Thinking and Inquiring* (*Siwen Lu* 思問錄), he said:

> There is universal principle, but no universal desire. Only after selfish desires are completely eliminated does heavenly principle prevail and the desires can be regarded as universal. If principle were to prevail in the world, it would be able to satisfy the desires of the whole world. But, if a person attempted to share their desires with others, they would fail miserably. (Wang 1996: 12:406)

On the surface, this quotation contradicts Wang's previous affirmation of the existence of universal desire. Actually, the statements do not contradict each other. In the preceding paragraph, universal desire just referred to the mind of compassion and the desire that matches humaneness or heavenly principle. In the last quotation, Wang insisted that "Only after *selfish* desire is eliminated does heavenly principle prevail, and then the desires could be regarded as universal." In essence, the desires would match heavenly principle insofar as they arose from the mind of compassion and supported the public interest.

What was the notion of "universal desire" that Wang denied here? It referred to yet another kind of desire, that is, to share one's desire with others without respect to principle. Wang Fuzhi identified it with sharing popular opinions and admonished a ruler for catering to the people's unreasonable and selfish desires. After quoting Mencius' words, "to help the people collect what they desire; stop the things that they dislike," Wang warned that one should not misinterpret the ordinary people's desires for short-term interest as universal desire. The pursuit of short-term interest looked like universal desire, and was presented as a universal opinion, but it seldom matched principle and always needed to be rectified. For this reason, Wang concluded, "There is universal principle, but no universal desire. Universal desire is only an illusory popular habit" (Wang 1996: 12:428).

4.4.2 The Inalienability of the Desires to Human Beings

Wang Fuzhi believed that, as the product of yin and yang and the Five Elements, human beings were born with inalienable desires. Indeed, he held that, without desires, human beings could not survive. As a human being, one had to live on the Earth, reside in an empty chamber, depend on fire for warmth, and drink water to stay hydrated. One had to eat grains and imbibe soup to keep hunger at bay. Otherwise, one could not survive (Wang 1996: 1:887). Certainly, human beings needed the desires to secure food, drink, clothing, and shelter, and to procreate. Wang did not accept the admonition he attributed to Zhu Xi and his followers that one must preserve principle and realize sagehood by eliminating the desires. He criticized Zhen Dexiu's 真德秀 (1178–1235) statement, "Master Yan (Yan Hui) had no desires while the others had few desires," with the implication that having no desires would be superior to having few desires. He noted that Confucius and Yan Hui both focused on preserving heavenly principle, and never regarded the desires as something poisonous, to be purged (Wang 1996: 6:673). Wang held that, once heavenly principle was preserved, one could enlist it to moderate the desires and satisfy the desires properly; therefore, it was not be necessary to purge the desires to realize sagehood.

Wang Fuzhi interpreted "no desires" or "being free of desire" as referring to desire meeting principle. "A noble person has no desire and does not deviate from principle. That is because their eyes, ears, mouth, and body pause at the proper place, and they do not bestow special favors upon others" (Wang 1996: 11:67). In this way, the expression "no desires" did not mean getting rid of desires, but rather it concerned the proper expression of desire according to principle.

Wang Fuzhi did not accept the notion of having "few desires," either. He regarded the desires as an impetus for making achievements. Without the spur of desire, one would be hard-pressed to make great contributions to the world. If a sage king lacked desire, he could not extend his humaneness and bestow benefits on the people. If Confucius had lacked the desire to establish a Zhou kingdom in the east, he would not have become the sage. What one should not have was selfish desires, such as seeking costly exquisite foods or lusting to enrich oneself at the expense of others. If one felt an ambition or desire like Confucius' and persistently endeavored to achieve it, one would stand shoulder to shoulder with the sages and worthies (Wang 1996: 6:899).

After justifying the desires as the inner impetus for making achievements, Wang drew a distinction between proper desires and selfish desires. Wang considered that selfish desires were focused on pleasures of the body or personal gain rather than concern for public welfare, while proper desires were those aimed to benefit both oneself and the public. One who had too few desires would lack the drive to benefit even oneself, not to mention serve the public interest. Wang warned, "I fear that those who look down on the desires would look down principle, as well, and those who decline to accept the world would be unwilling to undertake worldly affairs, as well" (Wang 1996: 3:374). Wang thus rightly pointed out a critical weakness of the Neo-Confucian vision, which decried worldly affairs and advanced pure moral virtues and having few desires. Because principle was originally one with the desires, how could one fail to look askance at principle when looking down on the desires? It took desire to tackle worldly affairs—how could a person with few desires boldly take them on? It equally took desire to engage in Confucian self-cultivation. This position distinguished Wang sharply from the previous Neo-Confucians, despite that he had inherited many of their ideas.

Wang Fuzhi insisted that the proper way to manage the desires was not to eliminate them, but to satisfy them properly. If a person managed their pursuit of profit with righteousness, and guided their desires with principle, they would manifest heavenly principle in their desires, and carry out their pursuit of sound, color, goods, and profit in due measure (Wang

1996: 1:355). As to grasping and abiding by principle, Wang recommended first moderating the desires by practicing ritual propriety. By practicing ritual propriety, one would enjoy the benefits befitting one's social status without taint of selfish desire. If one were an emperor, a splendid palace and beautiful concubines would befit his position. As to Confucius' refusal to sell his chariot to pay for Yan Hui's outer coffin (*Analects* 11.8), Wang did not regard Confucius' refusal as selfish because, as a low-ranking minister (*dafu* 大夫), Confucius needed his chariot to carry out his official and social affairs. In other words, if a person satisfied their desires according to their social status, they should not be deemed greedy, even if they used a lot of resources, nor be considered miserly even if they used little. "If it was good for him to consume bream fish, why should he reject it? If it was right for him to marry the beauty of the Jiang family, why should he decline her?" Therefore, "all things are created for some purpose, and all human desires have their due measure" (Wang 1996: 3:374). What a noble person could do was to weigh things up and assign them their proper place, and take care of their desires for food and sex, and satisfy them properly; they need not reject things and terminate desires. In a word, Wang took ritual propriety, not subjective or biological need, as the standard for determining what would be indulgence in things and the desires. One who sincerely observed ritual propriety could enjoy fine delicacies and lovely companions. Wang thereby appealed to ritual propriety in answering the problematic question of human desires, and turned the ontological principle-desire relation into a social ritual-desire relation.

Wang's appreciation of the desires distinguished him from most of his Neo-Confucian predecessors. He not only secured a proper place in human life for the desires, but offered students a way to deal with their material welfare. In Confucianism, there had been a tendency to praise having few desires or living a simple life. As a result, many in the Confucian school looked down on material goods and recommended a simple life. Dong Zhongshu 董仲舒 (179 BC–104 BC) even claimed, "A person should justify righteous conduct, not pursue their own interest; they should promote the Way, not concern themselves with achievement" (Ban 1962: 2524). Cheng Yi 程颐 (1033–1107) proposed, "A person's conduct will not match ritual propriety if they have the mind to do good" (Cheng and Cheng 2000: 190). Given this overly idealistic trend, discussions about benefits and profit became taboo among officials and scholars who pretended to live simple lives and look askance at material profit. In fact, however, this trend inclined people to become greedy whenever an opportunity to get benefits or realize profit arose. No wonder there were so many hypocritical scholars, although Zhu Xi had urged his students to repress their desires and be sincere. Wang's teaching that people acknowledge and satisfy their desires offers a way for people to manage their desires more judiciously, making social customs healthier.

Granted that heavenly principle resided in the desires, how could the desires deviate from heavenly principle and be selfish? Wang Fuzhi pointed out two reasons. One was popular opinions; the other was personal inclination. As to the former, he had in mind people who had discarded their own judgment and sense of principle and followed popular opinions in making decisions. Such people would savor exotic delicacies from the seas and mountains, not on the basis of their taste preferences, but in accord with popular opinion; they would don apparel made of pearls and jade, not from their need and comfort, but in accord with the fashion of the day. As popular tastes in fashion changed, their opinion would change unconsciously and they would ask themselves how they could have loved those old fashions before (Wang 1996: 11:67). Wang saw the impact of popular fashion on an individual's desires. He was critical of people's blind acceptance of popular fashion, and criticized their failure to apply good judgment and principle regarding such matters. In response, he suggested educating children with healthy habits and values, and shielding them from the influence of popular fashion. Once healthy habits and values had been instilled and become second nature, a person would not be easily swayed by popular preferences and be able to satisfy their desires in keeping with propriety and principle.

As to personal diversions, Wang Fuzhi was curious why "collectors" loved their "precious" curios and exotic pets so much. He frankly admitted that he could not understand why Duke Yi of Wei 衛懿公 loved cranes, Tang Emperor Xuan 唐玄宗 was so fond of the drums of the Jie 羯 tribe, or Song Emperor Hui 宋徽宗 indulged in flowers and stones. To Wang, such objects of adoration were no different than ordinary pottery and animals (Wang 1996: 11:67). Consequently, he regarded such people's love for their curios and exotic pets as excessive, and considered that such desires exceeded due measure and deviated from principle. He held that people seek the utility of objects. To desire more would be to deviate from heavenly principle and be selfish. To Wang, it would suffice if one's calligraphy conveyed its meaning and painting depicted the forms of mountains, rivers, trees, and animals. If Wang Xizhi's 王羲之 perfect calligraphy and Song Emperor Hui's beautiful paintings obsessed people to excess, they should be gathered up and burned (Wang 1996: 10:1150).

Wang's negative judgments regarding calligraphy, paintings, curios, exotic pets, and other fineries reflected his ignorance of aesthetics and his short-sighted pragmatism. He did not understand that art and aesthetics were also manifestations of nobility and civility. As Xunzi remarked, when people had deep emotions they expressed them through ritual propriety, for they wanted to express them, not only properly, but elegantly (Wang 1988: 26–27). Calligraphy, paintings, and other works of art were treasured because they embodied cultivation, elegance, and harmony, not just from an unhealthy thirst for new and exotic things, as Wang charged.

Wang Fuzhi also appealed to personal inclination in describing the behavior of Daoist hermits and Buddhist monks as selfish. His rationale was that aversion was the excess of dislike, as doting was the excess of like. As to Daoists who felt aversion for wealth and nobility but enjoyed poverty and humility or Buddhist monks who detested life and longed for death, Wang judged their aversions as forms of selfish desire (Wang 1996: 5:615). More positively, Confucian scholars would express their likes and dislikes in accord with ritual propriety and righteousness. If they were entitled to have wealth and nobility according to their social status, they would enjoy them; if the situation did not require them to die, they would live rather than throw their life away. From this perspective, Wang judged that the Daoist hermits who shunned the sages and delighted in poverty and humbleness, even in times of good governance, did so because they could not handle wealth and nobility, not because they were truly detached. It was their inability to handle wealth and nobility that led them to take delight in a simple dwelling with a string-bound door and jar-windows (Wang 1996: 5:614–615). Wang shed especially acidic venom on Zhuangzi, for disrespecting ritual propriety, indulging in excessive detachment, and thus making his desire for austerity selfish (Wang 1996: 6:769). In short, Wang did not condone either fondness or aversion in excess, but advocated that people moderate them with ritual propriety.

4.4.3 Preserving Principle to Moderate the Desires

Wang Fuzhi did not favor eliminating the desires to preserve principle, and advocated their basic unity. He compared the relation between principle and the desires to that between a fish and water. Without water, fish could not survive; without the desires, principle would have no place to prevail. Therefore, Wang advocated applying principle to moderate the desires on the faith that once a person understood and committed to principle, they would moderate their desires and express them in accord with ritual propriety (Wang 1996: 6:799).

Wang did not endorse the preservation of principle by repressing the desires, either. On his view, as a manifest sign of heavenly principle, the desires should not simply be repressed. If a person's desires were repressed in early childhood, they could be permanently weakened and lose the power to manifest heavenly principle (Wang 1996: 1:413–414). To illustrate, Wang compared a child's incipient desire to a sprout from a seed. The sprout should grow freely at the beginning. Only after some growth would the branches on the sides need to be trimmed to give the tree the proper shape. If the sprout were trimmed too early, its vitality would be sapped and it could possibly wither and die. Similarly, if a person's desires were repressed too early, their vitality would be sapped and they could not manifest principle. For this reason, Wang advocated moderating the desires after one had reached maturity:

> After the pliant yin (desire) has reached its proper stage, one extinguishes evil intention within, but it is not yet purely good without. Hence, one must adhere firmly to principle and avoid tiny, subtle mistakes. This is the right way to moderate desires. (Wang 1996: 1:414)

Wang Fuzhi's words reflected his contention that the desires, at root, were not bad and should not be repressed arbitrarily. They became bad or evil only when they had become excessive. The proper point to manage or control the desires was to grasp the right time to defer them from excess. This right time was before a person's evil intentions had arisen after their desires had begun to be influenced by things. Then, one would apply principle to moderate the desires to prevent their excess.

To moderate the desires, one first had to grasp principle and preserve it in mind, not simply repress the desires. "In learning, if one starts from repressing the desires and does it with zealously, on the surface, one may avoid the flaws of being competitive, boastful, resentful, and covetous; but, on a deeper level, one might fall into passive Nirvana" (Wang 1996: 6:793). Being competitive, boastful, resentful, and covetous were traits that Confucius advised his advisees and students to avoid. However, just eliminating such traits would not ensure that one would be humane. Nirvana was the supreme Buddhist realization, but, in Wang's view, it lacked vitality and humaneness. Instead, Wang claimed that in learning, one must strive to understand and preserve principle, then enlist it to moderate the desires.

Wang Fuzhi noted the damage that the Taizhou School 泰州學派, a branch of the Wang Yangming transmission, had wreaked by advocating repressing the desires before preserving principle. In Wang Fuzhi's view, these followers of Wang Yangming had held that the inborn knowledge of the mind transcended good and evil, and therefore made no cultivation efforts to rectify the mind. Initially, their preferred method of cultivation was to be circumspect about their mental state in solitude, but they soon found that new desires would arise after they had made efforts to repress the original ones. Even when they successfully repressed the desires, they found that this would result in a bland, vacuous mind. Moreover, this vacuous mind was an open door to new evil desires. In consequence, the followers of the Taizhou School could not stay focused on humaneness for even a month (Wang 1996: 12:412).

Wang Fuzhi's criticisms revealed that he wanted to go beyond the teachings of both Zhu Xi and Wang Yangming and establish a syncretic system of his own. Unfortunately, Wang did not shed the teaching of eliminating the desires completely, for he also sometimes contended that principle would prevail only after desires had been eliminated. Some might argue that Wang had advocated the elimination of *selfish* desire only. In the *Analects*, Confucius asked his disciples, Zi Lu 子路, Ran You 冉有, and Gongxi Hua 公西華 to state their ambitions. Some aspired to be high ministers, and some wished to be generals. Even though such ambitions may seem to be normal, Wang condemned them as desires. He argued, "Because they set up those goals in advance, they would feel satisfied only if they were to succeed, and would feel distressed if they were to fail. Their mindset was that of human desire" (Wang 1996: 6:761). He supported this assessment with Zhu Xi's assertions that "When there is no human desire, heavenly principle will prevail" (Zhu 1983: 130), and "One should first make one's mind empty of desire" (Zhu 2010: 23:2966; Wang 1996: 6:761).[6] Apparently, these remarks contradicted his previous argument that the sage also needed desires to make achievements (Wang 1996: 6:899). With desires to do something, the sage would be feeling disappointed if he failed. This was shown in Confucius' sighs when he failed to

---

[6] Zhu Xi's original text is 然須先理會要教自家身心自得無欲. Wang Fuzhi's citation makes some modification.

get appointment. Then how could Wang demand Confucius' disciples to do what Confucius himself could not do? Moreover, when Wang went on to praise Confucius and claim Confucius just did what was fitting in the situation and would not plan or desire anything in advance, or bear it in mind afterward (Wang 1996: 6:826), he started to sound like a Chan Buddhist, emphasizing pure spontaneity, and going against his own emphasis on cultivation and learning.

Returning to Wang Fuzhi's discussion on the preservation of principle, he adopted Mencius' method of cultivating the mind: do not neglect, do not help, but always be engaged (*wu wang, wu zhu, bi you shi yan* 勿忘勿助必有事焉). When a farmer sowed seeds, he did not neglect them, nor did he pull them to grow; rather, he always cultivated them. When the time was right, the crop would be ready to harvest. Similarly, Wang asked scholars to stay attentive to the indications of heavenly principle and not forget to apply it in life at the right times, nor should they just passively hold it or easily deviate from principle and the Mean when convenient. Then he would have filled his heart-mind with principle substantially and know it clearly, and he would avoid the invasion of selfish desires without wasting energy on driving them away (Wang 1996: 6:463). For Wang, once the mind was made replete with principle, leaving no space for *selfish* desires to take root, the selfish desires would be averted without having to make any additional efforts.

Lastly, Wang Fuzhi often discussed "moderating the desires by preserving principle" by means of "mastering the self by practicing ritual propriety (*keji fuli* 克己復禮)." In his view, if a person were to manage the desires with ritual propriety, they would be able to cope with all sorts of yin phenomena (desires, temptations, the petty minded, etc.) (Wang 1996: 1:363). As ritual propriety manifested principle concretely, cultivation by *keji fuli* amounted to moderating the desires by preserving principle. However, in fact, practicing the cultivation of *keji fuli* would be more concrete and easier to carry out because ritual propriety was recorded in texts and selfish desires were also easily recognizable in social intercourse.

First, just as preserving principle was a prerequisite of moderating the desires, practicing ritual propriety was prior to mastering the self, as well. If a person had practiced ritual propriety but had not yet mastered the self, they could proceed to master the self by undertaking introspection. One who mastered the self but had not practiced ritual propriety would encounter trouble for the rest of his life (Wang 1996: 12:477). "His trouble" would be the trouble that new selfish desires would arise right after the old ones have been controlled or purged. In Wang's view, ritual propriety was both the weapon to resist selfish desires and the standard to distinguish between selfish desires and less selfish ones. If a person were to practice ritual propriety, they would be set to overcome their selfish desires. "If ritual propriety is not practiced, a person will remain in the thrall of selfish desires. Yet, even if they have mastered their selfish desires, they may not yet have practiced ritual propriety" (Wang 1996: 6:765).

As to making efforts to practice ritual propriety, besides learning norms and rituals, Wang asked students to reflect on the nature, that is, the rule for the ears, eyes, mind, and bear in mind that Heaven endowed them with the power of introspection. Once a student had grasped this rule (principle), they would be able to determine what conduct was consistent with ritual propriety and what conduct reflected selfish desires. Such a student could begin to moderate their selfish desires (Wang 1996: 6:765). This rule was the principle of life or conscience, the source of righteousness and ritual propriety.

At the same time, Wang Fuzhi did not deny that mastering selfish desires, in turn, could facilitate one's practice of ritual propriety. He said, "Having mastered the selfish desires, one can practice ritual propriety; by practicing ritual propriety, one can master the selfish desires. These efforts are mutually supportive. It is wrong to stress mastering selfish desires alone" (Wang 1996: 6:683). But, Wang did not specify how mastering selfish desires could enhance practicing ritual propriety. In most of his discussions, he only stressed practicing ritual propriety. In fact, right after he proposed they were mutually supportive, he went on to say:

If there were no ritual propriety to serve as a standard of disposition and conduct, how could one recognize the selfish desires and master them? If one did not recognize heavenly principle in its companion—human desires— one would not grasp the rule that guides one's seeing, hearing, speaking, and moving with propriety, even though one appeared to be acting on principle. (Wang 1996: 6:911)

In short, ritual propriety needed to be part and parcel of whatever one did, whenever and wherever one did it. There could be no time when one neglected ritual propriety, so the notion of practicing ritual propriety only after purging the desires would be unfeasible. Ritual propriety as rule of conduct ran through all cases, having or lacking desire. In this way, once they could moderate their desires, Confucian scholars would be set to manage all sorts of affairs with moderation and propriety and set to avert any influx of new desires.

4.5   Humaneness and Other Virtues

4.5.1   Ritual Propriety: Concrete Manifestation of Humaneness and Righteousness

The reason why Wang Fuzhi recommended ritual propriety for moderating the desires was because it was the concrete pattern of heavenly principle. "Ritual propriety as the pattern of heavenly principle is fully contained in the mind before the emotions of joy, anger, sorrow, and pleasure are aroused, and guides the emotions to accord with the nature when they are expressed" (Wang 1996: 6:592). "If a person could practice and carry out ritual propriety in all of their seeing, hearing, speaking and acting, heavenly principle would prevail without obstruction. In this fashion, they would embody the Way or heavenly principle in themselves. Otherwise, they simply discuss the nature and the endowment (of Heaven) in vain" (Wang 1996: 12:218). By practicing ritual propriety, people could moderate the desires with propriety and embody heavenly principle in their conduct.

Besides moderating the desires, ritual propriety served as the means to express the sincerity of the mind and intentions. First, both ritual propriety and music originated in humaneness, and in turn could express the humaneness in the mind (Wang 1996: 7: 320). Wang Fuzhi elaborated: when the early sage kings found that humaneness was first manifested as people's love for their parents, they established ritual propriety to cultivate and expand on this. It was from the emotions of the human mind that ritual propriety arose; and it was found that through observances of ritual propriety the mind could be realized (Wang 1996: 8:302). Second, because ritual propriety depended on righteousness, and righteousness was the realization of humaneness in situations, ritual propriety offered the way to assign each thing its proper place (Wang 1996: 2:315). In that sense, ritual propriety was a concrete manifestation of righteousness in practical affairs and concrete things (Wang 1996: 1:297). Through proper observances of ritual propriety, one's righteousness would impress itself on others.

To avoid the ossification of ritual propriety, Wang Fuzhi emphasized adapting rituals to new and different situations. In making such adaptations, old rituals could be modified and new rituals could be innovated. "As to matters which were not addressed in the ritual classics, we must appeal to righteousness" (Wang 1996: 8:656). "If one's response meets the propriety of righteousness, even if it is not discussed in the rules of ritual propriety, a new ritual can be established on the basis of [this indication of] righteousness" (Wang 1996: 6:1048). At this point, Wang gave the cultivated mind the right and responsibility to adapt or innovate rituals according to situation, and praised the Tang emperors who established mourning rituals between brothers and sisters-in-law in keeping with the needs of Tang society.

Wang Fuzhi also discussed the relationship between ritual propriety and righteousness in terms of the relationship between norm (*jing* 經) and expediency (*quan* 權). He stressed that noble people could deploy righteousness and expediency in new or anomalous situations, but he did not accept that they could replace ritual propriety and convention completely—for righteous and expediency were deployed in this way in light of the system of ritual propriety for moral compass and bearings. He also spoke of assessing the importance of handling an event with expediency based on one's mastery of ritual propriety. "A noble person determines ritual propriety in accordance with the norms, and executes expediency in light of ritual propriety" (Wang 1996: 8:459). Wang offered two examples from the *Four Books* to illustrate this idea. As to convention, Wang cited Confucius' response to Duke Ai of Lu's summons. Generally, it was improper for a duke to summon a retired official. Nonetheless, according to ritual, once summoned, an official had to respond to the summons. Therefore, righteousness should defer to ritual and one should comply with convention and ritual in this case. As to expediency, Wang held that one should seize a drowning woman's hand to save her, even though ritual propriety demanded that a man not touch a woman's hand in public. One who failed to save the woman would have betrayed the original purpose of ritual propriety—the realization of humaneness.

4.5.2 Wisdom: Guarantor of the Proper Realization of Humaneness

Wang Fuzhi assigned to wisdom a crucial role in the realization of humaneness and the other Confucian virtues. In his view, wisdom ran through the other virtues and provided the clarity and insight to realize them perfectly in conduct. Specifically, a person with wisdom could be humane but not doting, righteous but not rigid, reliable but not overly restrained by promises made, and observant of ritual but not hypocritical (Wang 1996: 12:287). Wang's rationale was that being humane depended on the wisdom to love sincerely; observing ritual propriety depended on the wisdom to weigh degree of respect; righteousness depended on the wisdom to assess the feasibility and rightness of decisions; and reliability depended on the wisdom to distinguish the authenticity of sincerity (Wang 1996: 1:824).

Wang Fuzhi expressed this notion in his comment on Qin Shihuang, the First Qin Emperor (r. 221–206 BC). He observed that the first emperor's cruelty resulted from a serious lack of wisdom: Lacking wisdom, the First Emperor was inhumane, ignored righteousness, and disregarded ritual propriety. "People throughout the empire disparaged the First Emperor's lack of humaneness, despised his unrighteousness, and looked askance at his lack of rationality. Who then realized that all of these faults were results of his lack of wisdom" (Wang 1996: 3:370–371)? As to how Qin Shihuang's lack of wisdom had led to such inhumaneness, Wang responded that anyone so lacking in wisdom would be unable to weigh costs and benefits, distinguish truths from falsehoods, and be subject to whim (Wang 1996: 1:824).

What, then, was wisdom? Wang Fuzhi understood it as the power of perspicuity, and the clear discernment of truth and falsity. He said, "Human beings possess the truths and falsities of human beings; events possess truths and falsities of their own. As to these truths and falsities, one must keep perspicuous in the mind. This is wisdom" (Wang 1996: 6:393). He expanded the scope of wisdom to include the knowledge of good and evil, as well as the comprehension of humaneness and righteousness: "Wisdom is that one sharply distinguishes good from evil, truth from falsehood" (Wang 1996: 7:419). "The virtues in human nature are humaneness and righteousness. Wisdom is that one understands the principles of humaneness and righteousness" (Wang 1996: 8:478).

As righteousness sprang from the sense of shame and aversion, Wang Fuzhi observed that the greatest wisdom concerned the knowledge of shame and honor.[7] Based on this definition, he criticized Zhang Hua 張華 (232–300), a Jin dynasty prime minister, for not being truly wise. Zhang Hua was adept at noticing the incipient signs of events and catching the new trends in society. As to his official service, Zhang just aimed to be a timeserver and preserve his high position and glory intact. So, he did not

---

[7] Although one's sense of shame may not result from wisdom, no wisdom is higher than having the sense of shame (Wang 1996: 10:333). In many places, Wang Fuzhi identifies righteousness as the sense of honor and shame.

4 MORAL RECONSTRUCTION   141

defy the subversive Jin Empress Jia Nanfeng 賈南風 (256–300), nor did he support the patriots who struggled for the future of the empire. Consequently, after he passed away, the Jin Empire collapsed and central China was ruled by northern nomads. Inquiring into the cause, Wang found that Zhang's failure lay in the disconnect between wisdom and righteousness in his thought and conduct: "It was because Zhang Hua deployed his wisdom without regard for righteousness, and failed to grasp that one couldn't be wise without being righteousness" (Wang 1996: 10:439).

Wisdom without righteousness was called shrewdness. Its aim was to secure maximum selfish interest in one's endeavors. However, if a person wanted to be successful their entire life, they would have to uphold righteousness and use it to curb and guide their wisdom. Otherwise, their wisdom could shrink to shrewdness and eventually taint their renown and virtue. Wang concluded, "The highest wisdom is to practice righteousness and keep distance from harm … Whenever righteousness is established, harm will be kept at bay automatically" (Wang 1996: 2:278).

Clearly, Wang Fuzhi held that true wisdom involved upholding righteousness. To uphold righteousness, one had to grasp heavenly principle, on the one hand, and accept one's lot or fate, on the other. As to the former, Wang suggested applying one's mind to seek principle and, in turn, using principle to guide the mind. "If a person does not becloud their intelligence with selfish desires, but sharpens it with inquiry and questioning … when they reach the summit where no principle lies beyond their understanding, they achieve wisdom" (Wang 1996: 7:595). Again, principle included humaneness and righteousness; the method was to grasp ritual propriety and manage the desires accordingly. As to acceptance of one's lot and fate, Wang Fuzhi asked his students to cease asking about life and death, gain and loss, and to focus on humaneness and righteousness rather than selfish concerns. He said, "Know Heaven and do not change your mind regardless whether it is a matter of life and death—this is what is called the perfection of wisdom" (Wang 1996: 8:822).

Taking both righteousness and one's fate into account, Wang Fuzhi elaborated his view on achieving wisdom in his comment on Zhang Zai's statement, "Act when one must; stop when one cannot go farther. That is wisdom."

> "Act when one must" refers to when one cannot but uphold principle. That is righteousness. "Stop when one cannot go farther" means ceasing at what

should not be done, at that time. That is fate. Righteousness and fate are united by principle. One who upholds principle in bending and stretching, acting and resting hears wisdom in abundance. (Wang 1996: 12:168)

That is to say, achieving the wisdom involved upholding righteousness and accepting one's fate lay in prudent observance of ritual propriety.

Although Wang Fuzhi attempted to define wisdom with reference to righteousness and humaneness, he still maintained it was a kind of perspicuity, as the human mind was a discerning, perceptive mind. For this reason, Wang proposed that humaneness and wisdom were mutually supportive. In his view, a person who was not wise would not know how to be humane; for wisdom included knowing how to distinguish right from wrong and to bring things to completion. However, the wisdom of a person who lacked humaneness would lack principle and go astray; it would not be worthy of the name (Wang 1996: 8:822). In particular, as to rulers who lacked humaneness yet ventured to make shows of love and sustaining the people, their wisdom would only incur more harm (Wang 1996: 7:720). Hence, Wang urged people to strike a balance between humaneness and wisdom in their cultivation.

Although wisdom involved intelligence and perspicuity, and was determined by one's blood and bodily qi, Wang Fuzhi still insisted that one could overcome shortcomings of blood and bodily qi by cultivating wisdom. He urged:

> Spirit and wisdom rise and fall along with blood and bodily qi; they change three times as one proceeds from childhood to adulthood, then from adulthood to old age, and lack constancy. Consequently, if a person upheld the nature steadfastly, studied diligently, and make steady progress in cultivation, their spirit and wisdom would be preserved and ingrained. As a result, when blood and bodily qi prevail, their wisdom will not overflow; when blood and bodily qi decline, their wisdom will not ebb. (Wang 1996: 10:656)

Wang Fuzhi here distinguished wisdom from bodily qi, and assumed that wisdom could remain constant even when one's blood and bodily qi went into decline. Clearly, he exaggerated the impact of cultivation and underestimated biological determination. This distinction also ran counter to his qi-monism according to which wisdom or intelligence was a function of qi, and would rise and fall along with the condition of one's blood and bodily qi. On this score, Wang accepted the notion that true wisdom would be guided by righteousness and humaneness, and even asserted that a person's wisdom would not perish along with their physical body: "The noble person lays their foundation on humaneness and righteousness and makes their mind replete with learning. Even though they grow old, even die, their wisdom will not die with them" (Wang 1996: 10:657).

Pressing this argument, Wang added that it was not King Xuan of Qi's 齊宣王 lack of wisdom that caused his failure to carry out humane governance, but rather his lack of the will to carry it out. He grasped that the will played a crucial role in making choices. A reader may argue, a person who did not understand their own needs would be unable to establish an upright will. Moreover, even though people would become familiar with social customs and affairs over time, they could not stay immune from the impact of blood and bodily qi on their intelligence, for qi would not necessarily follow moral principle but would obey its own principles, and person's wisdom as a function of qi would be affected.

4.5.3   Courage: The Fortitude to Carry Out Humaneness and Wisdom

In Wang's view, although people were born with humaneness and wisdom, it would take courage for them to put humaneness and wisdom into practice. In a crisis, many people have known what must be done, but lacked the will to take action. This signified a lack of courage. Therefore, to be a noble person and carry out great feats, it would not be enough for one to be humane and wise; one would have to possess the courage to take action. For this reason, Wang assigned courage a high position in his system.

> All scholars know that, one becomes wise by following righteousness and humane by complying with ritual propriety. However, as to not abandoning righteousness at the point of death and not casting ritual aside in unexpected situations, a person needs courage to practice righteousness and ritual propriety. This challenge is unknown to the village wisemen who practice Confucian norms and rituals routinely, in an off-hand and leisurely manner .... Do not say that a warrior's courage has no relevance to the cultivation of a noble person, for what a noble person needs to cultivate is precisely this. In times of unexpected hesitation, doubt, horror, or sorrow, how could a person who is lacking in qi (courage, fortitude) be able to face them? (Wang 1996: 5:572–573)

Here, Wang Fuzhi stressed the role of courage in upholding humaneness and righteousness at critical junctures. Those who lacked courage would lose their heads in unexpected times of hesitation, doubt, horror, or sorrow. It took courage to uphold humaneness, righteousness, and ritual propriety, come hell or high water.

Wang Fuzhi supported this idea in his comment on the Song loyalist, Ma Shen 馬伸 (?–1128). In 1127, the Jurchens invaded the Northern Song capital Kaifeng 開封 and captured the two emperors. To govern the Song Empire, they installed Zhang Bangchang 張邦昌 (1081–1127) as a puppet emperor. Facing the threat of the Jurchen forces, only the official Ma Shen stood out to persuade Zhang Bangchang not to usurp the throne, but to welcome a Song prince to be emperor. Moved by Ma Shen's courage, Wang Fuzhi commented:

> As to people and righteousness, the question is not whether they grasp it, they do; the problem is that they lack the will to carry it out. Moreover, the question is not whether they have a will, they do; the problem is that they lack the expansive *qi* to express it forcefully. Zhang Bangchang should not be anointed as emperor; the Song emperor should not be chosen by the Jurchens; and the Song subjects should not honor Bangchang as their emperor. Everyone knew these truths and bore these thoughts in mind. However, their wills were obstructed, kept in check, unable to be expressed. This resulted from the lack of fortitude of their *qi*. (Wang 1996: 11:213)

In his writings, Wang used the terms courage and *qi* interchangeably. "The lack of their *qi*" meant their lack of courage. In contrast with his peers' timidity, Ma Shen upheld righteousness courageously. Such an expression of courage could not be supplanted by just humaneness or wisdom, nor did it arise from them.

In Wang Fuzhi's view, Ma Shen's courage was the product of the cultivation regimen he had practiced from youth. Moreover, he always confronted difficulties and threats head on and stood ready to die for his cause, thus he could stand out to scold Zhang Bangchang. In contrast, Wang criticized Zhang Hua for his cowardice in the face of Empress Jia's despotism (Wang 1996: 10:438) and denounced Wang Shengbian's 王僧辯 (?–555) surrender to the enemy after his vanguard was defeated (Wang 1996: 10:666). He concluded, "Without courage, a person will not maintain his integrity; this will ruin both his life and his renown. Isn't this pitiful? Therefore, if a person does not know righteousness, they can be informed. If they do know righteousness but lack the courage to carry it out, they will hesitate to act at a crucial moment—even if they are encouraged by a sage king or supported by close friends—and perish in infamy. Therefore, courage is a sort of heavenly endowed virtue, forming a triad with humaneness and wisdom" (Wang 1996: 10:666).

What, then, was courage? Wang Fuzhi first regarded it as a function of a person's *qi*, (Wang 1996: 5:571), a capacity of their blood and vital force. Courage was the impetus of a person's vital force and blood, not their decisiveness after deliberation. Citing two warriors of the state of Qi 齊, Wang noted their lack of wisdom and humaneness, but admitted their courage had emboldened them to hide behind enemy lines lying in ambush (Wang 1996: 5:572). Wang concluded that such courage arose from *qi*, and was a great function of *qi* (Wang 1996: 6:489).

Stressing that such courage stood on its own, Wang Fuzhi did not accept that the cultivation of humaneness and righteousness would give rise to courage. In his view, the so-called courage of the Way and righteousness (*dao yi zhi yong* 道義之勇) was wisdom if it deterred a person from improper acts and unrighteous ways, or it was humaneness if it inclined a person to adhere to the Way and righteousness. Neither one of them was courage *per se* (Wang 1996: 5:572). Wang proceeded to argue:

> Provided a person's courage could be subsumed under wisdom or humaneness, that would mean that his/her content of the mind and nature (i.e., wisdom and humaneness) would not need to depend on *qi* to be realized. That would come to an absurd conclusion that *qi* was a thing to run counter to the mind or nature, and Heaven and Earth had deliberately endowed human beings such recalcitrant *qi* to trouble them to no end. (Wang 1996: 5:572)

Here, Wang Fuzhi underscored the notion that, as a function of *qi*, courage was independent and could not be embraced by humaneness or wisdom. Otherwise, a person would be able to deal with everything with humaneness and wisdom, and *qi* would be redundant in the conduct of human affairs. Moreover, with the desires and emotions arising from *qi*, *qi* would be a spoiler for the cultivation of virtue. However, in the end, Wang found the reality to be the opposite; that is, courage and *qi* could help a person to undertake a righteous mission during a crisis. Wang Fuzhi concluded:

When rising, [courage] has its own substance, and does not depend on the Way or righteousness for its existence. When aroused, [courage] has its own function, and will help humaneness and wisdom to see their courses of action through. Courage thus forms a triad including wisdom and humaneness; the *qi*, the mind, and the nature are all precious endowments from Heaven and each plays its respective role. (Wang 1996: 5:572)

Wang Fuzhi maintained that the essence of courage lay not in displays of bravado, but in the steady maintenance of measure and propriety when facing the crises of life as well as matters of death, survival, and annihilation (Wang 1996: 10:216). To nurture courage, a person should develop it in times of peace and bring it into play in times of crisis—building their blood and *qi* with mental discipline. They should be resolved in mind at all times, ever ready to confront a crisis. The *Mencius* reports that, what Bei Gong You 北宮黝 bore in mind was his revenge for even a hostile look; what Meng Shishe 孟施舍 bore in mind was his struggles, regardless whether facing life and death, failure and success (Wang 1996: 8:183–184). Wang concluded that the greatest courage was a determined mental state, in which one forgets failure and success, life and death, and leaves the outcome to fate. A person of courage will think it righteous to confront disasters directly and stand ready to sacrifice their life in a crisis. Emboldened by this dedication, their courage would never erode.

Wang Fuzhi recommended that the noble person cultivate courage by guiding their *qi* with righteousness and the Way while distinguishing courage *per se* from humaneness and wisdom. He described the courage of the noble person in terms of Mencius' unperturbed mind (*bu dongxin* 不動心) and the broad and expansive *qi* (*Haoran zhi qi* 浩然之氣). Although he did not specifically identify courage with a noble person's unperturbed mind, he insisted that they both involved similar cultivation efforts. Specifically, both traits required having something to abide by. In the case of Meng Shishe, what he abided by was persistent nerve and morale; in the case of the noble person, what they abide by is righteousness, the cause that gives rise to resolve (Wang 1996: 8:185). With righteousness at its core, the noble person's courage will expand and be compelling such that they "would advance boldly regardless of difficulties, retreat not at threats to life and limb. They would carry out their will expansively, and abide by righteousness and principle without regret" (Wang 1996: 7:595). Specifically, Wang recommended directing one's *qi* or courage with the will, but in turn orienting will with righteousness and the Way. He defined the will as what the mind aspires to do (Wang 1996: 3:324). Once a person's will was established, they could go on to nurture their *qi* or courage and be forceful in the handling of affairs and dealings with others. In turn, courage would strengthen their will and make it more persistent.

4.6 *DAO* AND *DE* OR THE WAY AND ITS VIRTUE

While Wang Fuzhi placed emphasis on ritual propriety, the moderation of the emotions and desires, and the realization of humaneness and righteousness, he could not help but weaken the role of ritual propriety when he discussed the relationship between *Dao* 道 and *de* 德 or the Way and its virtue. In Wang's works, Dao had multiple meanings. In the present discussion, we focus only on its ontological and moral meanings, which were connected to virtue. Generally, Wang based his thinking about *Dao* and *de* on two Confucian classics, the *Book of Changes* and the *Doctrine of the Mean*, but he failed to resolve the discrepancies between these two books.

4.6.1 *The Meanings of the* Dao *and* De

Ontologically, Wang Fuzhi developed his understanding of the *Dao* on the definition given in the *Book of Changes*, "The alteration of one yin and one yang is called the *Dao*." As the *Dao* was manifested as the intercourse of yin and yang in Heaven, softness and firmness on Earth, and humaneness and righteousness among human beings, Wang called the Dao the Way to establish Heaven, Earth, and Humanity. Correspondingly, virtue was regarded as the function and capacity of the Dao (Wang 1996: 1:621). To realize this function, a thing had to follow and embody the Dao within itself, which was called "possessing virtue (*youde* 有德)" (Wang 1996: 1:821). In short, the Dao was the Way to produce and sustain the myriad things, while virtue was the state in which the Dao functioned and was embodied in the things it formed.

Wang Fuzhi endorsed the view that the Dao was one but its virtues (branches) were many and varied (*li yi fen shu* 理一分殊) (Wang 1996: 6:456), just as Aristotle's form was concretized with different forms of matter. Based on this proposition, Wang explained the differences among species, especially the differences between human beings and other creatures. In his view, all creatures had received their virtues from Heaven, but they differed in nature and the virtues due to their differing physical embodiments (Wang 1996: 12:195). On his view, virtue was a quality that was naturally endowed from Heaven. It was connected with and determined by the body and the nature, and in the case human beings had little connection with personal effort or social influence.

Wang associated the Dao with principle and virtue with the nature. He accepted Zhang Zai's notion that the Dao involved compliance with principle while virtue was the instantiation of principle under Heaven (Wang 1996: 12:194). Wang appealed to the *Book of Changes* in justifying his identification of the nature with virtue. The *Book of Changes* reads, "The alternation of yin and yang is called the *Dao*. What succeeds it is goodness and what is completed is the nature" (Shang 2016: 294). Based on this statement, Wang concluded, "To succeed goodness and obtain what the nature originally has, is called virtue" (Wang 1996: 12:132). "In my nature there are these virtues of humaneness and wisdom. If I can complete my nature, I will be able to complete my virtue" (Wang 1996: 7:196). That is, virtue was the original content of the nature. Since he regarded the nature and virtue as identical, it was no surprise he concluded that a person would be perfect in virtue if only they could maintain their nature whole.

Wang Fuzhi offered other definitions of the Dao and virtue as well, as in his comment on the following passage from the *Doctrine of the Mean*: "What Heaven has endowed is called the nature, and compliance with the nature is called the *Dao*" (Zhu 1983: 17; Wang 1996: 7:102). Unlike the definitions he gave in commenting on the *Book of Changes*, he here considered the nature as the origin of the *Dao* (Wang 1996: 7:105), and viewed the nature as hitting the mark or propriety (*zhong* 中) and the *Dao* as its function (Wang 1996: 6:458). As a result, the *Dao* here became the manifestation and function of the nature. If we compare "What Heaven has endowed is called the nature" with Wang Fuzhi's statement, "What has given rise to human life originally is heavenly virtue" (Wang 1996: 6:682), we can affirm that Wang identified the nature with heavenly virtue. This is confirmed by the following statements: "The *Dao* is an empty form while virtue is one's true attainment …Virtue is what makes the *Dao* prevail, while the *Dao* is what carries virtue" (Wang 1996: 6:683). In other words, the *Dao* became the manifestation and function of virtue, which contradicted the assertions in Wang's commentary on the *Book of Changes*.

To explain this contradiction, we must assume that Wang Fuzhi had different emphases in his commentaries on the two books. In the *Book of Changes*, he stressed that the *Dao* or the Way of Heaven had produced the myriad things in all of their variety, and so virtue became the *Dao*'s manifestation and function. In the *Doctrine of the Mean*, he stressed that virtue made a person as he was, and the manifestation of his virtue would become the *Dao* or the Way of humaneness. Therefore, from the *Changes* to the *Mean*, the Dao had evolved from the ontological and universal Way into the moral Way of humaneness, while virtue remained what made a person as he was. Virtue was identical with the nature, and became the link between the Way of Heaven and the Way of humaneness. It was the concrete embodiment of the Way of Heaven in human beings, on the one hand, and the origin of the Way of humaneness, on the other. But, Wang did not point out this change in the meaning of the Dao, which has led to confusion.

Corresponding to the Way of Heaven and the Way of humaneness, there were two kinds of principle in Wang's discussions. One was the pattern manifested by Heaven, Earth, and the myriad things; the other was the perfect principle of firmness, obedience, and the Five Constant Human Relationships, which were endowed by Heaven and received by human beings as their nature (Wang 1996: 6:716). Although ritual propriety originated from the latter (the nature), reflecting norms, it belonged to the former because of its objective and overt characteristics. Based on this distinction, Wang proposed two kinds of virtue—the virtue obtained by learning (*xue zhi de* 學之得), and the virtue obtained from the nature (*xing zhi de* 性之得). He said:

> Virtue is attainment. What is endowed by Heaven is the possession of the nature. What is attained by human effort is the possession of learning. The possession of learning is that man knows the Way and practices it; thus, it is also called virtue. The possession of the nature cannot be attained unless one perceives the mind of Heaven and Earth by silently preserving and actively investigating the nature. (Wang 1996: 6:821)

4.6.2   *Virtue Obtained from the Nature vs. Virtue Obtained by Learning*

When Wang Fuzhi embraced Zhang Zai's proposition, "Following principle in the world is called the Dao; and attaining principle in the world is called virtue," he was concerned about the virtue obtained by learning, for the Way in this respect referred to the manifest principle in events and things, and he believed that one could follow and grasp the manifest principle and attain virtue (Wang 1996: 12:194).

In this process, Wang Fuzhi emphasized actual experience in the practice of *Dao*, as he stated, "Virtue is that one practices *Dao* and has an actual experience of it in one's mind" (Wang 1996: 6:621, 649, 697). If a person were to routinely comply with the *Dao*, they would be lacking in genuine experience and not attain virtue. To have genuine experience, Wang recommended investigating things to grasp their principles, especially the moral principles of human society, and sincerely abide by them. At the same time, he deemed it crucial to know and awaken the nature (the virtue endowed by nature). He specified, "As to the *Dao*, it is the natural principle of Heaven, and the normative way of human beings … To embody the *Dao* and hold it in the mind, one has to rely on one's virtue, not on the *Dao* alone" (Wang 1996: 7:207). "One's virtue" referred to the virtue from the nature. If a person hoped to have genuine experience of the *Dao*, they first had to know their virtue from the nature. Obviously, this virtue differed from the virtue attained by learning and practicing the *Dao*.

Why was the knowledge of virtue from the nature so important for one's genuine experience of the Dao? First, Wang Fuzhi emphasized genuine experience over mere learned knowledge of the *Dao*. In his view, anyone could get to know and practice the Dao, but not everyone could truly understand the reason and necessity for doing so (Wang 1996: 7:830). To have an actual experience of the *Dao*, one had to realize that the *Dao* was originally from the nature and offered the way to recover the nature and realize the meaning of one's life. Second, once a person knew the nature (or virtue obtained from the nature), they would grasp the essence of wisdom, courage, and humaneness, and be able to carry out the universal Way in the world. Whenever such a person acted, the Way was practiced; when they stopped, they still bore virtue in the mind.

In contrast, if a person was just to practice the Way in the world to obtain virtue (by learning), they would only understand what they had done but not what they had not done (Wang 1996: 6:821). For this reason, Wang prioritized the virtue obtained from the nature over the virtue obtained by learning in practicing the *Dao*. He called the latter a virtue acquired from the outside, not a true inner knowledge of virtue (Wang 1996: 6:821). Wang criticized those who sought virtue by learning for "not believing in what their mind bears innately, but believing in the manifest rules of the *Dao*," and for abandoning their innate knowledge while relying on others (Wang 1996: 6:879).

By denying the possibility of knowing the virtue from the nature by practicing the Way, Wang Fuzhi weakened the role of the Way in attaining virtue. He considered that to conduct cultivation, one should seek it in the mind and recover the nature rather than simply practice the Way or rituals outwardly. As a result, like Wang Yangming, he made moral cultivation something mysterious and subjective, and contradicted his emphasis on realizing the nature by practicing ritual propriety.

Wang Fuzhi's basic contention was: a person ought to perform moral deeds out of their inborn knowledge of the good or conscience, not just follow the rules of society. Truly, this would be a good proposal to avoid the hypocrisies of social moral practice. But, when he emphasized the virtue from the nature or the conscience, while neglecting the bulwark of the Way or norms and rules, he stopped with "following nature is called the Way," but neglected "cultivation of the Way is called learning" in the *Doctrine of the Mean*. Moreover, he should have kept in mind that, with the exception of a sage, no person could know and exhaust the nature or virtue from the nature from the beginning. Even Confucius needed to set his will on learning before he could firmly take his stand at thirty. The process of Confucius' learning undoubtedly was the process of moral practice according to the *Dao* or ritual propriety. Therefore, if a person wanted to know the virtue from the nature, they had to do it by practicing the *Dao* that the sage had established. Only after prolonged learning and practice could a person awaken their virtue from the nature. For this reason, in the conduct of moral cultivation, a person could not just strive to realize the original mind or the nature but also had to endeavor to master and observe the rules of propriety. The inner and the outer were mutually supportive, as Wang Fuzhi always maintained.

4.7   Conclusion

Moral reconstruction formed the core of Wang Fuzhi's reconstruction effort of Confucianism. Starting with humaneness, he tried to confirm that everyone was born with the good nature which gave rise to the commiserating mind, stirred when one witnessed the suffering of others. In a person's life, the commiserating mind would be first manifested as filial piety and fraternal love. If a person sincerely treated their parents with filial piety, they would be set to cultivate humaneness and extend it to the myriad things, and thus complete their service to Heaven. However, a person's humaneness or commiserating mind may be overwhelmed by the emotions and selfish desires, so it would be necessary for them to moderate the emotions and the desires with principle (the nature).

Wang Fuzhi regarded the emotions as the mechanism of yin-yang intercourse, arising from the human mind. Desire was the degradation or turmoil of emotions. Therefore, once one's emotions were aroused, what mattered was to express them in due degree. As to the desires, the problem was how to restrain them to a socially acceptable range. For this reason, the relation between principle and the desires was also that between the nature and the emotions in Wang's works. The emotions pertained to the conative aspect of the mind, and were general and aesthetic; while the desires expressed biological needs and their fulfillment. To manage the emotions and the desires, a person would first need to rectify the mind with ritual propriety and make the intentions sincere. By practicing ritual propriety, they would develop good habits and reshape their nature. Once this was done, they would be set to express the emotions and satisfy their desires properly, without going to extremes.

Wang Fuzhi, however, ultimately downplayed the role of ritual propriety in moral cultivation when he claimed that righteousness was internal, and that the human mind was endowed with the nature (moral principle), which would help a person to avoid pretentiousness in their practice of ritual propriety. He also insisted that students first awaken to the nature. With this awakening, they would be set to grasp the master key of the principles of the myriad things to deal with them with propriety. Otherwise, they would grope in the darkness of human affairs and could deal with affairs only by following the set rituals. Wang elucidated this point with his distinction between the virtue from nature (*xing zhi de* 性之得) and the virtue from learning (*xue zhi de* 學之得). He argued that a person could not be called a person who had knowledge of virtue if they had attained virtue solely by learning and practicing ritual propriety. Rather, only if they knew virtue directly from their nature would they be competent to carry out the universal Way of the world and realize the great virtues of wisdom, courage, and humaneness.

Hence, by denying the possibility of knowing the virtue from nature by following the Way, Wang Fuzhi weakened the role of the Way or ritual propriety in the attainment of virtue. Like Wang Yangming, he came to make moral cultivation into something mysterious and subjective, and contradicted his own emphasis on exhausting the nature by practicing ritual propriety. Wang's prioritization of the virtue from the nature also ran counter to his proposal that the inner (heart-mind) and the outer (ritual propriety) were mutually supportive. This inconsistency demonstrates that he tried to construct a synthesis of Zhu Xi and Wang Yangming's teachings but was not entirely successful.

Wang Fuzhi's teaching of moral cultivation was aimed at promoting humaneness in the world. He traced the origin of humaneness to the Great Harmony or the harmonious *qi* in the cosmos. It was his faith that if everyone were to make efforts to cultivate humaneness, they would contribute their share of harmonious *qi* to the cosmos and thus reduce strife and increase harmony in the world. In this manner, everyone who cultivated and realized humaneness would achieve an eternal existence through their humaneness, or harmonious *qi*, and realize the meaning of human life.

BIBLIOGRAPHY

EARLY CHINESE TEXTS

Ban, Gu 班固, *Han Shu* 漢書 (*The History of the Han Dynasty*), Beijing: Zhonghua Shuju 北京: 中華書局, 1962

Cheng, Hao & Cheng, Yi 程顥, 程颐, *Er Cheng YiShu* 二程遗书 (*The Extant Works of the Two Chengs*), Shanghai: Shanghai Guji Chubanshe 上海古籍出版社, 2000

Li, Jingde, ed. 黎靖德, *Zhu Zi Yu Lei* 朱子語類 (*Conversations of Master Zhu, Arranged Topically*), Beijing: Zhonghua Shuju 北京: 中華書局, 1994

Li, Zhi 李贄, *De ye Ru Chen Hou Lun* 德業儒臣后論 (*A Post Comment on Confucian Scholars' Virtue and Achievements*), in *Li Zhi Quanji Zhu* 李贄全集注 (第六冊) (*An Annotation to the Complete Works of Li Zhi, Volume 6*), Beijing: Social Sciences Academic Press北京: 社會科學文獻出版社, 2010

Lu, Jiuyuan 陸九淵, *Lu Jiuyuan Ji* 陸九淵集 (*A Collection of Lu Jiuyuan's Writings*), Beijing: Zhonghua Shuju 北京: 中華書局, 1980

Shang, Binghe 尚秉和, *Zhou Yi Shangshi Xue* 周易尚氏學 (*Shang's Commentary on the Book of Changes*), Beijing: Zhonghua Shuju, 2016

Wang, Xianqian 王先謙, *Xunzi Jijie* 荀子集解 (*Collected Exegesis of the Xunzi*), Beijing: Zhonghua Shuju 北京: 中華書局, 1988

Wang, Yangming 王陽明, *Chuan Xi Lu Zhushu* 傳習錄注疏 (*Instructions for Practical Living*), annotated by Deng Aimin 鄧艾民, Shanghai: Shanghai Guji Chubanshe 上海: 上海古籍出版社, 2012

Wang, Yu 王敔, *Daxing Fujun Xingshu* 大行府君行述 (*A Brief Biographical Sketch of my Diseased Father*), in *Chuanshan Quanshu* 船山全書16 (*The Complete Works of Chuanshan*), Volume 16, Changsha: Yuelu Shushe 長沙: 岳麓書社, 1996

Zhu, Xi 朱熹, *Sishu Zhangju Jizhu* 四書章句集注 (*A Collected Commentary on the Four Books*), Beijing: Zhonghua Shuju 北京: 中華書局, 1983

Zhu, Xi 朱熹, *Huian Xiansheng Zhu Wengong Wenji* 晦庵先生朱文公文集 (Master Huian Zhu's Literary Works), In *Zhuzi Quanshu* 朱子全書, 第 23 冊(*The Complete Works of Master Zhu*) Volume 23, edited by Zhu Jieren, Yan Zuozhi, Liu Yongxiang et al. 朱傑人, 嚴佐之, 劉永翔等編訂, Shanghai: Shanghai Guji Chubanshe; Hefei: Anhui Jiaoyu Chubanshe, 2010 上海: 上海古籍出版社, 合肥: 安徽教育出版社, 2010

SECONDARY SOURCES

Chen, Lai 陳來, *Quanshi yu Chongjian: Wang Chuanshan de Zhexue Jingshen* 詮釋與重建: 王船山的哲學精神 (*Interpretation and Reconstruction: The Spirit of Wang Chuanshan's Philosophy*). Beijing: Peking University Press, 北京:北京大學出版社, 2004

Gadamer, Hans Georg, *Hermeneutics, Religion and Ethics*, trans. Joel Weinsheimer, New Haven: Yale University Press 1999

Hu, Shi 胡适, *Zhi Qian Xuantong* 致錢玄同 (*A Letter to Qian Xuantong*) in *Chuanshan Quanshu* 船山全書 (*The Complete Works of Chuanshan*), Volume 16, Changsha: Yuelu Shushe, 1996

Ji, Wenfu 嵇文甫, *Wang Chuanshan Xueshu Luncong* 王船山學術論叢 (*A Discussion on Wang Chuanshan's Academics*), Beijing: Sanlian Bookstore, 北京: 三聯書店, 1962

Watson, Burton, *The Complete Works of Chuang Tzu*, New York: Columbia University Press, 1968

Zhang, Binglin 章炳麟, *Chong Kan Chuanshan Yishu Xu* 重刊船山遺書序 (*A Preface for the Second Edition of Chuanshan Extant Book*), in Chuanshan Quanshu 船山全書 16 (Complete Works of Chuanshan), Volume 16, Changsha: Yuelu Shushe, 1996

CHAPTER 5

Cosmological Reconstruction

In diagnosing the decline of the Ming and the Manchu conquest, Wang Fuzhi identified causes first in the official misrule during the late Ming and then in the immorality and irresponsibility rampant in late Ming society. Finally, he concluded that disruption of the cosmic harmony brought about by these human disturbances was the underlying cause of the decline and fall of the Ming. Consequently, besides advocating political reform at the institutional level and self-cultivation at the personal level, Wang urged cultivating and preserving cosmic harmony and general ethics in society as necessary for preventing such disasters from recurring. He held that immoral conduct by anybody would undermine the harmony of their *qi* and add a parcel of disharmonious *qi* to the cosmos. In turn, such increases of disharmonious *qi* in the cosmos would lead to an increase of evil people and frequency of disasters. The way to stop this vicious cycle was for everyone to cultivate their own harmonious *qi* and thereby contribute to the general cosmic harmony. Wang based this position on his *qi*-monism, according to which all things were by-products of the flux of *qi*, as all shapes of ice were by-products of the waves of water. In the interconnected, resonant flux of *qi*, everyone's conduct would influence the state of Heaven, other people, and the myriad things, just as a wave would disturb the entire surface of a pond. Thus, "Anyone who intended to further the productive processes of *qi* would contribute their *qi* to promoting humaneness, thus raising humanity above the level of birds and barbarians. Otherwise, they would contribute their *qi* to the decline and fall of

M. Tan, *Wang Fuzhi's Reconstruction of Confucianism*, https://doi.org/10.1007/978-3-030-80263-9_5

civilized human life, for example, by putting themselves first, spreading evil, they would contribute to the destructive *qi* and undermine the resolute *qi* of others"(Wang 1996: 1:929). With line of reasoning, Wang, like his peer Gu Yanwu,[1] sought to heighten the moral responsibility of each person potentially to the cosmic level; for he held that every person was responsible to preserve general harmony and resist conflict and disaster.

Wang Fuzhi referred to the preservation of general harmony as "assisting Heaven (*xiangtian* 相天)." He spliced this expression from the *Zhuangzi* with the *Doctrine of the Mean's* call to "assist in the transforming and nourishing processes of Heaven and Earth." Wang held firmly that human beings could arrive at a perspicacious vantage point by "assisting Heaven", that those who protected their spirit and body from harm would contribute to the pure, harmonious *qi* of Heaven and Earth. Their precious parcel of harmonious *qi* would blend with the Great Void (Heaven) and brighten the sun, moon, and stars above, and nurture the creatures below (Wang 1996: 13:293). This vision of a perspicacious vantage point moved Wang to advocate that people cultivate their parcel of harmonious *qi* by moderating their desires and complying with principle. By cultivating their harmonious *qi*, a person could transcend the limitations of their physical allotment and perchance aspire to eternal life.

Wang's emphasis on assisting in the processes of Heaven distinguished him from his contemporaries who tended to advocate improving the general social morals by reform of political institutions, like Chen Que and Huang Zongxi, or by self-cultivation, like Gu Yanwu and Yanyuan. Focusing on the interface between Heaven (nature) and humanity, as discussed by Zhuangzi and Dong Zhongshu, Wang began to consider the impact of human conduct on the flux of heavenly or natural process. Just as we know today that cutting down the rain forests adversely impacts the biosphere, Wang believed that misrule by the ruler and officials and the untamed emotions of the people in society had disturbed the cosmic harmony, leading to the disruption of the seasons and proliferation of evil people. In this way, Wang offered a cosmic rationale for observing ritual propriety to moderate the emotions and the desires, and subsumed his approach to moral cultivation under the notion of cosmic harmony. In this, he emulated Guan Ning (158–241) who had also striven to preserve the Way of humaneness in chaotic times.

[1] Gu Yanwu once said, "To protect the peace of the world, even those as inferior as farmers have a responsibility" (Gu 1997: 594).

5.1 Wang Fuzhi's *Qi*-Monism

Wang Fuzhi, like most of his peers, appealed to *qi*-monism in explaining natural transformation and social change. This choice arose partly from a common disdain for the rigid, authoritarian worldview of Neo-Confucianism, but more directly it reflected their experience of resisting the Manchu invaders. On the battlefield, they found that the determinants of success and failure were superior intelligence, strategy, weapons, and fighters. Consequently, even the idealist Huang Zongxi based his concept of mind on *qi*, and a reluctant latter-day follower of Neo-Confucianism like Wang Fuzhi prioritized *qi* 氣 over principle (*li* 理) and objects (*qi* 器) over the Way (*dao* 道).

5.1.1 Qi *and Principle*

Even a cursory survey of the works of the Ming loyalists would show they shared the view that "What fills the space between Heaven and Earth is *qi* (*ying tiandi zhi jian zhe qi ye* 盈天地之間者氣也)" (Gu 1997: 36; Huang 2012: 1:57). Wang Fuzhi concurred, "Principle is not a thing, separate from *qi*. ...Principle can only be manifested by *qi*. What presides over and balances yin and yang is principle. Wherever *qi* exists, principle is attached therein" (Wang 1996: 6:726–727). "The marvelous function of *qi* is principle. After *qi* produces forms, principle resides therein" (Wang 1996: 6:716). Unlike his peers, Wang expanded the sweep of *qi*-monism and drew upon it in explaining the process of life and death, the unity of body and the nature, and the relationship between the Way and objects (*qi* 器).

First, Wang Fuzhi advocated that all things were at various stages of *qi* transformation. He pointed out that in the *Book of Changes*, the production of things occurred as gatherings and dispersals of *qi*, not as their simple birth and extinction. He aimed to replace the Buddhist concept of annihilation (Nirvana) with this conception, remarking, "In this way, I know the formation of human beings and other things depends on balanced yin-yang transformation and intercourse. When creatures die, they return to the harmonious state of yin and yang, to wait the next cycle of the gathering of *qi*. Still, the next gathering will be unpredictable and won't directly follow up the last cycle. Thus, the birth of things is not creation from Nonbeing, nor is their death pure annihilation. Things just follow the natural course of yin-yang transformation" (Wang 1996: 1:520).

Wang Fuzhi regarded yin and yang as the two basic phases of *qi*. They were mutually dependent complements whose intercourse gave rise to Heaven and Earth, the Five Phases, and the myriad things. "Yin and yang are the names of the two phases; they fill the space between Heaven and Earth.... From the perspective of unity and transformation, they unite as one to form the Great Ultimate. From the perspective of purity and turbidity, vacuity and substantiality, largeness and smallness, they separate as two" (Wang 1996: 1:659–660). In other words, all things were formed through yin-yang transformation and intercourse. Yin and yang naturally merged and were inseparable, but their features were distinct and contrastive: transparent vs. opaque, pure vs. turbid, vacuous vs. substantial. They were two interactive poles of *qi* activity.

Viewing things as transformation of *qi* and the human body as a stage in such transformations, Wang Fuzhi, like Zhuangzi and Zhang Zai, advocated that people identify with the flux of *qi* and not be attached to their human form. In this manner, they would become as open and vast as the cosmos in mind and body, their selfish concerns would vanish, and they would care for other human beings and creatures. Wang asserted, "As to *qi* transformation, my present body is the same as it was before my parents gave birth to me; hence, my original body is the transformative *qi* that fills the space between Heaven and Earth" (Wang 1996: 12:434). To Wang, a person's present form and their state before birth were both transformation of *qi*. Moreover, existentially free to assume other forms, every human being ought to take delight in the transformation of *qi* and not be attached to their present human form.

Viewing all things as different stages of *qi* transformation, Wang Fuzhi also held that the content of Heaven and human beings alike was nothing but *qi*. Moreover, while holding that principle directed *qi* to the right course, he denied it any existence apart from *qi* (Wang 1996: 6:1052). As the inner rule of *qi* transformation, principle depended on *qi* and had no existence beyond *qi*.

Wang Fuzhi posited the unity of *qi* and principle to rectify their bifurcation in Zhu Xi's philosophy. In *Tropically Arranged Conversations of Master Zhu* (*Zhuzi yulei* 朱子語類), Zhu Xi stated that principle existed independently of *qi* and things, remarking, "Before the rise of a certain matter, that principle already exists" (Li 1994: 2436). "If every mountain and river, even the Earth itself, were to collapse and vanish, their principle would persist" (Li 1994: 4). In response to questions raised by his students, Zhu Xi affirmed, not only that principle existed prior to yin, yang, and the myriad things, but that principle gave rise to *qi*: "The Great Ultimate is nothing but the principle of Heaven, Earth, and the myriad things … Before the emergence of Heaven and Earth, there was this principle, indeed. What moves and produces yang is this principle; what rests and produces yin is this principle, as well" (Li 1994: 1). "Before the emergence of Heaven and Earth, there was just this principle, indeed. With this principle came forth Heaven and Earth. Without this principle, there would not have been Heaven, Earth, human beings or anything else. Nothing could have existed. With this principle comes forth the flowing of *qi* and the production and nourishment of the myriad things" (Li 1994: 1).

Zhu Xi affirmed that principle existed prior to *qi* and gave rise to *qi*, to justify the priority and absoluteness of principle; by parity of reason, he held that society and government be arranged according to principle (norms and rituals). However, given Zhu Xi's insistence that principle was purely good, the foundation of cosmic order, and basis of moral social order, how could evil arise? How could evil be possible? Zhu Xi's only recourse was to attribute the existence of evil to imbalances in *qi* activity and intercourse. Because principle in itself was purely good and had no feelings, calculations, or activity of its own, it could not be the source of evil. In contrast, it was gatherings of *qi* that gave rise to wide spectra of things (Li 1994: 3), thus spontaneous *qi activity* could give rise to evil. However, since the yin and yang phases of *qi* reflected the basic motion and rest of principle, how could Zhu Xi deny that principle moved or produced? How then he did avoid attributing evil to principle? He drew an analogy between principle and *qi*, on the one hand, to father and son, on the other, and argued that principle could not control *qi* once it was produced. Once principle was manifested in *qi*, *qi* activities no longer followed pure principle but became conditioned by the proclivities of *qi*; after all, *qi* had energy and spontaneity, which principle lacked (Li 1994: 71). Zhu Xi thus was pressed to characterize the priority of principle as formal and concede that the proclivities of *qi* co-determined the shapes and ambiance of the myriad things.

Zhu Xi's bifurcation of principle and *qi* also led him to distinguish between the nature of heavenly endowment (*tianming zhi xing* 天命之性) and the nature of physical temperament (*qizhi zhi xing* 氣質之性), and to praise principle and deprecate the human body and the desires. This bifurcation made him accept that *qi* operated by its own proclivities, apart from principle. Hence, he could not close the gap between principle and *qi*, nor could he avoid the conclusion that *qi* followed proclivities of its own, apart from principle, although he insisted that "principle and *qi* could not separate from each other, principle existed in *qi*, and was not a separate thing" (Li 1994: 3).

Additionally, by separating principle from *qi*, Zhu Xi made principle insubstantial, something like Buddhist Emptiness (Sunyata). By ascribing the appearance of evil to *qi*, Zhu was led to denigrate the physical endowment and enter the Buddhist path of deprecating the human body and the desires in a quest for emptiness and quietude. For example, when explaining why some people could not awaken to the luminous virtue (*mingde* 明德), Zhu Xi asserted they were handicapped by their physical embodiment so that their inner virtue was obscured by their desires (Li 1994: 271, 264). It was no wonder that Zhu Xi taught his students to preserve heavenly principle by extinguishing the desires.

Sharply critical of Zhu Xi's bifurcation of principle and *qi*, Wang Fuzhi advocated *qi*-monism. On his view, "Principle serves to put *qi* in order and act as the rule of *qi*. Principle did not first stand outside of *qi* and then enter *qi*" (Wang 1996: 6:1076). His idea was that principle took shape in the course of *qi* activities, transformations, and formations. Second, Wang did not accept the Cheng-Zhu claim that it was human physical embodiment (*qi bing* 氣稟) that gave rise to evil. He countered that there was nothing wrong with human embodiment, there was nothing inherently evil about it (Wang 1996: 6:1131). Wang noted that, in explaining the emergence of evil, Cheng Yi had compared the physical embodiment to a glass and principle (the nature) to water. Principle or the nature was manifested differently in different embodiments just as water was shaped differently in different glasses (Wang 1996: 6:961). Zhu Xi had made the claim that principle (nature) was to embodiment as a pearl was to water. A pearl's luster would vary with the purity of the water (Li 1994: 73). Wang criticized that, in their analogies, Cheng and Zhu had divided principle from *qi* and embodiment, and imagined principle in a pure state in empty space free of material conditions (Wang 1996: 6:961).

Wang Fuzhi also criticized that Zhu Xi's bifurcation of principle and *qi* contradicted the *Doctrine of the Mean* assertion, "What Heaven endows is called the nature." According to Wang, this 'endows' (*ming* 命) meant that Heaven bequeathed each person with a parcel of *qi* bearing the principle of *qi*. 'The nature' (*xing* 性) signified that humanity received this principle of *qi* from Heaven … Hence, since the endowment consisted of *qi* as the content and principle as its rule, this parcel of *qi* and principle could never be separated from each other (Wang 1996: 6:1139).

Elsewhere, Wang asserted, "Heaven endowed humanity and things with *qi* and principle ... Wherever there was *qi*, there would be principle. Hence, every heavenly endowment included both *qi* and principle" (Wang 1996: 6:726–727). One may still wonder how Wang could account for the appearance of evil. His new explanation was that evil arose from "habit (*xi* 習)," that is, human choices and practices, as discussed in Chap. 4.

5.1.2   Bodily Organs and Their Functions Are One with the Nature Conferred by Heaven (xingse ji tianxing 形色即天性)

For centuries, the Neo-Confucians discussed the relationship between *qi* and principle to justify their account of the human body and human nature (*xing* 性). Their view of the relationship between *qi* and principle would shape their grasp of the relationship between the human body and the nature. Cheng Yi and Zhu Xi endorsed the bifurcation of principle and *qi*, so they distinguished sharply between human nature and the physical embodiment, as well as between the nature of heavenly endowment (*tianming zhi xing* 天命之性) and the nature of physical temperament (*qizhi zhi xing* 氣質之性). Based on his *qi*-monism, Wang maintained the unity of the human body and the nature and rejected the Cheng-Zhu distinction between the nature of heavenly endowment and the nature of temperament. He insisted that the nature of temperament was simply the embodied "nature." "This nature is principle; the principle of this embodiment" (Wang 1996: 6:863). Hence, the nature of temperament did not differ from the nature of heavenly endowment. He asserted, "The embodied 'nature' is indeed the original nature from Heaven" (Wang 1996: 6:858).

Since Wang Fuzhi proposed the unity of *qi* with principle and the unity of human nature with physical temperament, he could not entertain the possibility that human nature was good while the physical temperament was evil. Wang affirmed that both *qi* and principle were good, and both human nature and the physical temperament were good, as well. "If principle is good, *qi* will be good, too. If *qi* is not good, principle will not be good, either" (Wang 1996: 6:1052). "Mencius found the metaphysical principle in those forms, so he regarded the body and its organs as marvelous and replete with the Way from Heaven, indeed. Evil did not come from the bodily organs and their functions" (Wang 1996: 6:961). "The bodily organs and their functions" referred to the human body and the physical temperament. Since the physical temperament and the human body were replete with the Way from Heaven, they were basically good, as well. Thus, Wang was in basic disagreement with the Buddhists and Zhu Xi who denigrated the human body and the physical temperament.

Having declared the goodness of *qi* as well as of principle, Wang Fuzhi still had to explain the origin of evil. First, he proposed that evil arose from *qi*. "Principle has no error or mistake, but *qi* commits errors and makes mistakes. The living human being commits errors and creates evil because of its *qi* embodiment" (Wang 1996: 6:617). He offered that *qi* could commit errors and cause evil because it sometimes ran counter to and deviated from principle, due to vicissitudes of time and circumstance (*shi shu zhi ou ran* 時數之偶然) (Wang 1996: 6:861). This view was no different than the Cheng-Zhu account, which ascribed the rise of evil to *qi*, even though Wang tried to qualify that *qi* gave rise to evil by accidental deviations from principle.

Holding that the embodiment (*zhi* 質) was produced by *qi* intercourse through which "*qi* follows principle to form embodiment" (Wang 1996: 6:861), Wang had to concede the embodiment gave rise to evil, if he was to hold that it was *qi*'s errors that gave rise to evil, even if by accident. He, indeed, made this concession. He said, "In my view, human beings receive the nature from the same origin, Heaven. While close, their manifestations of human nature are not the same. The source of differences in their manifestations of human nature is differences in their embodiments (*zhi* 質), rather than their *qi per se*" (Wang 1996: 6:859). That is, human beings received the nature from Heaven. If some of them were kind while others were evil, it was due to differences in their embodiments. Once a person's embodiment was set, it would change little. It would bear the imprint of past mistakes and the evils that their *qi* embodiment had committed, giving rise to differences in the nature of different people. Elsewhere, Wang maintained that a person's embodiment was set at birth. Also, different embodiments meant having different capacities. For example, a large embryo would tend to have more capacities than a small one (Wang 1996: 6:676). Hence, the differences in the natures of different people were caused by differences in their embodiments. Consequently, Wang was unable to defend his monistic view that "Bodily organs and their functions are one with the heavenly nature (*xingse ji tianxing* 形色即天性)," blunting the force his criticism of the Cheng-Zhu view, which ascribed evil to the embodiment.

In an effort to make his argument consistent, Wang Fuzhi proposed the possibility of changing one's embodiment (*bianhua qizhi* 變化氣質) to rectify their defects in bodily form and embodiment. He suggested that a person could modify their embodiment by adjusting their breath, food, and social relations. Although the human form was basically set at birth, it could still be changed by a person's choices and habits as they grow up and mature. "As to those who change their bad embodiment to a better one, they need to cultivate their *qi*, as well. Having cultivated good habits for a while, they will be able to modify their embodiment. As Mencius said, 'One's dwelling alters one's character, and one's nutrients affect one's body.' A person's body will change along with changes of their *qi*" (Wang 1996: 6:861). For example, gluttony causes obesity, which in turn changes a person's character. Fasting causes a fit body and a warm character. Wang claimed that once a person's embodiment had changed, their embodied nature would change, as well. In this way, a person could develop a new "nature." In Wang's formulation, "A person's *qi* changes along with their habits, and their habits participate in the formation of their nature" (Wang 1996: 6:860). Wang believed this was the way to preserve *qi*-monism, maintain the unity of *qi* and principle, and avoid the path of Zhu Xi and the Buddhists of denigrating the human body and the embodied nature.

While Wang Fuzhi finally accepted that the embodiment gave rise to evil, he did open the possibility of one's changing a bad embodiment into a better one. However, he still faced a contradiction between the possibility of changing one's embodiment and his stated view that "As to the embodiment of human beings, there simply is no evil" (Wang 1996: 6:1131). To resolve this inconsistency, he proposed that neither the human body nor material things were the cause of evil; evil arose from the transactions between human body and material things. He asserted, "Thus, Mencius regarded all of these bodies and shapes as lovely and beautiful. All so-called bad bodies and shapes are not bad in themselves. The cause of evil lies in the untimely and imprudent actions of human beings interacting with material things" (Wang 1996: 6:960). Elsewhere, he asserted that the origin of evil was not the human body or its functions, or the material things themselves, but the time and circumstance of intercourse between the human body and material things (Wang 1996: 6:963). In order to avoid improper intercourse, a person should act according to the nature (principle). The concrete manifestation of the nature was ritual propriety and righteousness. "A person must discipline their seeing, hearing, speech and action. After Master Yan 顏子 had practiced ritual propriety, he could be said to have made his body perfect" (Wang 1996: 6:1132). At this point, Wang confidently asserted, "If a person were not distracted or tempted by material things, even though their embodiment was not perfect, it would still be good" (Wang 1996: 6:960). In other words, if a person cultivated their body and conduct with ritual propriety and was immune to the attractions of material things, their embodiment would not give rise to evil despite its imperfections.

5.1.3   Objects and the Way (Qi he Dao 器和道)

Based on his *qi*-monism, Wang Fuzhi proposed that "Under Heaven, only objects (*qi* 器) exist. The Way is the way of objects; objects cannot be said to be the objects of the Way" (Wang 1996: 1:1027). With this, Wang tried to clarify that objects were the body and bearer of the Way, not the converse. He saw the Way as the principle of objects, and insisted that the Way could not exist beyond the objects. Objects determined the existence of the Way. Moreover, Wang asserted that all norms and rituals arose from the needs of human beings. Without human beings and their needs, such norms and rituals would not have come into existence. He said:

> In remote antiquity, the Way of courtesy between host and guest did not exist. At the time of Yao and Shun, the Way of condolence and punitive expedition did not exist. During the Han and Tang, the Way of the present did not exist. At present, we do not have the Way of the future. (Wang 1996: 1:1028)

Wang Fuzhi realized that the ways, norms, and rules then in use had been established in response to the needs of time and circumstance. As society developed and evolved, new ways, norms, and rules were established. Wang further placed the Way on a material foundation with the claim that all ways depended on objects for their existence. He continued:

> Without bow and arrow, the Way of archery would not exist. Without chariot and horse, the Way of charioteering would not exist. Without sacrificial meat, wine, jade and silk, and bells and stringed instruments, the Way of rituals and music would not exist. Moreover, without a son, a person would not practice the Way of being a father. Without a younger brother, a person would not practice the Way of being an elder brother. There are many other cases for which a Way could be developed but has not. Hence, without the

suitable objects and circumstances, a certain Way will not appear, indeed. (Wang 1996: 1:1028)

With this eloquent statement, Wang Fuzhi sought to show that all "ways" arose from the needs of time and circumstance and depended on their objects. If a person had no son, he would not have to call to develop the way to nurture a baby. Hence, for Wang, the Way was established by observing and using objects, and then it was applied to manage such objects. Wang drew the conclusion that "The sage is simply one who is good at managing objects" (Wang 1996: 1:1028).

Wang Fuzhi also realized the transcendence of the Way to objects. Although the Way was formulated by observing and analyzing objects, it was relatively stable and constant and would not change with objects from moment to moment. For this reason, Wang proposed that "There are no constant objects, but there is a constant Way (*wu heng qi er you heng dao* 无恒器而有恒道)" (Wang 1996: 12:454). With these words, he did not mean to suggest that the Way could exist before the objects. Even though inventions could seem to come into existence directly from the inventor's subjective ideas, they were actually the product of the inventor's grasp of existing objects and seeing room for improvement. Wang still affirmed that "Under Heaven, there are only objects," and asserted, "Some people may not be able to make objects because they do not know their way. But, such cases do not falsify my basic proposition that objects exist prior to their way" (Wang 1996: 1:1028).

Since Wang Fuzhi endorsed the unity of objects and the Way, he rejected seeking the Way beyond objects. He argued that under certain given objects and circumstances, the Way would emerge accordingly. If the objects were abandoned, their Way would perish along with them (Wang 1996: 1:861). At the same time, he conceded that a person who observed and analyzed objects from the past with care would be able to recover their Way (盡器則道在其中矣) (Wang 1996: 12:427). In comments on the *Appendices to the Book of Changes* (*xi ci* 系辭), Wang exemplified his notion of seeking the Way through its objects:

> When it was said, "Those who can invent are called sagacious," it referred to the invention of objects (utensils). When it was said, "Those who narrate are called luminous," it referred to the narrations of objects. When it was said, "Spiritual but elucidated, would depend on someone," it referred to objects that were spiritual yet could be elucidated. Therefore, once a person had

recognized a category of objects, identified their distinctive patterns, improved their function, and defined their shapes, he would do all of this quietly and fulfill this mission implicitly. Such a person could do this because they had a solid grasp of the object in mind, on which they could depend for inspiration. Indeed, the noble person's Way would be perfect once the proper function of the corresponding objects had been thoroughly carried out. (Wang 1996: 1:1029)

In short, whenever a sage invented something or commented on a classic, they focused on the function of the object. They would seek to identify the category of the object and explore its patterns, to grasp its function. Therefore, the Way of the sages could not go beyond, or abandon, the objects. On this point, Wang Fuzhi criticized Laozi for seeking the Way in vacuity (*xu* 虛), and the Buddhists for seeking the Way in silence (*ji* 寂). He ridiculed them for not knowing that vacuity and silence only made sense against the backdrop material objects (Wang 1996: 1:1029). Without any material object for context, no one could understand vacuity or silence.

As a corollary to his statement, "bodily organs and their functions are at one with the nature conferred by Heaven," Wang Fuzhi affirmed that humanity was the object that carried the Way (*ren jie zai dao zhi qi* 人皆載 道之器). He defined the Way in this sense as the principle of *qi* transformation, running through Heaven, Earth, and the myriad things. He noted that people often referred to the soaring of a bird and the swimming of a fish as manifestations of the Way, but questioned whether the smile or word of a human being didn't go beyond the Way. He observed, "The Way never abandons any person. It is manifested in human deeds as much as in the flight of birds and the swimming of fish. Every moment and situation, a person embodies the Way, just as does a bird soaring in the sky and a fish diving into the depths" (Wang 1996: 6:501). This was Wang's reading of the statement, "Heaven is the Way and humanity the object (*tian zhe dao, ren zhe qi* 天者道, 人者器)."

As a Confucian, Wang Fuzhi could not rest satisfied with this Daoist sort of account of the relationship between Heaven and humanity, the Way and object. Hence, he sought to promote the Way of humaneness, and stressed the human role of "assisting in the nourishing and transforming power of Heaven and Earth." He proposed the view that "Heaven is the object, while man is the Way (*tian zhe qi, ren zhe dao* 天者器, 人者 道)." He cited passages from the *Book of Odes* to illustrate the noble person's effort at conducting moral cultivation and promoting the Way of humaneness. "The fish dives deep and stays at the bottom, but it remains visible." "Though only the ceiling looks down upon you, stay free of shame even in the recesses of your own home." Rather than take these as examples of the dictum that a noble person would be circumspect when alone, Wang read them as illustrations the practice of the Way of humaneness in all situations. He raised the question, "Don't these sentences express a thing (the Way of humaneness) that is invisible and inaudible but still immanent in all things? All objects under Heaven take the Way of humaneness as their substance, without exception. This is to say, the Way of humaneness is ubiquitous, presiding over Heaven and Earth and bestowing meaning on all things without leaving a trace. Therefore, I say, 'Heaven is the object, while humanity is the Way'" (Wang 1996: 12:405). In other words, Wang insisted that people practice the Way of humaneness to manage Heaven, Earth, and the myriad things, and nourish them with the Confucian virtues. Humanity should not rest content with being natural creatures and manifest the Way of Heaven; they should manifest the Way of humaneness, to make the cosmos more significant. In making this point, Wang followed up Zhang Zai's aspiration, "to establish the will of Heaven and Earth, and to establish the Way of humaneness" (Zhang 1978: 320).

5.2　Harmony and the Great Harmony

Wang Fuzhi's promotion of universal harmony prompts the question, what were general harmony and the Great Harmony (*taihe* 太和)? In early Chinese texts, harmony (*he* 和) originally meant a proportionate, balanced blend of various ingredients. In the *Recorded Sayings of the States* (*Guoyu* 國語), Shi Bo 史伯, a diviner of the Western Zhou, proposed this concept. "Harmony truly sustains a thing, while sameness (*tong* 同) is not sufficient for it to survive. Using one thing to balance another thing is called harmony" (Xu 2002: 470). Shi Bo meant that it was the interdependence and collective energy of different factors that helped a thing to sustain its vitality while the addition of "the same" would weaken it. Later, Yan Ying 晏嬰 (578–500 BC) enriched this idea when he advised his lord to accept different opinions, comparing the synthesis of different opinions to the blend of sugar, vinegar, sauces, and other ingredients to produce a tasty broth. If his lord were to only accept ideas that were the same as or similar to his own, it would be like adding water to water and no tasty broth (adequate decision) would be produced. He also compared harmony to melodies as combinations of various notes (Yang 1981: 1419–1420).

This notion of harmony as balanced fusion of various elements and essences, aimed to sustain the vitality of things, greatly impacted traditional Chinese philosophy and was a basic concept in Confucianism and Daoism. Confucius expressed this notion in remarking, "The noble person is harmonious but not adulatory; the petty minded are adulatory but not harmonious" (Analects 13.23). In this remark, harmony referred to the due measure achieved through tolerance and openness to other views. Laozi also invoked this concept to explain the rise and resilience of the myriad things in saying, "The ten thousand things carry the yin on their back and embrace the yang; by blending them, they achieve harmony" (Laozi 42). The *Zhuangzi* speaks of "harmony of yin and yang (*yin yang zhi he* 陰陽之和)" and invokes the Great Harmony, that is, the heavenly blending and transformation of the myriad things (Guo 1961: 502).

In the Great Appendices of the *Book of Changes,* these two expressions from the *Zhuangzi* were enlisted to explain yin-yang intercourse within and among the sixty-four hexagrams. However, in the Great Appendices *taihe* 太和 was presented as *dahe* 大和 in a description of the way of *Qian* 乾as to achieve the perfect harmony and bring all things to their proper nature: "The principle of *Qian* transforms each thing, and each thing realizes its upright nature and endowment accordingly. All of them remain united with the Great Harmony and achieve their right course" (Shang 2016: 8). Since a basic axiom of the *Book of Changes* was that *Qian* initiates a thing and Kun 坤 completes it, it is apparent that the Great Harmony was the fusion of yin and yang in perfect proportion. It was this perfect proportion that was thought to make and sustain the myriad things.

Based on the foregoing, the Great Harmony as the perfect fusion of yin and yang should be a mass of harmonious *qi* guided by its principle or *Dao* 道. This principle or *Dao* would make the fusion of yin and yang perfect and guide further movements of yin and yang. Zhang Zai interpreted the Great Harmony in this way to explain cosmic processes. On the one hand, he viewed the Great Harmony as Dao or principle, which contained the propensity of *qi* to rise and fall, float and sink, move and rest, and interact, and to give rise to fermentation, agitation, victory and defeat, and bending and stretching. On the other hand, he described the Great Harmony as a mass of fermenting *qi*. When it dispersed into perceptible forms, it was called *qi*; when it remained pure, transparent, and indescribable, it was called spirit (*shen* 神). When it was not as misty and murky as the wild horse-like clouds, it could not yet be called the Great Harmony (Zhang 1978: 7). In sum, Zhang Zai presented the Great Harmony as a mass of fermenting *qi* with its principle or Dao.

Wang Fuzhi adapted Zhang Zai's concept of the Great Harmony, regarding it as a harmonious fusion of *yin* and *yang*.

> The Great Harmony is the perfect state of harmony. The Way or Dao is the universal principle of Heaven, Earth, human beings, and all things; it is also what is called the Great Ultimate (*taiji* 太極). Although yin and yang have different essences, they blend in the Great Void, unite, and do not harm each other, co-existing without distinction and reaching a perfect harmony. Before the appearance of form and object, there is no original disharmony; after the appearance of form and object, the original harmony is not lost. Consequently, it is called the Great Harmony. (Wang 1996: 12:15)

The Great Harmony was the unity of *Dao* and the harmonious mass of *qi*. *Dao* ran through *yin* and *yang* making them a mass of harmonious *qi*. It was such harmonious *qi* that penetrated both form and formlessness, making possible the formation of the world. Notably, Wang adapted this account of *Dao* from the *Laozi* in which *Dao* was presented as a harmonious fusion of yin and yang and a nameless mass before the appearance of the myriad things (Laozi 42). However, as to the relationship between *Dao* and the myriad things, the *Laozi* described it as natural and amoral, discounting human interference. Wang insisted that the Great Harmony was the origin of the Way of humaneness and the spirit of all things, the cultivation of which would "assist in the nurturing processes of Heaven."

Wang Fuzhi identified the Great Harmony and the Great Void (*taixu* 太虛) with Heaven. If the Great Harmony reflected Heaven as a harmonious unity and intercourse of yin and yang, the Great Void reflected its containing yin and yang in their primal formless state, as in his claim that the space between sky and earth was filled with transformative, harmonious *qi* (Wang 1996: 1:409). Because yin and yang permeated everywhere, the Great Harmony and the Great Void were ultimately identical. Wang remarked:

> The Great Void is *qi*, the substance of the transforming mass of yin and yang. Yin and yang blend in the Great Harmony, so the Great Harmony is *qi* in actuality. But, the Great Harmony cannot be simply called *qi*. As to its rising and falling, floating in the air, and acting as the initiator of the myriad things without knowing how, it is called Heaven. (Wang 1996: 12:32)

In this context, "Heaven" refers to the space between sky and earth rather than to the entire cosmos. In this sense, Heaven was considered to be replete with harmonious *qi* and not completely vacuous. This was the portion of the cosmos that human beings could utilize and should be concerned about.

Notably, "Heaven" carried several meanings in Wang Fuzhi's writings, which need to be grasped before attempting to convey how the Great Harmony was identical with Heaven and how humanity could "assist in the nurturing processes of Heaven."

5.3   Heaven

Building on his *qi*-monism, Wang Fuzhi described Heaven as a body of accumulated *qi* (Wang 1996: 6:1110). As a body of accumulated *qi*, Heaven was "the pure, vacuous, one, and great (*qing xu yi da* 清虚一大)," an objective and natural body:

> Above the sky, the *qi* of earth cannot reach; the illumination of the sun, moon, and stars do not illuminate that part of Heaven. The color of that part of Heaven is the original color of Heaven. This original color is colorless. Having no color, no substance, no form, and no quantity, that part of Heaven is called pure, vacuous, one, and great (*qing xu yi da* 清虚一大), and is the source of principle. (Wang 1996: 12:457)

"The pure, vacuous, one, and great" is similar to Zhang Zai's the Great Void (*tai xu* 太虚) and refers to the entire cosmos, that is, the "outer space" of contemporary astronomy, beyond the Earth's atmosphere. Due to limitations in his knowledge of astronomy, Wang thought the sun, moon, and stars were revolving in the atmosphere of the Earth, and that their light did not illuminate "the pure, vacuous, one, and great." Nevertheless, he assumed that this region was replete with principle and *qi*. Because "the pure, vacuous, one, and great" transcended even the illumination of the sun, moon, and stars, and had no rain, wind, thunder, or dew, Wang held that even the spirit and transformation of *qi* did not happen there (Wang 1996: 12:406) and that there was no benefit in devoting one's thoughts to "the pure, vacuous, one, and great."

Second, for Wang Fuzhi, the Great Harmony referred to that part of Heaven where the *qi* of Earth interacted with the *qi* of Heaven to produce wind, rain, dew, and thunder, and where the spirit and transformation of

Heaven produced the myriad things. This part of Heaven corresponded to the Earth and its surrounding atmosphere. He called the Great Harmony "the heaven of humanity (*ren zhi tian* 人之天)," while "the pure, vacuous, one, and great" "the heaven of Heaven (*tian zhi tian* 天之天)." He insisted that while these two Heavens were fundamentally one, interactive, and inter-transformative, people could only make use of the heaven of humanity, having no access to the heaven of Heaven (Wang 1996: 3:463). Therefore, the noble person should devote himself to the heaven of humanity and be responsive to heavenly phenomena that are related to humanity. If a noble person were to lose their way in aspiring to the heaven of Heaven, they would come to their wit's end (Wang 1996: 5:134).

Wang Fuzhi approached the Heaven of humanity, that is, the Great Harmony, from two vantages: its objectivity and impersonality, on the one hand, and its relation to humanity, on the other.

5.3.1   Heaven as an Impartial, Impersonal Agent

Wang Fuzhi followed Daoism and the *Book of Changes* in regarding Heaven's production of the myriad things as an impersonal, natural process. Heavenly transformation produced only what was "due" at specific times and places, without cognizance of what would be produced. It had no concern whether the weeds would harm grain sprouts, nor whether carnivores would prey on herbivores. One thing it produced might be successful while another one a miserable failure; one person might be benefited but another one harmed regardless of their virtue or vice. Heaven never shared in the concerns of the sages. The heavenly process was the natural way, the flux of nature (Wang 1996: 6:1138). Producing all things by natural impulse, Heaven did not heed the wants and expectations of human beings. As to the subjective human concerns of "gain, loss, success, and failure," they were not part of Heaven's Way. In this, Wang adopted the impersonal Heaven propounded in the *Laozi*, "Heaven and earth are not humane, but regard all things as straw dogs" (Laozi 5), and Xunzi's notion that "Heaven has its own constancy, it does not plot Yao's 堯 survival, or arrange the execution of Jie 桀" (Wang 1988: 362).

As Heaven does not share in the sage's concerns, that is, the well-being of humanity, Heaven's operations may not always be deemed good or righteous. At the same time, Wang held that anything that was produced by Heaven was "true and right" by that very fact; any artifice or falsehood was the result of human machinations. "Principle is heavenly principle.

Whatever is in Heaven matches principle. Heaven goes back and forth freely; it is interactive with what it meets, unconcerned about the success or failure of things. What humanity deems false or absurd (*wang* 妄) is not false to Heaven anyway" (Wang 1996: 1:235). This view is reminiscent of the Daoist conception that, while Heaven was perfect, human machinations and constructions gave rise to disaster and chaos. Again, since Heaven was always good, Wang placed responsibility for the emergence of evil on the shoulders of humanity. He denied that Heaven contained any evil elements or impulses. People who regarded Heaven as evil just did not understand Heaven. Evil arose only after human emotions and talents had come into play (Wang 1996: 6:1059).

The problem was: if Heaven was always right and righteous, why did the sage have any worries or concerns, and how would it be possible for humanity to facilitate the nurturing processes of Heaven or improve the general harmonious *qi* if human beings were the source of evil and error? This dilemma forced Wang to accept that Heaven had shortcomings in provisioning human welfare, so human beings needed to step up to make up for Heaven's insufficiencies (see below). For example, since Heaven produced weeds as well as crop plants, human beings had to select and cultivate the plants that could be crops (Wang 1996: 12:317). However, even with this proviso, Wang could not render his theory of Heaven consistent.

While Wang Fuzhi insisted whatever was in Heaven was consistent with principle, he did not accept Cheng Hao's 程顥 proposition that "Heaven is principle" (Cheng and Cheng 2000: 178). Wang viewed Heaven first and foremost as an accumulation of *qi*. Through transformations of *qi*, principle was manifested. Accordingly, Heaven could be called "that from which principle comes forth," but it could not be considered to be identical with principle (Wang 1996: 6:1110). Heaven was broader than principle; it was the origin of principle. In this way, Wang dethroned principle from its dominant position the Cheng-Zhu School held.

Wang Fuzhi also denied that human intelligence could know Heaven completely. He admitted that humanity could discover some principles by observing and analyzing heavenly processes, but he also warned that such principles were partial and should not apply to Heaven unconditionally. He criticized Zhang Zai for falsely holding that the moon moved more slowly across the sky than did the sun, based on the principle that yang was more active than yin.[2] He asserted that "Principle comes out of Heaven, and what is in Heaven is naturally consistent with principle. But, it is not feasible to blindly believe in principles that human beings obtained from Heaven" (Wang 1996: 12:438). In other words, Heaven must possess more principles than could be discovered by human beings; therefore, if human beings attempted to blindly apply the principles they had discovered to predict the movements or transformations of Heaven, they would encounter obstacles and errors (Wang 1996: 12:53). However, Wang did not mean to imply that humanity should lose hope about the possibility of knowing Heaven. He just wanted to warn people not to become limited and partial out of obsession for the principles they had discovered. Wang held that the only way humanity could know and interact with Heaven was by knowing principle.

5.3.2   Heaven as the Initiator of the Myriad Things and the Origin of Humaneness

Although Wang Fuzhi registered the impersonal and impartial qualities of Heaven and came close to the Daoist conception of Heaven in that regard, he never considered himself a Daoist. Rather, he embraced Confucian humanism and held that the primary characteristic of Heaven was humaneness. Consequently, he was pressed to explain how an impersonal Heaven could be characterized as humane. Wang solved this problem with an arbitrary assumption; that is, he proposed that Heaven expressed its humaneness by producing the myriad things. He argued that, since humaneness was the great virtue of Heaven and Earth, their properties of initiating and producing life were evidence of the humaneness of Heaven (Wang 1996: 6:704).

Having justified humaneness as Heaven's primary characteristic in this way, Wang Fuzhi went on to maintain this was Heaven's essence, and drew the conclusion that it was humaneness in this sense that made Heaven significant and creative. In this context, he identified the movement of yang with the productive process of Heaven. "Regarding the activation of yang … it is through the continuity of this activation that Heaven and Earth have four seasons, create the manifold varieties of things, and operate ceaselessly forever. Evidently, it is not a remote and pure, dead and still

---

[2] According to the Book of Changes, the sun belongs to yang, while the moon to yin, yang is active while yin is passive.

mass that is called Heaven and Earth" (Wang 1996: 1:229). As yang stood for life and vigor, when yang moved or was activated in the human mind, it was expressed as the mind of compassion; when it was activated in Heaven, it was expressed as the productivity of Heaven and springtime. Wang thus proclaimed, "Heaven is the whole body of humaneness, while humaneness is the mind of Heaven. Heaven and humaneness are one" (Wang 1996: 12:66).

Moreover, because humaneness was a characteristic that human beings had attributed to Heaven, and it was only after human beings had realized humaneness that they could regard Heaven's productivity as evidence of its humaneness, Wang Fuzhi eulogized the role of human beings, concluding that human beings were the mind of Heaven. He argued that we might think that Heaven and Earth are mindless when judging from their separate forms. But, "after we see human beings, we find that the mind of Heaven and Earth is there (in humanity) ... Therefore, it is human beings that make Heaven and Earth marvelous and intelligent. Without human beings, Heaven and Earth are just those forms and images in the void" (Wang 1996: 13:693). The mind of Heaven and Earth in human beings is humaneness or compassion. As to humaneness and compassion, Heaven is supposed to be alive and intelligent, and is considered to be humane. Hence, it was human beings that registered the virtues and transformations of Heaven and Earth and realized its humaneness. In this way, Wang transferred the governance of Heaven and Earth into the hands of human beings and asked human being to seek Heaven in their own minds, that is, to discern their compassion and conscience:

> Heaven has its established forms. It renders spring as spring, autumn as autumn, human beings as human beings, and things as things. All these phenomena have their order and nomenclature without disarray; these are manifest expressions of Heaven that human beings can put into words. As to its subtle transformations and various accomplishments, its knowledge of the great beginning and storehouse of perfect humaneness, where is Heaven? It resides in the mind of human beings. Therefore, the sages discern Heaven in their minds, and establish the Heaven that they discovered [within] as the master of their spirit. (Wang 1996: 11:161)

Fundamentally, the Heaven that the sages discovered within were the humaneness and conscience in their own mind, through which they appreciated the creativity of nature in a moral way. These features were categorically unlike the objective, physical cycles of Heaven, such as the alternation of seasons. Rather, they expressed the mind's inborn sense of compassion. Therefore, the union of Heaven and human beings laid in the cultivation of humaneness.

However, in what sense could Heaven be said to reside in the mind? To answer this question, we have to go back to Heaven's creativity. In Wang Fuzhi's view, Heaven as the Great Harmony continuously created the myriad things, including human beings. In the course of this process, the Great Harmony resided in the body as spirit or mind. "Heaven is what is consolidated in human beings and thus produces the human mind" (Wang 1996: 5:247). Wang further indicated that Heaven provided the mind with order, prescribed the measure for its activities, and would be realized through the quiescence of the human mind (humaneness) (Wang 1996: 5:543). He not only pinpointed the Heaven or Great Harmony in the human mind, but he also identified Heaven as the peace at the center of the human mind. Therefore, whenever a person decided whether or not a course of action would be right, the standard they would consult would not be some remote, objective Heaven; it would be the Heaven or humaneness in the mind. Therefore, as to the human mission to assist Heaven, we need not commence doing it by manifest conduct, but rather by cultivating the mind; for example, by striving to purify the mind by reducing the desires in order to realize our parcel of harmonious *qi*.

Wang Fuzhi did not overlook the impersonal character of Heaven. He noted that while the humaneness of Heaven was creative and productive of life forms, it was a blind or indiscriminate productivity, so Wang cautioned being cautious in emulating Heaven. The noble person should uphold principle and propriety, "The Way of Heaven is indiscriminate, but the Way of humaneness has distinctions" (Wang 1996: 1:529). Wang thus conceded that Heaven's provenance was not an all-encompassing goodness, nor could it meet all human expectations, and began to stress that human beings should assist in the nurturing processes of Heaven. From this perspective, he criticized what he deemed to be the blind emulation of Heaven encouraged by some Neo-Confucians. For instance, when Zhang Shi 張栻 (1133–1180) identified the mind of Heaven and Earth with the sage's mind, Wang replied that the genuine sage could only judge and complement Heaven by following the right course of heavenly principle. Moreover, he asserted that the genuine sage would never take the productive mind of Heaven and Earth as their mind. If the sage was to take the productive mind of Heaven and Earth as their own mind when, say, fishing or hunting, they had better give up fishing and hunting altogether. As all-encompassing, Heaven and Earth did not need reciprocal support from the myriad things; however, human beings did (Wang 1996: 6:709). Therefore, Wang stressed the difference between the sage's mind and the mind of Heaven and Earth, despite that humaneness was their common essence. Human beings ought to emulate Heaven's humaneness, but with discrimination and consideration of human needs, and not follow the Daoist teaching of emulating Heaven indiscriminately.

Having registered this indiscriminateness of Heaven, Wang Fuzhi preserved Heaven's features of impersonality and impartiality while conceding that heavenly transformation and production would not always be in accord with human expectations. Moreover, he offered a rationale for human beings to assist in the nurturing processes of Heaven by the exercise of moral judgment and choice. He honored and praised Heaven as the source of humaneness and goodness for its creativity and nurturing; in this light, he insisted that human beings emulate Heaven's unselfishness and nurturing. It was by such ethical emulation that human beings could realize the meaning of their life. He concluded, "What the sage shares with Heaven and Earth is the same origin [the Great Harmony, humaneness]; what distinguishes the sage from Heaven and Earth is their different applications and considerations" (Wang 1996: 6:710).

5.4   THE NECESSITY OF ASSISTING HEAVEN

Wang Fuzhi discussed the necessity of assisting Heaven from two perspectives: the insufficiency of Heaven and the blame of human beings. The former referred to both the mismatch between heavenly transformation and human expectation and the anomalies that arise in the operation of heavenly processes. Wang's focus for the latter was overflows of human emotions and desires. However, as a philosopher, he attempted to exculpate the liability of Heaven for the emergence of evil, and urge human beings to assist in the nurturing processes of Heaven by moral cultivation and related practices.

5.4.1   The Insufficiency of Heaven

As noted, Wang Fuzhi admitted that Heaven did not share in the sage's concerns. Heaven did not provide everything that human beings needed. Thus, to provide for the well-being of humanity, it was necessary for the sages to build upon and augment the provisions of Heaven, such as by cultivating crops, domesticating animals, and inventing tools and techniques. In this way, assisting Heaven meant to provide for human well-being by deliberate human effort. This meant carrying out what Heaven could not do and thus making the cosmos more complete.

By raising human efforts and inventions to the level of the productivity of Heaven and Earth, Wang Fuzhi made human beings stand shoulder to shoulder with Heaven and Earth, to "Form a triad with Heaven and Earth (*yu tiandi can* 與天地參)." Wang corroborated this view in his comments on Hou Ji 后稷, a legendary king of early Chinese history. Hou Ji was reputedly the first person to conduct experiments and select species of wild plants, including suspected weeds, to be domesticated as crops, thus exerting human intelligence and effort to make up for what Heaven and Earth did not carry out. Wang commented, "Heaven can produce it, earth can complete it, but it is human ability that selects and cultivates the creatures to realize the fine, pure potential of yin and yang" (Wang 1996: 12:317). Wang compared the efforts of the sages to those of Hou Ji: in his view, they all made improvements in human living by following Heaven to the benefit of humanity.

Based on such human efforts to complement what Heaven had not completed, Wang warned against sacrificing the Way of human beings to the Way of Heaven. He remarked, "The Way of human beings is a branch of the Way of Heaven; but the Way of Heaven cannot be simply regarded as the Way of human beings. As to the great accomplishments of assisting Heaven, human beings must rather emulate the sages" (Wang 1996: 5:617). According to this view, if human beings were just to follow their instincts like a fish's swimming or a bird's soaring, and give free rein to whatever Heaven bestowed (the instincts), human beings would have no need to establish a ruler or teacher, or to make efforts to utilize things to improve human life; nor would there be a need for human beings to establish or abide by ritual propriety or righteousness. Needless to say, there then would be no human civilization, either. Wang further mounted an ontological defense of the Way of human beings: "Yin and yang give rise to human beings and bestow them with life; yin and yang govern human behavior, but they cannot substitute for human governance completely. Once a person was born into the world, they would manifest the nature and the emotions that Heaven had endowed in them. Although Dao (Heaven) had endowed them with these things, Dao cannot take the place of human beings in making efforts to manage their lives" (Wang 1996: 1:992). So from birth, a person bears the principles by which to discipline and govern their conduct. Human beings' autonomy from Heaven allows them to choose and invent things to improve their life. If human beings did not utilize their intelligence but just passively followed natural processes, they would lose sight of the full meaning of human living and thriving. Therefore, Wang insisted that human beings should not simply heed Heaven, but rather strive to fulfill their distinctively human needs and aspirations.

Wang Fuzhi also ascribed the insufficiency of Heaven's productivity to the differences between Heaven and human beings. To explain these differences, he offered two reasons: the intercourse and transformation *of yin and yang* and the occasions when Heaven and human beings meet.

First, Wang Fuzhi noted that the bending and stretching of *qi* could be abnormal (*wang* 妄) (Wang 1996: 6:617). Such abnormality would result from contingencies and swerves in *qi*'s movements. Given such contingencies or swerves in *qi*'s movements, human beings had no assurance that the productions of Heaven would all be perfect. Wang held that the only creations of Heaven that could be regarded as perfect were human beings; other species, such as dogs, sheep, and so on, were relatively imperfect (Wang 1996: 6:1052). Wang conceded that there were people who were born evil or sagacious and differed from others in nature and capability. As to the sagacious, rather than be influenced by bad customs, they would choose the right course according to their judgment, even under the most unfavorable circumstances. As to those who were born evil, unmoved by a good social milieu, they would ply their wiles even under the threat of draconian laws and strict enforcement (Wang 1996: 7:902–903). Wang thought that such evil persons were immune to training, education, reform, or correction, and felt resigned that the only way was to leave them alone. He urged students to emulate Shun 舜 and accept whatever Heaven bestowed to them and earnestly practice self-cultivation.

Second, Wang Fuzhi attributed the differences to improper meetings between Heaven and human beings. Specifically, these sorts of differences would arise when the productions of Heaven did not accord with human needs or expectation, that is, Heaven disposed or did not dispose at certain times or places. For example, when farmers needed to irrigate their crops, rainfall had to be timely and plentiful, and when they needed to harvest their crops, rainfall had to be occasional and sparse. Hence, Wang stated that discord and improper meetings would arise when yin-yang intercourse and transformations did not occur at the right time and place, and such improper things would, in turn, give rise to bad things (Wang 1996: 6:962). Undoubtedly, it was human beings who had judged what times and places were timely, and it was human evaluations that concluded whether things were improper and bad, even though the occurrence of such things was beyond human prediction or control.

Then, as to the possibility of humanity's assisting in the nurturing processes of Heaven, Wang Fuzhi had to answer two questions. First, since good and evil people were born from Heaven, could human beings prevent Heaven from producing evil people through yin-yang intercourse and transformation? Second, since success and failure, good fortune and misfortune were determined by time and place, how could human beings strive to improve the general harmonious *qi* through human effort? Wang's reply was that human beings should accept whatever Heaven disposed, and strive to change themselves by observing ritual propriety, noting the distinction between heavenly endowment (*tianming* 天命) and human occasions (*yu* 遇). While heavenly endowment was always right, human occasions could be untimely and bring failure and misfortune. To offer an analogy, heavenly endowment was to human occasions as rain was to the rainwater that each plant received. The rain itself could not be called bad, but whether a plant was desiccated or drenched would depend on the rainfall and the plant's setting and capacity. Based on this, Wang asserted that Bi Gan's 比干 death and Confucius' and Mencius' straits were not caused by their heavenly endowment, but by the time and circumstance in which they encountered these calamities (Wang 1996: 12:368). However, without human occasions, there would be no heavenly endowment at all, for they were essentially one. When a student asked Cheng Yi 程頤 what the difference between them was, Cheng said, "Whether or not the occasion arises for a person to encounter something is a matter of endowment, indeed" (Cheng and Cheng 2000: 253). In the end, Wang could not provide us with a convincing account of the rise of evil by this uncompelling distinction.

5.4.2 The Blame of Human Beings

Since Heaven had no mind to bless or punish any human being, and the appearance of misfortune and good fortune depended on the uncontrollable occasions of human beings' meetings with Heaven, the logical conclusion should have been that Heaven and human beings alike bear blame for misfortune. However, Wang simply exculpated Heaven and blamed human beings for the occurrence of good fortune and misfortune. He stated:

The Way of human beings originally sets human beings in a triad with Heaven and Earth. When human beings uses or misuses the firmness and softness of the Earth, they interact with the partial *qi* of yin and yang in favorable or unfavorable ways. Therefore, misfortune is always caused by their improper actions, while good fortune is always caused by their proper actions. (Wang 1996: 1:612)

Obviously, Wang Fuzhi tried to ascribe the cause of good fortune and misfortune to human conduct. However, his argument was ambiguous. If it was the case that human beings' proper or improper utility of firmness and softness caused them to interact with the partial *qi* of yin and yang in favorable or unfavorable ways, the emergence of good fortune and misfortune should be the result of the joint action of human beings, Earth, and Heaven, and it would be unfair for Wang to ascribe the cause to human beings alone. This quotation also implied another one of Wang's presumptions; that is, if human beings always acted according to the Way of humaneness, they would always have good fortune and never misfortune. However, Wang could not explain why a sage like Confucius had met with misfortune; after all Confucius was recognized by all as a sincere and reflective practitioner of the Way. The source of Wang's inconsistency was that he regarded human performances as the basic cause of fortune and misfortune, and demanded that human beings be held responsible even for the results of heavenly processes beyond their control.

Let us see how Wang Fuzhi tried to explain the rise of good fortune and misfortune due to human actions alone. He divided human life into the prenatal part and the postnatal part. He insisted that the prenatal part was controlled by heavenly transformation and always good. However, postnatal, with the rise of human emotions and talents, bad things would begin to arise (Wang 1996: 6:1059). Specifically, bad things would begin to arise because people began to indulge their desires (the emotions), and interact with the material things which attracted their senses, instead of according to principle (Wang 1996: 12:366). After locating the emotions and the desires as the origin of evil, Wang advocated promoting humaneness by moderating the emotions and the desires with principle and ritual propriety (see Chap. 4). By moderating the emotions and the desires, a person could transform their disharmonious *qi* into harmonious *qi*, and avert the rise of disharmony and evil.

5.4.3   The Feasibility of Assisting Heaven

According to Wang Fuzhi, the unique relationship between Heaven and human beings supported the feasibility of assisting Heaven with human contributions. On the one hand, human beings had originated from Heaven and shared with Heaven the same principle and *qi*. On the other hand, human beings differed from Heaven because human beings were the most intelligent of living creatures and had to devise tactics of survival from birth. Wang said, "The respect in which the sages are the same as Heaven and Earth is that they share the same origin (*yiben* 一本), and the respect in which they differ from Heaven and Earth is that they are differently manifested (*fenshu* 分殊)" (Wang 1996: 6:710). The same origin referred to bearing the same *qi* and principle; their different manifestations referred to Heaven's mindless transformations versus human intelligence and positive contributions. These similarities and differences made it possible for human beings to assist in the nurturing processes of Heaven.

First, Wang accepted Zhuangzi's idea that human beings were only one stage of heavenly transformation and were never separated from Heaven; human beings always exchanged their *qi* with Heaven. From the birth of each person, they differed in *qi* from other kinds of creatures, but as to the process of heavenly transformation, a person could always be at one with all *qi*, whether of the cosmos, other creatures, or things. Wang asserted, "From the perspective of transformation, the present I is identical with the I before my parents conceived me. All the fermenting *qi* between Heaven and Earth is my original state. Its mechanism is *qi*, while its spirit is principle" (Wang 1996: 12:434). In other words, "the present I" and the "I before conception" were of the same mass of general harmonious *qi* and at one with Heaven, partaking with Heaven of the same *qi* and principle. He justified this conception by reference to productive process. Wang envisioned *Qian* 乾 and *Kun* 坤 as the virtues of Heaven and Earth, respectively, with one's father and mother as their counterparts and representatives in the human world. He observed, "Father and mother carry the powers of Qian and Kun to conceive and give birth to me … So, my bodily form and nature are no different than those of my parents, nor are they different from those of Heaven and Earth" (Wang 1996: 12:354).

Second, although human beings were never completely separate from Heaven, they were distinguished from Heaven by their intelligence. This difference reflected that Heaven was mindless and indiscriminate in the production of things, while human beings could always distinguish good from evil. Wang elaborated:

> What fills the space between Heaven and Earth is my body, but my body does not use all of it (*qi*). Therefore, I utilize the myriad things for the benefit of human beings, but I will not love things in the same way as I love human beings. That which directs Heaven and Earth becomes my nature, but after my nature is established, I can alter my *qi* by maintaining a strong will, prolong my life by prudent choices, and realize the great function of the Way of humanity. I don't again use what directs Heaven and Earth as my sole guide, but have to moderate my joy, anger, sorrow and pleasure, and refrain from nurturing or killing living things heedlessly. (Wang 1996: 12:407)

Therefore, the things that human beings shared with Heaven did not preclude human beings' independence and autonomy; that is, once a person was born, they would become increasingly different from Heaven and fashion their own ways of living and conducting themselves. In this regard, the Way of humanity differed from the Way of Heaven. On this basis, Wang criticized the Daoist teaching of following the natural way, and supported the Confucian teaching that human beings should exert their intelligence and skills to make up for what Heaven had not provided:

> The Way of Heaven belongs to Heaven, and the Way of humanity belongs to humankind. Human beings have their own way, and the sages completely fulfill it and then realize their heavenly endowment by fulfilling the nature and disciplining their conduct. Therefore, the teachings of the sages and the worthies are what distinguish human beings from the things below, without allowing human beings to become equal to Heaven above. Heaven is natural, things and creatures are natural. The righteousness of bees and ants and the ceremonies of rats do not have to be deliberately learned by them, for they follow their natural instincts. If human beings were to stress following natural instincts to unite with Heaven, Heaven would become a concrete particular thing. That would be dangerous. (Wang 1996: 6:1144)

According to Wang, the Way of Heaven was natural, and all things and creatures, with the exception of human beings, behaved with naturalness. However, human beings could not be completely natural and follow natural instincts. Inevitably, they would have to apply human efforts to complement natural processes. They would not only choose preferred aspects of natural processes to emulate and follow, but would alter those aspects of natural processes to produce what they needed or desired. "It is only after uniting Heaven and Earth with human efforts that the capacities of the Way or *Dao* will be made comprehensive" (Wang 1996: 7:131–132). "What is natural is Heaven and Earth and what presides over Heaven and Earth is human beings; for human beings are the mind of Heaven and Earth" (Wang 1996: 1:885).

By what standard could human beings evaluate Heaven's performance and act as the mind of Heaven and Earth? Wang Fuzhi's answer was, human well-being: "It is only when we cannot fulfil our needs by depending on Heaven that we start to depend on ourselves; it is only after we cannot handle a state of affairs in timely fashion that the Way of humanity will be brought into play" (Wang 1996: 2:238). To provide for human well-being, human beings had to work with heavenly processes in response to human needs; therefore, assisting in the nurturing processes of Heaven was, in essence, a way to begin to provide for and maintain human well-being.

Wang Fuzhi appreciated the following proposition from the *Book of Changes*: "Heaven and Earth occupy their positions; the sages exert their abilities." He still insisted that human ability was at one with Heaven: "When Heaven wants a rest, it is human beings that give it rest; when Heaven wants to rise, it is human beings that activate it. In this way, I know the Way of humanity. How great is the Way of humanity! It matches Heaven and makes its distinctive contributions" (Wang 1996: 3:446). With the intervention and assistance of the sages, yin and yang could be made harmonious, the Five Phases could be balanced, and human relationships could be made orderly and upright. The sages' assistance extended the functions of the Way of Heaven and Earth; their knowledge brought their teachings to fruition (Wang 1996: 6:832).

In summary, Wang Fuzhi advocated that Heaven and human beings stood in a relation of interdependence and mutual influence. On the one hand, human beings originated from and was never completely separate from Heaven; on the other, human beings was partly independent of Heaven due to human's intelligence and ability to influence and alter heavenly processes. Wang held that if either Heaven or human beings were to change, the other would be influenced: "When the qi of Heaven prevails, it can transform human beings; when the qi of human beings prevails, it can, in turn, influence Heaven" (Wang 1996: 10:974). Thus, it was incumbent on human beings to enhance their harmonious qi by exercising moral judgment and conduct, thereby enhancing the harmonious qi of Heaven.

5.5   THE MEANS OF ASSISTING HEAVEN

5.5.1   To Transform Disharmonious Things with Harmonious Ones

According to Wang Fuzhi, although harmony characterized the core of Heaven, the actions of yin and yang sometimes deviated from their harmonious course and became imbalanced and produced disharmonious phenomena. In such situations, human beings had to carry out harmonious actions to transform the disharmonious phenomena. He noted that the early sage kings had employed physically challenged people as musicians to play harmonious notes to correct their imbalanced *qi* and restore them to peace and harmony. The underlying assumption was that by producing and hearing music the physically challenged could enhance their inner harmony. When these disharmonious challenged people were infused with music, they would disperse their chronic sorrow and depression and begin to take delight in living and cease thinking of death. As a result, their unhappy imbalance of yin and yang would be righted and the principle of life would be extended (Wang 1996: 1:940). In a word, Wang held that challenged people suffered from imbalances of yin and yang, and held out the possibility that the harmony of music could dispel their imbalances of yin and yang and restore their peace and harmony of mind and body.

Second, human beings should avoid disharmonious phenomena and embrace harmonious ones. They should preserve the harmonious *qi* of Heaven through their conscious moral choices and actions. Wang admitted that under normal conditions, the varieties of yin-yang intercourse were bound to produce cold and warm spells, respectively; however, people would call it excessive or even perverse if it caused extremes of cold and heat. Wang counseled that on such occasions people should ameliorate these extremes of heat or cold by taking practical measures to enhance their *qi* harmony and follow the cycle of seasons. People should drink cool water and stay in the shade during the sweltering summer heat, while drinking hot fluids and staying near the fire to offset the bitter winter cold. In this way, they would preserve their life and maintain the harmonious *qi* of Heaven under such extreme conditions. Wang asserted that avoiding the excesses but embracing the harmony was a positive way to serve Heaven (Wang 1996: 1:956–957).

To embrace Heaven's harmonious *qi* while avoiding its perverse excesses, it would be necessary for human beings to be able to predict the time and place that an event would take place or a person should act. For this purpose, early sages composed the *Book of Changes* so that users could grasp the signs and indications of events and act at the right time. By interpreting the movements of the strokes and the changes of the sixty-four hexagrams, the sages instructed people as to how to use objects, choose the right time to act to achieve human well-being, and avoid unfavorable situations. According to Wang, first, the *Book of Changes* let people know their lot in life, so they would accept it as a natural occurrence. Second, it inclined people to be concerned about their situation while offering guidance to dispel their concerns by following the Way. Finally, it encouraged people to seek good ends and sought to eliminate unanticipated disasters by bringing the user closer to the Way. In this manner, the sages sought to extend the harmony of Heaven and help human beings (Wang 1996: 1:993). The Way here referred to both the natural, impersonal heavenly processes and the Way of humanity. The sagely authors asked the users of the *Book of Changes* to calmly accept whatever Heaven had wrought, then apply their own intelligence to manage it. By grasping the Way, people would thus be empowered to avert disaster and achieve good ends.

In explaining this function of the *Book of Changes*, Wang Fuzhi suggested that the *Book of Changes* offered ways to manage human affairs based on the Way of Heaven. By cultivating and mastering this book, one would be able to grasp and apply the principle of Heaven. They would be able to predict the proper time and place to act by divination and cautiously deal with uncertain matters of grave concern. Despite unfavorable situations and worries, the user would be counselled to keep their activities in accord with the principle. For this, they would gain the blessings of Heaven and tend to have propitious results without incurring disadvantages (Wang 1996: 1:516). In this fashion, Wang asserted human beings could predict affairs and manage heavenly processes by practicing divination using the lines and hexagrams.

5.5.2   Preserving Spirit to Maintain Harmony

Since spirit was the principle of the Great Harmony, Wang Fuzhi taught preserving spirit (*shen* 神) to achieve and maintain harmony. "In the Great Harmony, there are *qi* and spirit. Spirit is nothing but the principle of the pure, penetrating yin and yang" (Wang 1996: 12:16). If human beings were to preserve spirit and fully enfold the nature, they would maintain their unity with the Great Harmony and guide yin and yang to follow principle. They would thus contribute to the harmony of Heaven and their *qi* would be under the control of their will (Wang 1996: 12:44). In this fashion, human beings could transform their disharmonious *qi* into harmonious *qi*. Wang supported this view by claiming that the early sages had devoted themselves to preserving spirit and contributing harmonious *qi* to Heaven, adding that people should devote themselves to this mission, as well. A person who has done so would be at one with heavenly transformation and never disturb the Great Harmony, in life or in death. As to the space between Heaven and Earth, such a person would not bequeath one iota of disharmonious *qi* that would spur perversion, disaster, wickedness, turbidity, and chaos (Wang 1996: 12:22). If everyone were to devote themselves to carrying out this mission, evil conduct and disasters would cease and the world would have less conflict and more peace.

The question, then, was how to preserve spirit? Wang Fuzhi suggested two approaches. The first was by observing ritual propriety and grasping the essence of righteousness. "The principle of spirit and transformation becomes patterns (*wen* 文) when it disperses into the myriad things; it is manifested as ritual propriety when human beings properly conduct affairs" (Wang 1996: 12:159). In this way, one's dedicated observances of ritual propriety would support the preservation of spirit. Wang further held that righteousness was based on managing the vitality and compliance, movement and rest, of yin and yang; a person who upheld righteousness would maintain the principle of spirit, as well.

The second approach to the preservation of spirit was to unfold the nature. The nature was spirit or the Way of Heaven endowed in human beings. "Heaven uses spirit as its Way. The nature is the substance of spirit. The nature and the Way of Heaven are spirit, nothing else" (Wang 1996: 12:95). "The nature is what spirit gathers in human beings; the Way of Heaven is the transformation of spirit" (Wang 1996: 12:55). Since the nature was the gathering of spirit in the human body and spirit in turn was the Way of Heaven; a person would be able to assist Heaven if they were to unfold the nature. As the good nature was, in essence, the principle of harmonious *qi*; by developing the good nature, a person would be set to contribute their portion to the universal harmonious *qi* or the Great Harmony. If the cosmos could thus be made replete with harmonious *qi*, there would be fewer selfish people, and people's social ethics would be enhanced. A person who was born into such a positive social milieu would more likely nurture and maintain the nature to be a noble person. Wang thusly connected Heaven, society, and the person, advocating that everyone contribute their part to the harmony of the world.

Wang Fuzhi also defined spirit as a mass of harmonious *qi*: "Spirit is the fine, pure part of the cosmic *qi*" (Wang 1996: 13:207). He thus regarded spirit as the essence of both the Great Harmony and the harmonious *qi* of the human body. Therefore, by making efforts to preserve spirit, a person would be improving their own harmonious *qi* and, in turn, contribute to the general harmonious *qi*. As to preserving spirit (the harmonious *qi*), Wang suggested that a person "maintain their will by cultivating reverence and consolidate their spirit by maintaining their will (*yi zhuan chi zhi, yi zhi ning shen* 以專持志, 以志凝神)" (Wang 1996: 13:296).

In order to moderate unruly tendencies of bodily *qi* and spirit, a person should uphold their will as the master of mind and body. With a tranquil mind and a steady will, a person would make their spirit and *qi* stay the course and accumulate their energies over time. In the end, spirit would dwell in their body in perfect ease (Wang 1996: 13:301). In this condition, the spirit would be concentrated and free of attachment or disturbance.

As to upholding the will with reverence, Wang Fuzhi suggested forgetting material things. Human desires were the first things a person ought to forget. "How can material things disturb my will, sway my spirit, harm my body, transform me into a slave of objects, and make me indulge in material things? Or, what opens up my will, spirit, and body to being overwhelmed by material things? It is caused by the impulse of my desires and mind seeking gratification" (Wang 1996: 13:299). To uphold a steady will, the prescription was to make the mind vacuous, be satisfied with one's lot or fate in life, not distinguish between self and other, and cast away the disturbances of the desires.

With a firm will, a person could preserve spirit and strive to unite with the Great Harmony. Having cast off their disharmonious *qi*, they would no longer encounter disasters and conflicts. In contrast, a person who failed to preserve spirit and let the turbid and perverse *qi* prevail in their mind and body, and by extension, between Heaven and Earth, would face multiple disasters and evil people (Wang 1996: 12:44). Wang thus affirmed that a noble person's duty was to maintain the pure, firm part of Heaven, eliminate the disastrous *qi* produced by things and affairs, promote the Way of humanity, and make it lasting (Wang 1996: 1:929). Unquestionably, the pure, firm part of Heaven was harmonious *qi*.

Wang Fuzhi's two definitions of spirit could be united, because if a mass of *qi* followed the principle of yin-yang, it would be harmonious. In this way, spirit as a mass of harmonious *qi* could be considered a concrete embodiment of the principle of yin-yang. Therefore, to preserve spirit, one had to observe ritual propriety to moderate the emotions and the desires, on the one hand, and one would accumulate harmonious *qi* by maintaining the will, on the other hand. Consequently, Wang requested that students preserve spirit by purifying mind and pacifying *qi*; he even advocated cultivating a vacuous mind to attain a sharp intelligence in this context. He also proceeded to request students to ponder principle deeply and maintain a reverent attitude for cultivating harmonious *qi* (Wang 1996: 12:93). In this way, he worked out a practical synthesis of Confucian and Daoist methods of spiritual cultivation.

5.5.3   To Cultivate Harmony by Being Reverent

As observing ritual propriety conduced to preserving spirit, Wang Fuzhi regarded ritual propriety as the guide to the proper conduct of human relationships and affairs and preventing the decrease of harmony. The presumption was that people who observed ritual propriety would moderate their desires for food and sex and achieve the mean in their conduct of affairs, which was termed harmony in the *Doctrine of the Mean*. Therefore, "As ritual propriety has its due measure, it is used to cultivate harmony in the human mind and avoid untempered expressions of the emotions. It is through such measures that harmony is achieved" (Wang 1996: 7:268).

As reverence is the essence of ritual propriety,[3] Wang Fuzhi took reverence as a key approach to cultivating harmony. When criticizing Zhuangzi's cultivation of harmony, he stressed that the best way to achieve harmony was none other than cultivating reverence. If a person were to maintain a reverent attitude and make the mind tranquil, spirit would master the mind and body. Spirit would guide their body and *qi*, and sustain the smooth operation of their bodily functions. If such were the case, how

---

[3] Wang Fuzhi regarded reverence as the spirit of rituals, claiming when a person's reverence ran through the ceremonies and texts he practiced, he would rest in them smartly and people in the world would trust him (Wang 1996: 12:215).Therefore, to prevent rituals from becoming mere gestures, one should prudently practice rituals with respect (Wang 1996: 7:338).

could a person's health fail before their time? How could they not reap the blessings of Heaven (Wang 1996: 5:556)?

How to maintain a reverent attitude? What should a person reverence? According to Wang Fuzhi, "Being reverent involves human effort; harmony is a heavenly virtue. To achieve heavenly virtue by human effort, one must grasp reverence as the essence of ritual propriety and achieve harmony in that way" (Wang 1996: 6:592). Taking this approach as a standard, Wang criticized the Daoist method of cultivating harmony. He enumerated the ways to achieve harmony offered in the *Zhuangzi* and observed, "[In order to achieve harmony,] one ought to be like Ji Xing's 紀渻 wooden rooster, or Shu Shan's 叔山 treatment of his toe, or Nan Guo's 南郭 loss of his ego, or Ju Baiyu's 蘧伯玉 innocent baby. If a person were to achieve harmony in these ways, they truly would be harmonious, but their intention in achieving such harmony would be beyond reckoning (*ran qi suo you yi he zhe bu ke wen yi* 然其所繇以和者不可問已)" (Wang 1996: 5:554–555). In Wang's perspective, saying "his intention in achieving such harmony would be beyond reckoning" meant that Zhuangzi's intention in achieving such harmony was tainted with selfish desires.

In the *Zhuangzi*, the fundamental approach to achieving harmony was to forget the artificial distinctions among things, realize that all things were transformations of the same mass of *qi*, and follow natural transformations without preferences or attachments. Abandoning distinctions and attachments, the rooster raised by Master Ji Xing would lose its fear and appear like a wooden rooster before the other game roosters; realizing the Oneness of all things, Shu Shan Wu Zhi and Nan Guo Zi Xu would not mind the loss of a toe or even their ego-self. Forsaking preference and attachment, Ju Baiyu could act the innocent baby before others. In such ways, a person could maintain a tranquil mind and achieve harmony. To certain extent, these were better ways to achieve harmony than just by observing ritual propriety. Because if a person were to observe ritual propriety to cultivate harmony, they would already be drawing distinctions among things and find it difficult to maintain peace and harmony when witnessing improper conduct and corrupt affairs.

After explaining how Zhuangzi's intention to achieve harmony was beyond reckoning, Wang Fuzhi continued, "As to sleep, he [Zhuangzi] desires it to be sound; as to sitting, he tends to spread his legs; as to going abroad, he does not want to defy other's smiles and faces; and as to returning home, he intends to let his ears and eyes rest. If he were to achieve all of these results, he would feel harmonious; otherwise, he would feel disharmonious. Don't common people tend to act and respond in pre-cisely this way?" (Wang 1996: 5:555). That is to say, in Wang estimation, Zhuangzi was a person who sought to fulfill his desires, avoid defying other people, and enjoy a harmonious life. However, Wang's judgment of Zhuangzi contradicted the earlier examples he cited from the *Zhuangzi*; for if a person were to achieve the mindset of the wooden cock or the baby, they would not have any desire for comfort or concern for other things.

Wang Fuzhi's mistake lay in that he took ritual propriety as the exclu-sive path to achieving harmony. Truly, without the restraints of ritual pro-priety, most people would tend to indulge in the emotions and the desires to achieve peace of mind. But it is improper that, by exaggerating the role of ritual propriety, he denied the validity of other approaches to cultivating harmony. In this way, he contradicted the truth that it was the Great Harmony that gave rise to humaneness, righteousness, and thus ritual pro-priety, not vice versa. Ritual propriety as one branch of harmony could be one approach to reaching harmony, but clearly it was not the only one.

5.5.4   *To Assist Heaven by Knowing One's* Ming 命

One main cause of disharmony was the complaints of human beings to Heaven. If a person was to accept whatever they encountered in life with equanimity, the emotions of joy, anger, sorrow, and pleasure would not be aroused in their mind at the sight of gain and loss, life and death. And they would not easily incur disharmonious *qi*. This mentality was termed "being content with one's time and accepting one's status (*an shi chu shun* 安時處順)" in the *Zhuangzi*, and "knowing one's fate (*zhi ming* 知命)" in the *Analects*. *Ming* was interpreted as natural destiny or what came about beyond human control. As a worshiper of Confucius, Wang asserted that if a person were to awaken to their destiny (*ming* 命), they would enjoy whatever fate Heaven offered. They would be moderate and never exces-sive in utilizing the myriad things; they would seek to improve the welfare of human beings, whether by killing or rescuing others. In this way, they would establish their destiny (*liming* 立命) and assist in the processes of Heaven (Wang 1996: 12:125). Obviously, Wang continued Confucius' and Zhuangzi's line of thought, but he specified *ming* as a person's social role or whatever they encountered (*yu* 遇). He argued, "Oxen are pierced through their noses to plow fields, horses are bridled to be ridden, silk-worms are boiled for their silk, wood is cut for firewood, ordinary people serve the nobles with their labor, and defend their ruler and state with their lives. Are they born for these purposes? No, it is their destiny or fate that makes it so" (Wang 1996: 12:125). In this way, Wang identified social role as a person's fate or destiny, which differed from the nature or what Heaven had endowed. He realized this difference and distinguished the species nature of oxen in themselves from their utility to human beings. But, if the utility or use value of human beings was regarded as their fate, their assisting Heaven through awakening to fate would be tantamount to improving human well-being by utilizing things. As a result, Wang's goal of preserving harmonious *qi* by assisting Heaven would be in question, because human well-being was not necessarily the same thing as general harmony. After all, driving oxen and horses and cutting trees for firewood could only destroy natural processes or general harmony in the grand scheme of things.

Among the types of fate that Wang Fuzhi advocated heeding, he recognized that life and death played a key role in a person's cultivation of harmonious *qi*. He suggested that people know the principle of life and death, to make contributions to Heaven. He considered that life and death were the gathering and dispersal of a mass of *qi*, and human body was just a temporary stage in the transformation of this *qi*. A person should seek identity with this ongoing mass of *qi* rather than with its temporary stage as his body. If they were to awaken to this long-term reality, they would no longer be attached to this corporeal life, but accept the death of this body and all such natural and social occurrences with equanimity. He asserted:

> I won't change my normal manner when *qi* gathers to form my body, so after birth I can recover my vigor and deferential nature by persistent cultivation, though I be fettered in physical embodiment or shackled by desires for material things. I will retain my cosmic body after the dispersion of *qi*, so the pure and turbid parts of my bodily *qi* will return to their respective kinds after my body disappears, though I encounter good and evil, chaos and order during my life. (Wang 1996: 12:19–20)

Having grasped the principle of life and death, we consign life and death to the gathering and dispersal of *qi* and do not anticipate longevity or good fortune. We thus become at peace, free of complaint or regret. Our *qi* becomes harmonious. This would be a passive approach to preserving the Great Harmony.

Wang Fuzhi, however, was no fatalist and advocated human effort, so his understanding of *ming* carried a further dimension: to cultivate humaneness by grasping the principle of life. He called this dimension of *ming* the portion that a person is to establish by self-cultivation (*ming zhi keyi xiushen er li zhe* 命之可以脩身而立者), as distinguished from pure fate:

> As to the aspect of *ming* that is beyond human control, such as, longevity and early death, success and failure, fortune and misfortune, they arise by their own principles and hit a person seemingly by chance. None of them is not determined by Heaven, and thus are called destiny (*ming* 命). Yet, viewed from the aspect of *ming* that is established by self-cultivation, as to longevity and early death and the like, some are called proper (*zheng* 正) when Heaven causes them but I encounter them by chance; some are not proper if Heaven does not produce them but I incur them by my own deeds. (Wang 1996: 8:825)

Just as Mencius did not think a person knew his fate who got harmed while standing near an unstable wall (Mencius 7A.2), Wang Fuzhi first did not think it a proper case if a person got harmed while giving up to their fate or not avoiding harm when they could. He also denied that such results were proper if a person got them by reckless conduct, such as obtaining benefit by taking a risk or sheer luck, or indulging the desires regardless of threat to life and limb. In particular, a person who committed a crime and was sentenced to death was improper and should not blame Heaven.

Nevertheless, Wang Fuzhi thought it proper if a person followed the norms or ritual propriety in managing their life because he regarded the norms and ritual propriety as concrete forms of the principle, which Heaven endowed in human beings. In other words, a person's observances of ritual propriety would be tantamount to their conscientious acceptance of Heaven's endowment. In this way, Wang drew a distinction between proper and improper in terms of ritual propriety and the Way of humanity. He argued, "Heaven has its time to kill or give life, and its fortune and misfortune. Yet, human beings receive their endowment with the Way of humanity; regardless of fortune, misfortune, disaster and blessing, human beings can achieve humaneness and righteousness despite them, having no impropriety" (Wang 1996: 12:127). To be precise, a person would achieve their proper fate if they were to practice the Way of humanity by conscientiously reducing their desires and being circumspect about their words in ordinary times, while exerting their loyalty and filial piety and upholding their purity and integrity in times of crisis.

Wang Fuzhi identified the Way of humanity with the principle of life, and deemed it the key to knowing and establishing one's proper fate by adhering to the principle of life. If a person knew that Heaven had produced them by this very principle and faced by the vicissitudes of *qi* with equanimity, they would regard life and death, bending and stretching as all the same (Wang 1996: 8:823). As the principle of life was identified with human nature in Wang's works, he went on to develop Mencius' approach: know Heaven by knowing the nature. He assumed that from birth, everyone took Heaven's endowment as their nature, so they could make their fate proper by upholding the Way of humanity (Wang 1996: 8:824). To be precise, a person should uphold the principle of life in word and deed, and develop their steadfastness and integrity. Whether faced with long life or an early death, such a person would uphold principle heart and soul, and await Heaven's decree without second thought. They would be set to make a real contribution to Heaven by upholding principle (Wang 1996: 8:823–824).

At this point, Wang Fuzhi seems to be prioritizing knowledge of principle over knowledge of the mass of *qi* in the process of transcending life and death and assisting Heaven. His claim was that the knowledge of human life did not lie in knowing the living, existent body, but lay in preserving the principle of life without fail. He insisted that only after a person had guided their actions by the nature (principle) could they avoid being blind to the meaning of human life (Wang 1996: 8:647). By upholding principle, one could transcend the human preferences for life, wealth, and nobility, and extinguish human complaints about unfavorable situations or death, regard everything as products of natural processes, be at one with the principle of the bending and stretching of *qi*, and unite with Heaven (Wang 1996: 12:206). Having entered this sphere, one could "return Heaven and Earth a principle with a mass of vigorous, compliant *qi*, and finish life without bequeathing disaster to the Great Void (Heaven)" (Wang 1996: 12:207).

5.5.5   To Assist Heaven by Transforming One's Temperament (bianhua qizhi 變化氣質)

Wang Fuzhi admitted that heavenly transformation could produce people with some disharmonious *qi* and make them different in appearance, shape, and virtue. "The Way of Heaven completes and nurtures human bodies at random, so there are the differences of beautiful and ugly, partial and fully formed, tall and short among people" (Wang 1996: 10:404). However, he did not think that human beings were powerless with respect to the bodies that Heaven had endowed to them. He insisted that with effort, they could change their bodies from bad to good, partial to complete, impure to pure (Wang 1996: 10:404).

He justified the possibility of such change on the basis of cosmic process and human effort. As to cosmic process, although at birth a human body had been formed with a defect or imbalance in temperament because of impure *qi*, it kept breathing and exchanging its *qi* with that of Heaven from birth. Under normal conditions, such postnatal exchanges would not change a person's temperament, for the exchanged *qi* would come and pass through the body at random. That was why different creatures had differently shaped bodies and the most foolish and wise people could not be changed. However, if this exchange was deliberately guided, it would be possible for a person to change their temperament. Wang thus made the following claim:

> After a body is formed, it continuously grows and decays without cease. In the beginning, the growth and decay remain within the body itself. But, the body will alter once it becomes fond of receiving disorderly *qi*. Likewise, the transformation from evil to good lies in the cultivation of good *qi*. When one continues such cultivation of good *qi* at length, one's temperament will change. Thus, it is said, "One's dwelling changes one's *qi*, and one's food changes one's body," for one's body too will change with the change of *qi* ... This is human capacity. It is habit. (Wang 1996: 6:860)

In other words, while the repetitive absorption of disorderly *qi* could alter the formed body for the worse, and likewise, the persistent cultivation of good *qi* could improve one's temperament. But, was it really possible to transform a challenged person into a normal person just by their cultivating good *qi*? Wang did not directly address this question. To a certain extent, this reflected the limits of his grasp of the problem of transforming one's temperament.

As to human effort, Wang Fuzhi emphasized the role of habit. Habit was the good habits developed while observing ritual propriety. Cultivating good habits involved one's moderating the emotions and the desires and being prudent about one's choices of food and drink. By carefully choosing their food intake, a person could nourish not only their blood and *qi* but also their virtues of softness, purity, firmness, and elegance. Once their blood and *qi* had turned pure and clear, their nature and emotions would also incline toward uprightness. By not carefully choosing one's food intake, one could render one's *qi* turbid and mind confused if the food and drink had been carelessly prepared, stale, or impure (Wang 1996: 7:619).

Wang Fuzhi firmly believed that by effort and perseverance, a person could transform the partiality of their or even the temperament of other people. He called this "being sincerely concentrated on one mission (*zhi qu zhi cheng* 致曲之誠)." Yet, whether a person would be successful in this mission would depend on the intensity and sincerity of their effort (Wang 1996: 7:657). If a person were to strive to the utmost, they would sooner or later overcome the partiality of their or the other's bodily temperament. Wang further elucidated this idea by discussing legendary emperor Shun's 舜 success at transforming his evil father:

> We cannot disobey our parents, but sometimes we cannot make them cooperate. Shun exhausted his sincere efforts and finally made his father cooperate and change his evil nature. Thus, we know that the growth and decay of Heaven and Earth are changeable, and the great man can transform a chaotic condition into an orderly one. Therefore, by rectifying oneself and being sincere in one's intentions, the partiality of one's *qi* can be overcome. (Wang 1996: 12:356)

What Shun used to transform his father was his virtues of sincerity and filial piety. When he did that to the utmost, his father felt moved and was transformed. In this fashion, a truly great man could transform others with their sincere observances of ritual propriety.

In the end, Wang Fuzhi reminded us that Heaven could not spontaneously transform bad or perverse *qi* into good, harmonious *qi*, even though it did produce human beings mostly with harmonious *qi*. For this very reason, everyone should be cautious not to bequeath corrupt, disharmonious *qi* to the world. Wang pointed out that the good *qi* of the early sages and the bad *qi* of the early tyrants, such as King Zhou of the Shang 商紂王 and King Jie of the Xia 夏桀王, still lingered in the cosmos (Wang 1996: 12:23). The reason for this was, in effect, that birds of a feather flock together: the good, harmonious *qi* and the bad, disharmonious *qi* of each king or emperor came and went, bent and stretched according to its respective course, and did not mingle (Wang 1996: 12:19). Consequently, Wang assigned an important duty to human beings: transform evil *qi* into good *qi*. He stressed this mission with his affirmation that humanity was the mind of Heaven and Earth.

5.6   CONCLUSION

Although Heaven and humanity differed in the scope of their *qi*, Wang Fuzhi insisted that humanity could assist Heaven because the *qi* and principle of human beings came from Heaven. If human beings could uphold principle or humaneness, they would contribute their share of harmony to assist in maintaining the Great Harmony. Specifically, if a person were to maintain their spirit and body intact, they would return to Heaven and Earth a mass of pure, harmonious *qi* and benefit the world forever. He envisioned:

> If both (spirit and body) are not harmed, then the pure, clear *qi* of Heaven and Earth will be molded by me. When they (body and spirit) disperse and return to their original state, their purity and clarity will marvellously match the void. They will enhance the luminosity of the sun, moon, and stars above, and nurture the fecundity of all things below. They become the breeze blowing between Heaven and Earth, and their life-principle will gather good *qi* to form more good people. In this way, although the body changes, the pure and clear harmonious *qi* does not change, but becomes the focus of goodness and good fortune and greatly benefits the living creatures under Heaven. They thus assist in the transformation of Heaven and persist forever, spreading throughout the cosmos and mingling with the myriad forms. No benefit would be greater than this. (Wang 1996: 13:293)

This bright vision inspired Wang Fuzhi to cultivate harmonious *qi* by moderating the emotions and the desires and complying with principle. However, Wang also admitted that Heaven transformed all things randomly, and might gather pure, clean *qi* to produce sages and worthies, or disperse the previous sages' *qi* to generate common, foolish people (Wang 1996: 1:1045). But, this should not discourage anyone from attempting to increase the total amount of cosmic harmonious *qi* by practicing moral cultivation.

To purify one's impure *qi* or change the partiality of one's bodily temperament, Wang Fuzhi proposed various methods, including infusing oneself with harmonious *qi*, observing ritual propriety, preserving spirit, and knowing one's *ming*. However, the most important method laid in transforming one's temperament by cultivating good habits. Such habits would include choosing food and drink wisely according to ritual propriety and focusing on performing good deeds. If a person were to perfect their performance of good deeds, as Shun displayed utmost filial piety to his father, they would not only affect change within themselves, but even change others. Otherwise, if a person were irresponsible and bequeathed disastrous, disharmonious *qi* to the cosmos, it would be difficult for Heaven to transform it into harmonious *qi*. Therefore, as a human being, everyone should accept the duty to cultivate their harmonious *qi* to make the cosmos better.

Consequently, as to cultivating harmonious *qi*, Wang Fuzhi identified a way to connect an individual's efforts and behavior with maintaining cosmic harmony. If a person were to cultivate their harmonious *qi* by promoting Confucianism in chaotic times, they would preserve a seed for the recovery of social harmony and human civilization. Implicitly, Wang expressed his own ambition to preserve the Ming culture under the harsh control of the Manchu invaders in this way. He did not believe that the Manchus were capable of mastering the essence of Confucianism or promoting humaneness given the massacres they had carried out in Yangzhou and Jiangyin. For this reason, Wang dedicated himself to preserving the light of humaneness for later generations and hoped that a future sage king or emperor would appear and discover the Confucian Way presented in his works and strive to extend the firm, pure *qi* Wang had preserved, and return the throne to the Han Chinese.

BIBLIOGRAPHY

EARLY CHINESE TEXTS

Cheng, Hao & Cheng, Yi 程颢, 程颐, *Er Cheng YiShu* 二程遗书 (*The Extant Works of the Two Chengs*), Shanghai: Shanghai Guji Chubanshe 上海古籍出版社, 2000

Gu, Yanwu, *Record of Daily Accumulated Knowledge* (*Ri Zhi Lu* 日知录), Lanzhou: Gansu Minzu Chubanshe, 1997

Guo, Qingfan 郭慶藩, *Zhuangzi Jishi* 莊子集釋 (*Collected Commentaries on the Zhuangzi*), Beijing: Zhonghua Shuju 北京:中華書局, 1961

Huang, Zongxi 黃宗羲, *Huang Zongxi Quanji* 黃宗羲全集 (1–22 冊) (*The Complete Works of Huang Zongxi*), Volume 1–22, Hangzhou: Zhejiang Guji Chubanshe 杭州:浙江古籍出版社, 2012

Li, Jingde, ed. 黎靖德, *Zhu Zi Yu Lei* 朱子語類 (*Conversations of Master Zhu, Arranged Topically*), Beijing: Zhonghua Shuju 北京: 中華書局, 1994

Shang, Binghe 尚秉和, *Zhou Yi Shangshi Xue* 周易尚氏學 (*Shang's Commentary on the Book of Changes*), Beijing: Zhonghua Shuju, 2016

Wang, Xianqian 王先謙, *Xunzi Jijie* 荀子集解 (*Collected Exegesis of the Xunzi*), Beijing: Zhonghua Shuju 北京: 中華書局, 1988

Wang, Yu 王敔, *Daxing Fujun Xingshu* 大行府君行述 (*A Brief Biographical Sketch of my Diseased Father*), in *Chuanshan Quanshu* 船山全書16 (*The Complete Works of Chuanshan*), Volume 16, Changsha: Yuelu Shushe 長沙: 岳麓書社, 1996

Xu, Yuangao 徐元誥, *Guo Yu Jijie* 國語集解 (*Collected Notes on the Records of States*), Zhonghua Shuju, 2002

Yang, Bojun 楊伯峻, *Chunqiu Zuozhuan Zhu* 春秋左傳注 (*Annotations on the Zuo Commentary Tradition on the Spring-Autumn Annals*), Beijing: Zhonghua Shuju 北京: 中華書局, 1981

Zhang, Zai 張載, *Zhang Zai Ji* 張載集 (*A Collection of Zhang Zai's Works*), Beijing: Zhonghua Shuju 北京: 中華書局, 1978

Heresies: The Causes of the Fall of the Ming and the Obstacles to Implementing the Kingly Way

In Chap. 4, we addressed Wang Fuzhi's analysis of the political and administrative defects that led to the fall of the Ming and the Manchu conquest, which the historian Wu Han 吴晗 (1909–1969) ascribed to official corruption, heavy taxes, factional struggles, and natural disasters, which together ignited widespread peasant uprisings (Wu 1956: 1–38). Wang Fuzhi, however, placed most blame on the declining social ethos, which he believed had been spawned by faulty, misleading interpretations of the Confucian classics and seductive heretical teachings. In particular, he blamed the general decline in social ethos on the teachings of Wang Yangming and his followers, accusing their teachings of stirring the common people to lose their sense of shame and honor, the proliferation of bandits and thieves, and the invasion of the Manchus (Wang 1996: 12:371). To make sense of Wang Fuzhi's criticisms, it is necessary to consider his attitude toward Buddhism, Daoism, Legalism, and the other teachings he denounced as heretical, and understand how he reconstructed Neo-Confucianism in his effort to make it resistant to the heretical teachings.

© The Author(s), under exclusive license to Springer Nature
Switzerland AG 2021
M. Tan, *Wang Fuzhi's Reconstruction of Confucianism*,
https://doi.org/10.1007/978-3-030-80263-9_6

6.1   WANG FUZHI'S REFLECTIONS ON MING
CONFUCIAN SCHOLARSHIP

Although Wang Fuzhi advocated transforming the people by ritual propriety and music, he did not think the official version of Ming Neo-
Confucianism had served this purpose. The problem, in his view, was that
mainstream Neo-Confucianism had been adulterated with Buddhism and
thus had departed from the original teachings of the early sage kings. He
therefore dedicated his efforts to rectifying the commentaries of the
Cheng-Zhu School and criticizing the Chan Buddhist elements in the
teachings of the Wang Yangming School. Specifically, he criticized Zhu Xi
and his followers for interpreting the Confucian classics with Buddhism
concepts. He also assumed that the teachings of Wang and his followers
had disinclined the people from practicing Confucian ritual propriety and
encouraged them to pursue their selfish desires by urging to realize their
inborn knowledge of the good. In consequence, Wang charged that these
misguided Neo-Confucian teachings had led people to abandon loyalty
and trust, lose their sense of shame and honor, and accept the Manchus as
their rulers despite the blow to their ethnic dignity.

Concerning Wang Yangming's teaching of inborn knowledge of the
good, Wang Fuzhi remarked that Wang Yangming's teaching, "The
inborn knowledge of the good, which is neither good nor bad," had misled the people and caused the Confucian moral system to collapse. With
its avowed transcendence of good and evil, this teaching enabled the criminals and eunuchs to erase their sense of evil and shame and for this became
their treasured creed (Wang 1996: 12:11). Wang Yangming's disciple
Wang Ji 王畿 (1498–1583) went so far as to abandon all moral principles
and advocate the Huayan 華嚴 Buddhist doctrine, "No obstruction
between principle and phenomena, nor between phenomena and phenomena" (Wang 1996: 12:642). People could interpret this Buddhist
doctrine as eradicating the contradiction between evil actions and moral
principle, and weaken the moral conscience of wrong-doers. Another follower of Wang Yangming, Li Zhi 李贄 (1527–1602), sought to identify
one's selfish desires with their inborn knowledge of the good and reduced
human relationships to nothing more than basic biological needs. He
affirmed, "Beyond wearing clothes and eating meals, there are no human
relationships. All things in the world are nothing but clothes and food"
(Li 1975: 4). Such teachings of Wang Yangming and his followers not
only contradicted Mencius' proposition that human nature is good, but

also betrayed his distinction between human beings and the birds and beast by the standards of ritual propriety and humaneness. Consequently, Wang Fuzhi declared that "Wang Yangming's teachings were first passed down to Wang Ji, and then to Li Zhi. After such reckless teachings were disseminated, the people lost their sense of shame and honor, bandits and thieves proliferated, and China was invaded by the Manchus" (Wang 1996: 12:371).

Wang Fuzhi pointed out that Wang Yangming's original purpose was to subsume action under knowledge and to regard knowledge as action when he proposed the teaching of inborn knowledge of the good. Because Wang Yangming and his followers "mistook knowledge for action, they easily fell into the error of regarding inaction as action. As a result, they would not put heart and soul into fulfilling human relationships or following the principles of affairs, despite the little knowledge they did have" (Wang 1996: 2:312). Between confusing knowledge for action and denying the distinction between good and evil, they brought about the disintegration of the Confucian moral order and stirred the formation of an unsustainable social ethos of irresponsibility and contentiousness.

Attempting to rectify Wang Yangming's account of inborn knowledge of the good, Wang Fuzhi indicated that inborn knowledge of the good (*liangzhi* 良知) and inborn ability to do good (*liangneng* 良能) had been presented as inseparable complements in the *Mencius*. In effect, *liangneng* referred to each person's capacity to realize *liangzhi* in practice. Without such practical efficacy, one's inborn knowledge of the good would be no better than ignorance. Wang Yangming's error was that he had ignored the ability to realize goodness in action by focusing solely on knowledge— and thus fell into heresy (Wang 1996: 12:121). Wang Fuzhi proposed rather that knowledge and action should be mutually supportive and active. "Knowledge and action each have their function and achievement, and thus should be mutually supportive. Wang Yangming did not realize this, so he misled the people throughout the empire with his faulty teaching of the unity of knowledge and action" (Wang 1996: 4:1256).

As a matter of fact, Wang Fuzhi misunderstood Wang Yangming's teaching of knowledge and action. When Wang Yangming proposed the unity of knowledge and action, he was thinking of a person's true knowledge of a cognitive event, in the sense of a person's true knowledge when facing the risk of being devoured by a tiger. He remarked, "When a person knows something clearly and sincerely, their response will be a true action; when a person does something with keenness and discrimination, they truly know it" (Wang 2012: 95). He indicated that he wished to correct two types of people: (1) those who were inclined to do things recklessly, such as jump into a lake before ascertaining the water's depth, and (2) those who were inclined to hesitate for lack of complete knowledge (Wang 2012: 11). Wang Yangming had not replaced action with knowledge at all, but in fact had proposed that knowledge and action were mutually supportive (Wang 2012: 94), a view which, as we saw, Wang Fuzhi also endorsed.

Wang Fuzhi further revealed ways in which Wang Yangming had misunderstood Confucianism and misled the world. Wang Yangming had these misunderstandings because he had adulterated Confucianism with Chan Buddhism. He derided Wang Yangming's handing down his teachings to Wang Longxi 王龍溪 and Qian Xushan 錢緒山 at Tianquan Bridge as mimicking the fifth Chan Master's handing down his teachings to Hui Neng惠能 and Shen Xiu 神秀 (Wang 1996: 12:488). Wang Fuzhi showed how Wang Yangming had interpreted some expressions and phrases from the Confucian classics in Chan Buddhist terms. The essence of his inborn knowledge of the good was Buddhist in spirit: to sever the path of language, annihilate rational mental functioning, rise above worldly affairs, and stay unattached to any idea or opinion (Wang 1996: 12:370).

Nonetheless, it would not be persuasive to classify Wang Yangming as a Chan Buddhist just because the Tianquan Bridge story had Chan Buddhist overtones. Moreover, Wang Yangming's teaching of inborn knowledge of the good would not fit into the Buddhist constellation of ideas, either. After all, Wang Yangming defined inborn knowledge of the good as the essence of the mind, that is, the nature and heavenly principle (Wang 2012: 121, 146). This principle was the principle of life, and distinguished the mind from a pound of flesh, by endowing mind with the virtue of humaneness (Wang 2012: 82). Wang Yangming also made clear what he meant by "neither good nor evil (*wu shan wu e* 無善無惡)" in his discourses: "The Buddhists understand 'beyond good and evil' rigidly, leaving every affair unsettled, and are incapable of governing the world. The Confucian sages understand 'beyond good and evil' to mean free of preference and aversion, and free of emotional agitation. Additionally, they practice the Kingly Way and know their purpose, hence they always heed heavenly principle, and assist Heaven and the emperor in giving rise to and sustaining all life" (Wang 2012: 66). It is noteworthy that Wang Yangming characterized ritual propriety as the concrete expression of heavenly principle. "Ritual propriety (*li* 禮) is tantamount to principle (*li* 理). When principle is manifested, the visible aspect is called pattern (*wen* 文); when the pattern becomes invisible, the invisible aspect is called principle. They are one and the same" (Wang 2012: 16). Based on these quotations, it is apparent that Wang Fuzhi misunderstood Wang Yangming when he accused him of advocating Chan Buddhism in the guise of Confucianism. However, when Wang Yangming proposed that inborn knowledge of the good was beyond good and evil, and asked people to heed their inborn knowledge in taking action, he had neglected that people still needed to rectify their mind and make their intentions sincere before proceeding to identify their intentions and actions, in other words realizing the unity of knowledge and action. Some people took advantage of such mixing of intentions and action, to justify satisfying their selfish desires.

Wang Fuzhi also pointed out that Wang Yangming had confused instinct with cultivated virtue when he compared one's moral practice with one's love of beauty and dislike of filth, which he had cited in support of his identification of knowledge and action. By such faulty analogies, Wang Yangming had tried to explain a person's truthfulness in their moral behavior. But, he did not realize that lazy, evil, hypocritical people would use this identification as a pretext to replace moral practice with pure knowledge. It was for this that Wang Fuzhi attacked him and his followers, for basing Confucian practice on subjective whim without any standard, such that anyone who said they had awakened to their inborn knowledge could claim that they had achieved sagehood. As Wang Yangming's teachings were disseminated around China, evil, lazy people took advantage of these teachings to justify their evildoing and negligence. Lazy scholars wanted to have achievements without making any effort and neglected their human relationships and investigating real things.

Wang Fuzhi spat less venom on the Cheng-Zhu School, but this did not mean he absolved it from blame for the fall of the Ming. In his view, in their quest to obtain solid knowledge of the Confucian classics, Zhu Xi's followers had metamorphosed into bookworms—preoccupied with counting words and copying lines but hesitant to put Confucian ritual propriety into practice. Their negative influence had also contributed to the decline of the Ming social ethos, despite their different teachings and practices. Consequently, Wang Fuzhi sought to discourage practitioners of the Confucian Way from entering either path (Wang 1996: 2:313). Wang accused Zhu Xi's followers of putting knowledge before action and prizing asceticism and pedantic book learning, unlike his criticisms of Wang

Yangming's and his followers' teachings of the unity of knowledge and action and indulgence of the desires.

Besides his criticism of Zhu Xi's pedantic book learning, Wang Fuzhi denounced the ascetic and repressive character of his teachings. Zhu Xi had proposed repressing the selfish desires to preserve heavenly principle, but his followers went to the extreme of purifying their minds of any intention or calculation. They tried to achieve a mental state like Zhuangzi's "perfect mind," which Zhuangzi had likened to a mirror—going after nothing, welcoming nothing, responding but not storing (Watson 1968: 97) and to the stillness of parched wood and the cold cliff of Buddhism (Wang 1996: 6:770). Such extremes ran counter to Zhu Xi's own avowed goal of ordering the state and pacifying the world. The practice of one of Zhu's followers, Wu Yubi 吳與弼 (1391–1469) provides a good example of this excess. In Theodore de Bary's words, "The search for sagehood proved for Wu Yubi to be incompatible with an official career… This inner drive to achieve a kind of sanctity—in Confucian terms characterized by a state of purity (*chun* 醇), integrity (*zheng* 正), serenity (*dan* 澹), or composure (*jing* 靜)—was accompanied by symptoms of alienation from ordinary society and the established forms of social intercourse, which one does not normally expect to find in a model of traditional virtue or pillar of orthodoxy" (De Bary 1975: 20).

If being a sage in the Cheng-Zhu School meant keeping away from society, human relationships and an official career, then that form of sagehood would be different than the sagehood envisioned by Confucius and Mencius. Rather, the Cheng-Zhu sage was more reminiscent of the Buddha or a Bodhisattva than a sage in the Confucian pantheon. For this reason, Wang Fuzhi stressed the Buddhist character of Zhu Xi's antithesis of heavenly principle and the human desires, arguing that "Master Zhu said, 'There is no mental state that belongs to neither heavenly principle nor the human desires' (Li 1994: 1047). I would rather say that while the mental state in which a person has no thoughts and stays like dead wood and a cold cliff does not belong to the human desires, nor does it reach heavenly principle" (Wang 1996: 6:770). Dead wood and cold cliff rather characterize the state of Nirvana to which practitioners of Buddhists aspire.

Unlike Zhu Xi, Wang Fuzhi regarded heavenly principle as the fulfillment of the human desires, and the human desires as the embodiment of heavenly principle. "Although rituals are the forms and details of heavenly principle, they must be manifested through the human desires … Therefore, there will never be a Heaven beyond human beings, nor will there be principle beyond the desires. It is only Buddhism that insists on principle beyond the desires, so a Buddhist will reject the rules of things and disregard human relationships" (Wang 1996: 6:910). He proceeded to warn Zhu Xi's followers that the main focus of Confucius' and Yan Hui's teachings in the *Four Books* and the *Six Classics* was to preserve heavenly principle. When did they begin to treat the human desires as a snake and scorpion, and draw a clear line demarcating them (Wang 1996: 6:673)?

Wang Fuzhi also criticized Zhu Xi's practice of quiet-sitting, a method to prevent the rise of excessive human desires. Quiet-sitting, according to Zhu Xi's master Li Tong 李侗, referred to the mental state before the emotions of joy, anger, sorrow, and happiness were aroused (Li 1994: 2773). By quiet-sitting, Zhu Xi and his followers believed that they would achieve an empty mind by avoiding human affairs, the mental state of equilibrium (*zhong* 中) in the *Doctrine of the Mean*, capable of responding to external affairs spontaneously. Wang Fuzhi observed, "When someone says, the sage's mind is like the Great Void. I counter that this could only be the teaching of a heretical sage who would turn their mind into the Great Void, to wait for external interaction and response, but not proactively use their will and spirit (*qi* 氣) to make achievements" (Wang 1996: 3:309). Since the Great Void meant empty space. Wang Fuzhi accused Zhu Xi of neglecting the Confucian mission of making achievements to benefit the people and falling into the realm of Daoist non-action or Buddhist Nirvana. This was why Wang Fuzhi called Zhu Xi's form of sagehood "the heretical sage." Wang further remarked, "Later Confucians ... adulterated Confucianism with Buddhist and Daoist ideas, and advocated the cultivation of spirit by quiet-sitting. This teaching is harmful, indeed" (Wang 1996: 6:937).

Elsewhere, he criticized Zhu Xi's follower Yun Feng 雲峰 of mistaking the Confucian sagely mind for the Daoist or Buddhist mind. Concerning Yun Feng's remark, "Once a person uses their mind to judge and deliberate, they have departed from their original mind," Wang criticized it as heretical and a betrayal of Confucianism. He pointed out that Mencius had asked students to expand this very mind and apply it to governance, and never denied the necessity of moral deliberation and judgment. Moreover, the training of the sages, the worthies, and the ancient kings had never included cultivating a passive state of mind—aloof like a blank slate. Indeed, the virtue of being non-judgmental was the virtue of a Buddhist going forward without returning, while being free of deliberation was a vestige of Zhuangzi's teachings (Wang 1996: 6:943).

One may wonder how Zhu Xi's teaching had won the favor of Chinese rulers, despite its many defects and betrayal of the Confucian Way. The most obvious reason was that its repressive teaching aimed at calming down people's unruly desires could, by the same token, be adapted to consolidate the ruler's power. Were the people in the empire to have their desires repressed and their personal thoughts eliminated, even an idiot would be able to enjoy his pleasure on the throne. This suggests why Mao Zedong campaigned under the slogan "Utter devotion to others without any thought of self (*hao bu li ji zhuan men li ren* 毫不利己, 專門利人) (Mao 1991: 659)," a Communist version of Zhu Xi's "purge the human desires to preserve heavenly principle." However, despite its usefulness for consolidating imperial power, this teaching weakened the vitality of society, and by encouraging people to deny their selfish desires, it only led people to become hypocritical. The resulting loss of social vitality and rise of a hypocritical social ethos surely weakened the Southern Song's ability to resist the Mongol invasion and led to its downfall. The reflections of Zhou Mi 周密 (1232–1308), a Song loyalist, are illuminating.

> The Learning of the Way (*daoxue* 道學)[1] arose during the Yuanyou period 元佑 (1086–1094) and became prevalent in the Chunxi period 淳熙 (1174–1189). [It praised moral cultivation while debasing all other professions.] … It regarded tax collectors as wealth accumulators, frontier defenders and expanders as uncouth people, readers and writers as ill-spent youths, responsible officials as vulgar clerks … Its scholars were bigoted and befuddled in their discussions, pretending to be morally clean and indifferent to wealth and fame by sitting on a wrecked palanquin. Prime Minister Jia Sidao 賈似道 (1213–1275) took advantage of these scholars' pedantry and incapability, and assigned them to important posts. As a result, the myriad imperial affairs were not carried out, the Song dynasty collapsed, and these pedants lost their lives. (Zhou 2015: 40)

The very same accusation against the Cheng-Zhu School was leveled once again 400 years later. This time, it was sounded by Li Zhi and echoed by Huang Zongxi, who pointed out the disastrous effects of the Cheng-Zhu teaching. Li Zhi claimed that these Neo-Confucian scholars knew only how to bow and salute to one another. In peaceful times, they would sit all day in an upright position like clay images, thinking they would be

---

[1] *Daoxue* or the Learning of the Way is the original name of the Cheng-Zhu School and Neo-Confucianism.

sages and worthies once they had surpassed all trains of thought. But, when a crisis loomed, they would look at each other, pale and speechless, trying to pass the blame to one another (Li 1975: 156). Li Zhi's observation was soon verified by the collapse of the Ming. After the fall, Huang Zhongxi, now despondent, indignantly interrogated the character of the Neo-Confucian scholars. He stressed that the original Confucian scholarship had been meant to guide proper governance and put the empire into order, not just to study the words and dialogues of Cheng Yi and Zhu Xi. Scholars of the Cheng-Zhu tradition regarded tax collectors as wealth accumulators and defenders and expanders of the frontier as uncouth people, while bragging that they themselves had "set the highest standards for the people, established the mind of Heaven and Earth, and put the world in order forever." However, whenever real crises loomed and the ministers had to deal with complicated state affairs, they just stared into the darkness, mouths agape, as if lost in dense fog (Huang 2012: 20:450).

The moral cultivation instructed in the Cheng-Zhu School acquired its reputation because of its claim to turn its practitioners into sages. However, what it produced was far removed from effective sages of the caliber of the Duke of Zhou or Confucius who had the true grit to face difficult political and social affairs. Instead, it produced scholars who were narrow, rigid, incapable, hypocritical, and irresponsible. As a result, the Cheng-Zhu styled of personal cultivation, not only encouraged the practitioner to abandon the ambition of an official career, but failed in its basic aim—to enhance social customs. In fact, ever since it became the imperial ideology, Neo-Confucianism began to plant the seeds of the moral and political crises that would plague the Ming dynasty. It is regrettable that the Ming scholars and officials did not take Zhou Mi and Li Zhi's criticisms seriously and came to realize the defects of the Cheng-Zhu School only after the Manchu overthrow.

6.2   Wang Fuzhi's Overall Attitude Toward Heretics

Wang Fuzhi regarded all philosophies that differed from Confucianism as heretical, but he mainly focused on Daoism, Buddhism, and Legalism. He accused these schools of "going against the principle of Heaven and Earth, betraying the early kings' decrees, obscuring the meaning of the *Six Classics*, misunderstanding the content of the mind and the nature, and destroying the principle of right and wrong" (Wang 1996: 10:279–280). By inquiring into these accusations, we find that Wang presented the following general criticisms of heretics.

First, Wang Fuzhi criticized heretics for their failure to understand Heaven, the Way, and the nature. He regarded Heaven as a concrete body, affirming that "Heaven is a body of accumulated *qi*" (Wang 1996: 6:1109), and that "Heaven is the principle and *qi* that sustain the myriad things" (Wang 1996: 1:244). He disagreed with the Buddhists who regarded emptiness as the primary state of the world, condemning them for neglecting the principle manifested by Heaven in plain sight while seeking Heaven in a remote place (Wang 1996: 2:383). He did not think that the Daoists truly understood Heaven, either, declaring, "It is absurd that Laozi, Zhuangzi, and their ilk regard as Nothingness that which they cannot perceive" (Wang 1996: 12:272).

Because Wang Fuzhi did not think that any of the heretical thinkers knew the true state of Heaven, he did not believe they could emulate Heave, either. He viewed Qian 乾 as the virtue of Heaven, representing vigor and resolve. A Confucian nobleperson would strive to emulate Heaven's vigor and resolve, and apply them in fulfilling human relationships and practicing moral cultivation; they certainly would not just strive to love all creatures impartially. So, Wang did not endorse the Buddhist adage to feed one's body to a tiger, remarking, "The Buddhists and Mohists 墨 propose universal affection and resolve to benefit other creatures without leisure or rest, thus they do not know how to emulate Qian" (Wang 1996: 1:697). Similarly, he viewed Kun坤, the virtue of Earth, as the representative of accommodation and passivity. The right way to emulate the tolerance of the Earth was to be accommodating and magnanimous, not to accept one's fate passively. Wang stated, "Zhuangzi and Liezi 列子 followed trends and situations passively, abandoned their efforts and were lacking in resolve; they did not know how to emulate Kun" (Wang 1996: 1:697). Because these heretics did not know how to emulate Heaven, Wang criticized them for being unable to grasp the manifest principle of Heaven or promote the welfare of the people, and viewed their destructive impact on human society as equal to that of a tyrant.

Wang Fuzhi did not think that the Mohists or Catholics could emulate Heaven, either. He considered that Heaven was a mass of transforming *qi*, which produced each living creature through the agency of its parents. That was why a child should respect and love its parents first, and only afterward extend its love to Heaven. If a child were to forsake its parents and directly love Heaven, it would grow up to be a barbarian who knew only Heaven but did not care for its parents. Wang criticized this Mohist teaching for leading people to abandon their fathers and just venerate the great root—Heaven (Wang 1996: 8:394). He also criticized Catholicism in his comment on the Jesuit Matteo Ricci, "The Western barbarian Matteo Ricci worshiped Heaven as his Heavenly Lord, and dared to approach God while abandoning his own parents without scruple. He was a barbarian plain and simple, although he adorned his belief with aplomb" (Wang 1996: 1:1015).

Wang Fuzhi also accused heretical scholars of misunderstanding of the Way and the nature. He argued:

I suspect those scholars who discuss the Way solely with reference to the natural world. They identify the Sage's Way with heavenly transformation, assume that Heaven's humaneness is the same as human beings', degrade human beings to the level of birds and beasts, and do not establish their heavenly endowment to benefit the people. My doubts grow concerning their teachings on the nature. They identify the nature of things with heavenly endowment, and hold that following the nature of things is the same as following the Way of things. Yet, they are blind to their own nature and go against Heaven. (Wang 1996: 13:677–678)

Wang Fuzhi had the several heretics in his mind in making this statement. Mozi 墨子, who had elevated the sage's Way to heavenly transformation, thus mistook Heaven's indiscriminate love as his impartial love. The Daoists did the same thing but proceeded to degrade human beings to the level of the birds and beast, thus ignoring the uniqueness of human nature. Zhuangzi thought that heavenly endowment became the nature of things, so following the natural process of things would accomplish their Way. But, in these ways, Wang charged, they had forgotten the distinction between human beings and Heaven and other kinds of creatures, and failed to see the unique place and role of human beings in the cosmos. In Wang's view, with his intelligence, man distinguished himself from Heaven who produced and loved the myriad things without discrimination. Man also differed from other creatures in nature. The duty of human beings lay in following human nature and improving human welfare, not blindly following the nature of things to become one with Heaven.

Second, Wang Fuzhi assumed that the heretical thinkers had discarded the moral function of mind and passively accepted fate:

The reason why the charge of heresy is leveled is that while the heretical thinkers still uphold their mind as the master in their actual responses to things, after they realize the depths of their mind, they strive to elevate their mind above gain and loss and right and wrong, leave the fluctuations of gain and loss and right and wrong to their lot, and avoid interacting with external things. Consequently, their minds become increasingly irresponsible and ignorant. (Wang 1996: 8:181)

As a Confucian, Wang observed that human beings lived in the real world and had no choice but to interact with things and other people, so the distinctions between good and evil, truth and falsity, gain and loss, were valid and inescapable. The right way would not be to maintain a detached mind, avoid human affairs, and neglect the complexities of life, but to interact with things actively yet prudently. Consequently, Wang insisted that Confucian scholars make their minds upright and their intentions sincere to judge the gains and losses under Heaven, and investigate things to extend knowledge, to distinguish between truth and falsity.

Wang Fuzhi held that since the heretical thinkers did not engage their minds to inquire into the principles of things, the matters they held to be true were most likely false. He argued that heretical thinkers might pretend discussing on the mind, but they definitely could not pretend discussing on the truth. To obtain genuine truth, a true scholar would have to persistently inquire, without doubts or hesitation. Although the principles of things may be easy to grasp once understood, the effort to understand them was often painstaking, and the rewards of anyone's inquiries could come very slowly. In contrast, heretical thinkers tended to desire quick results and were averse to persistent effort. That was why they were unable to catch hold of solid truth (Wang 1996: 8:202). On this point, Wang set his sights on Zhuangzi and the Chan masters who had recommended casting books and sutras aside to achieve sudden enlightenment. He also targeted Wang Yangming's followers who favored inborn knowledge of the good and discarded all book learning and social norms. Wang concluded that neither Buddhism nor Daoism could offer a comprehensive teaching; not only did they fail to inquire into things, they did not make efforts to fulfill human relations or conduct social affairs but rest content with "setting their mind at ease in a cozy and lazy realm, leaving a big section of social affairs unsettled" (Wang 1996: 6:795).

Third, Wang Fuzhi blamed the heretical thinkers for their betrayal of the decrees of the early kings and undermining of the social ethos. He compared the heretical teachings to the chirpings of birds, able to disturb the human mind and nature, and degrade human beings to the level of birds and beasts. Like Mencius, he criticized the Daoist Yang Zhu 楊朱 for his non-interference approach. "Yang Zhu thought, 'Each person cares for himself only. Although they live together with others, they actually forget each other and act in their own ways. Thus, Heaven, Earth and the myriad things will not be able to disturb the peace of their mind.' This means that Yang Zhu thought the world did not need a ruler and would be more peaceful without a ruler" (Wang 1996: 8:394). Mencius and Wang Fuzhi were both firm supporters of emperors and imperial rule, so they misunderstood the Daoist teaching of non-interference as the denial of rulers and then falsely condemned this teaching's supposed undermining of the social order. Besides Yang Zhu, Wang condemned the Mohists for abandoning their fathers, concluding that they had "led even some intelligent, capable people to the Way of birds and beasts" (Wang 1996: 8:394). Wang obviously exaggerated the negative effects of their teachings. In fact, Yang Zhu's teaching did not necessarily entail the elimination of the ruler or other superiors just as modern individualism has not wiped out social rank and differentiation. Mozi's impartial concern would not necessarily lead people to disrespect their fathers, either; for nobody could transcend the principle to extend love from close people to distant ones. In brief, Wang's criticisms showed his sensitivity toward teachings that appeared to threaten the basic human relationships prioritized by Confucianism.

Wang Fuzhi was even more indignant about Buddhism's destructive impact on human relationships. Wang criticized the Buddhists repeatedly for disregarding and abandoning human relationships and thus undermining inborn human virtues. He once asserted that the Buddhists confused truth with falsity and regarded existing things and human life as illusions. In the end, they sought to discard their bodies to achieve purity, took death as a joyful end, and saw the elimination of human relationships as purity (Wang 1996: 1:885). Wang elsewhere condemned the Buddhists for purging the desires and breaking off interactions with things. By denying their body and things, the Buddhists held an insensate emptiness and simply trod the path to death. In this pursuit, they freely donated their property, wives, and children without second thought, abandoning all of their human relationships and destroying the principle of things (Wang 1996: 2:239).

In his effort to refute Buddhism, Wang Fuzhi began by emphasizing that what human perception could not discern was not necessarily illusory.

Human perception and experience were limited, just as a dog from the tropics could not recognize snow and would bark at it. Therefore, it was not right for the Buddhists to draw the conclusion that the Great Void (Heaven) was empty (Wang 1996: 12:374). Second, he argued that as a living creature, every person depended on material things to live. Without such things, they could not live as a human being. Wang went on to list the sort of material stuffs on which human survival depended, such as space, soil, wood, fire, water, and grains, and asserted that these necessities could not be deemed illusory (Wang 1996: 1:887). He concluded that the Buddhists, as human beings themselves, also depended on such material things for survival, which contradicted their teaching of purging both the desires and things. "Sleeping or eating, they must use things; moving or speaking, they must refer to things. Unable to break off from them but stubbornly trying to do that, they put themselves in dire straits when either the things move back and forth or they do not deal with things properly" (Wang 1996: 2:239).

As a remedy, on the one hand, Wang Fuzhi asserted that the human body manifested heavenly principle. "The human body is composed of qi, while the nature is principle. Qi is indeed the qi that bears its principle; therefore, the human body manifests the nature that Heaven endows it with" (Wang 1996: 6:1132). Now, since the human body is one with the nature, it would be improper to indiscriminately condemn the five organs and the human desires as evil. In fact, if a person were to prudently satisfy their desires, they would cause no evil. Concerning this point, Wang also was indignant about Laozi's teaching that "The five colors cause one's eyes to go blind; the five tones cause one's ears to go deaf; the five flavors cause one's palate to go numb" (Laozi 12). He refuted Laozi's teaching with the recommendation that Laozi simply excise his eyes, ears, and tongue to avoid those troubles. He concluded, "Laozi regarded the body as a big trouble; the Buddhists regard people's love of their parents as craving and foolishness. Their evil is thus far worse than that of the Xia tyrant King Jie 桀 and Bandit Zhi" (Wang 1996: 2:407).

Wang Fuzhi's counterproposal was that people just acquire things and satisfy their desires in due measure. While the Buddhists held that eating delicious foods was like feeding a hungry ulcer, and enjoying pretty women was like cooking sand for one's meal. Wang responded that the Buddhists hadn't realized that fine foods and pretty women were natural bodies from Heaven (nature), which bore principles of their own. How would they harm the human mind if they were appreciated and used properly (Wang

1996: 6:1086)! Wang's general point was that people accept and respond to things, including colors, tones, and flavors, according to their nature.

Moreover, a person should realize their own limits when receiving things. They should not be greedy or accept things beyond their capacity. That is, they should have the wisdom of the mole that drank water at the riverside: it would drink no more than a bellyful. They also should acquire things as needed for their purpose and utility but not accumulate things without limit (Wang 1996: 2:409). In short, Wang advocated interacting with things in accordance with one's nature and the Way of things, to hit due measure thereby and avoid excess or insufficiency. In this way, even though one's eyes gazed at a sheer black and yellow dress, one's ears listened to throbbing drums and bells, one's mouth savored succulent, sweet food, one would still always hit the due measure and cause no trouble.

6.3   WANG FUZHI'S CRITICISM OF BUDDHISM

Wang Fuzhi set out to evaluate Buddhism on the basis of Confucian values. He censured the Buddhists for not fulfilling Confucian righteousness and responsibility, and criticized their quest for Nirvana at the cost of life and their resulting failure to realize the meaning and duty of human life. He charged that the Buddhists did not accept the reality of Heaven, spirit, and human nature as truly existent (*shi you* 實有), but regarded them as insubstantial and empty. Based on his *qi*-monism, Wang held that life and death as the respective gathering and dispersing of the flux of *qi*, which in his view amounted to a rebuttal of the Buddhist doctrine of karmic retribution and reincarnation. Moreover, he noted the paradox between the Buddhist teaching of undifferentiated love and their doctrine that all things were empty and illusory, which in his view revealed the inherent self-centeredness of many Buddhist practices.

Wang Fuzhi blamed the widespread dissemination of Buddhism for the decline and ruin of the Ming dynasty. In the Preface to *Zhangzi Zhengmeng Zhu* (*An Annotation on Master Zhang's Correcting the Ignorant* 張子正蒙注), Wang denounced Wang Yangming's teachings as heretical, that is, as promoting Buddhist thought and practices in the guise of Confucianism (Wang 1996: 12:10). He charged that "Recently, Wang Yangming's teaching of the inborn knowledge of the good has been like this: it includes Buddhist ideas as its themes. It recommends severing the path of language and avoiding the path of intellectual inquiry to transcend one's cognitive faculties and their objects, and establish no ideas or knowledge" (Wang

1996: 12:370). Consequently, Wang accepted the duty of purging Confucianism of Buddhist elements by preparing a reinterpretation of the Confucian classics, proclaiming "The Six Confucian classics require me to initiate something new" (Wang 1996: 15:717).

First, Wang Fuzhi criticized the Buddhist concept of emptiness and its destructive impact on social ethos. For example, the Buddhist conception that all things were essentially empty, permitted evildoers to regard their crimes as nothing and set their minds at ease. Consequently, "a person can achieve Buddhahood whether in a brothel or a bar. Though a person's evil may fill a room, they can purify it with one thought and feel no shame or remorse" (Wang 1996: 10:639). This "one thought" meant viewing one's crimes as empty and illusory, thus wiping out one's sense of remorse or guilt.

Viewing the essence of all things as empty, the Buddhists regarded the nature of things as universally empty, as well. However, surprisingly, the Buddhists based their teaching of universal love on the empty nature. According to Wang's analysis, the Buddhists believed that the nature had originated from Heaven and was shared equally among human beings and other creatures. Regarding every person as essentially same as everyone else, a Buddhist would love their nephew no more dearly than they would love their neighbor's son. Regarding every person as the same as every other creature, the Buddhists considered that the myriad things and human beings shared the same natural endowment (*ming* 命). As a result, since that they drew no basic distinction between human beings and other creatures, from the perspective of the great origin (*daben* 大本) (Heaven), how could they love their next-of-kin more than other people or creatures (Wang 1996: 6:974)? Consequently, "The Buddhist could jump off a cliff to feed the hungry tiger with their body because they had been led astray by the teaching of universal love" (Wang 1996: 6:980).

In his effort to criticize and rectify the Buddhist conception of the nature as empty, Wang Fuzhi appealed to the Neo-Confucian adage, "The root is one but its branches are many (*yi ben wan shu* 一本萬殊)." He clarified, "From the perspective of Heaven, all things share the same origin; but, from the perspective of endowment (*ming* 命), they differ from each other in nature" (Wang 1996: 6:1118). Although their endowment came from the same Heaven, it was not the same as Heaven. It was a concretization of the principle of Heaven in their specific *qi*, which was formed as the nature of a specific kind of thing. The nature was the endowment that a thing consolidated within itself, the principle that made it what it was

(Wang 1996: 6:1117). Therefore, while it could be said that all things shared the same root, it cannot be said that all things shared the same nature. It was therefore appropriate to love and treat other human beings and other creatures with different degrees of affection.

Second, as to the Buddhist teaching of emptiness, Wang Fuzhi criticized its justification of interdependent causation (*yuanqi* 緣起). In his view, the Buddhist doctrine of interdependent causation entailed the view that all things were like the foam and ice that form on the surface of water, formed by the interdependent causation of various factors equally. He went on to attack the notion of the equality of the various factors in the formation of things. He appealed to the Daoist conception of self-so-ing (*ziran* 自然), saying, "self-so-ing means a thing has the potential to be so of itself (*you suo zi er ran zhi wei ye* 有所自而然之謂也) ... When the peach tree and the plum tree are in bloom, they blossom spontaneously. This happens because the peach tree and the plum tree bear the potential to blossom within. Given this potential, they will blossom without failure, without depending on anything else" (Wang 1996: 6:1019). Wang meant that such self-so-ing referred to examples like seeds in which the plant and blossom were determined within and were not decided by external factors. A certain kind of seed would sprout into a certain species of plant. If a peach tree were to propagate, it would produce peach blossoms regardless of external factors. Wang contrasted this argument with his account of how foam and ice were formed. In the case of foam and ice, they were formed because the waters had been agitated by external forces, such as wind, temperature, and snow. The formation of foam and ice could not be considered as examples of self-so-ing, and were not relevant to explaining the birth of human beings or other species (Wang 1996: 12:415). Wang further suggested that the rise of human beings was owing to the marvelous function of *qi*, that is, the natural transformations of yin and yang. The process was "inherently and naturally composed of yin and yang, and not dependent on interdependent causation" (Wang 1996: 2:265). Wang had found the Achilles' heel of the Buddhist doctrine of interdependent causation by indicating the natural inborn potential of all things; however, his further denial that the formation of foam and ice was a natural process also narrowed the scope of his teaching of self-so-ing.

Wang Fuzhi criticized Buddhist interdependent causation in terms of epistemology, as well. In providing an explanation of the emergence of things from emptiness, "the Buddhists assumed that all things arose from nowhere but depended on the arising and ceasing of the human mind. So they established the twelve links of interdependent causation and regarded nescience as the root of life and death" (Wang 1996: 12:155). Having proposed that "the variety of things depends upon the arising and ceasing of the mind," the Buddhists confused human ability (*neng* 能) with external objects (*suo* 所), and made the claim that all phenomena were nothing but consciousness, that they were mind-dependent. Regarding this doctrine, Wang simply drew the distinction between seeing a mountain and the mountain itself to disclose the Buddhists' absurd confusion of the human ability to perceive (*neng* 能) with the thing perceived (*suo* 所). He argued, "There are mountains in Yue 越; therefore, it cannot be said that there were no mountains there before I arrived there and saw them. Moreover, it cannot be said that my arriving and seeing the mountains is the mountains themselves" (Wang 1996: 2:378).

Third, Wang Fuzhi realized the importance of the notions of life, death, and karmic retribution in the dissemination of Buddhism in China. He noted that the tales of the revenge exacted by spirits in the *Zuo Commentary on the Spring and Autumn Annals* had paved the way for the Chinese people's acceptance of Buddhist karmic retribution, for they both frightened people to deter them from doing evil.[2] He found that "when people could not achieve justice but could only pray for supernatural intervention, they behaved like the poor crying out to Heaven. Consequently, when the Buddhists appealed to the doctrine of karmic retribution in desperate situations, the agitated common people took comfort in hearing it" (Wang 1996: 5:235–236). He inferred that the Buddhists had agitated the people with their teaching of karmic retribution in life and death, fortune, and misfortune. Consequently, he reasoned that what was needed to stop people from believing in Buddhism was a more reasonable and compelling explanation of life and death. In his words, "If a person did not know the process and causes of life and death, they would not consider it their duty or nature to do good and repel evil. On the personal level, they would abandon human relationships and pursue their selfish desires. On a general level, they would regard worldly things as fleeting and all names and honors as so much foam" (Wang 1996: 12:11). Wang admired Zhang Zai's

---

[2] For example, after King Xuan of the Zhou executed Minister Du Bo 杜伯, it was said that he was shot with an arrow by Du Bo's spirit. After the prince of State Jin Shen Sheng 申生 was wronged and killed, he could sue his criminal brothers in heavenly court, and get them punished with death by Heaven (Wang 1996: 5:553).

explanation of the process of life and death in terms of the waxing and waning of *qi* and followed his line of thinking to resist Buddhism.

Wang Fuzhi reasoned that the life and death of all things was just a matter of the gathering and scattering of *qi*. This was natural process determined by principle and situation, impervious to human intervention (Wang 1996: 12:20). He indicated that the life and death of things did not follow a fixed route because the bending and stretching of *qi* was not definite and the gathering and scattering of *qi* did not follow a uniform process (Wang 1996: 12:55). Unlike the Buddhist cycle of life and death, Wang denied the existence of an afterlife and accepted the fact of the dissolution of body and soul. He admitted that a person's dispersed *qi* would regroup sometime later to form a new person or other creature, but the new lifeform would not be a new incarnation of the deceased person. That is, it would not be the same person (or soul) who had died here that would be reborn there. He hypothesized that, after death, a dying person's *qi* could be dispersed to several newborns, and that the *qi* of several dying people might gather in one newborn. He deemed that such dispersions and gatherings of *qi* were dependent on situation and principle, and unpredictable. On these grounds, Wang concluded that Buddhist doctrines of incarnation and retribution were not operative in the world (Wang 1996: 1:1045).

Wang Fuzhi also denied the existence of the sorts of spirits (*shen* 神) and ghosts (*gui* 鬼) that common people believed in, and explained that the visages of ghosts and spirits that people saw were just the retreating and stretching motions of *qi*. If people understood the transformation between human being and spirit as a natural process, they would not be partial toward either life or death, or follow in the footsteps of the gullible who prayed for help from mysterious supernatural forces, let alone listen to Buddhist words on karmic retribution (Wang 1996: 5:235).

Wang Fuzhi insisted that the meaning of human life came from bringing benefits to humanity and harmonious *qi* to the cosmos. He proposed that "a person should be able to transform their own *qi* and assist Heaven (*neng yi yi xiang tian* 能移以相天)." That is to say, a person should be able to improve their moral character and harmonious *qi* by rectifying their mind and practicing ritual propriety. Afterward, when they died, "their pure, harmonious *qi* would match the Great Void perfectly, make the sun, moon and stars above shine more brightly, and make the creatures below thrive, as their well-cultivated body and spirit disintegrated and was dispersed" (Wang 1996: 13:293). Wang thus recommended that people

focus on cultivating proper conduct during their lifetime. "A truly compassionate person is one who is concerned to comply with the principle of
life, without concern about their own life or death … They do not take
their own death as important or prepare for it in advance. Their attitude
differs greatly from that of the Buddhists who are preoccupied with death"
(Wang 1996: 6:828). In other words, Wang advocated that if a person had
fulfilled their duty in society and did no harm to the world, they would
realize the meaning of life and die a worthy death, as well.

However, Wang Fuzhi was overconfident about the attractiveness of his
theory of life and death. He hadn't grasped that the people's basic trepida-
tion about death was not just that their afterlife might resolve into the
dispersal of *qi*, but how to conquer their existential fear and foreboding in
the face of imminent suffering and death. It was the sort of spiritual con-
solation offered by Buddhism that people longed for, not the sort of rational explanation of life and death proffered by Wang. Regrettably, Wang
could not provide any balm for their spiritual needs. Nevertheless, Wang's
notion that a person could achieve a sort of eternal life by moral cultivation and service to society offered a new way for future generations to
think about life and death.

Some scholars have argued that Wang Fuzhi softened his criticisms of
Buddhism and even endeavored to study and transform Buddhism in his
later years (Xu 1991). Their principal evidence was Wang Fuzhi's commentary on a sutra, *Veins and Arteries of Dharmalaksana* (*Xiang Zong
Luo Suo* 相宗絡索), and *Praise of the Precepts on the Eight Cognitions by
Master of the Tripitaka* (*Sanzang Fashi Bashi Guiju Lunzan* 三藏法師八識
規矩論贊), both of which he composed in later life. However, it would be
a stretch to think that Wang wanted to transform Buddhism, even though
he did try to borrow some of its treasures. While he was hostile toward the
Chan doctrine of sudden awakening, Wang was likely in sympathy with
the gradualist teaching of *Dharmalaksana* cultivation; for he advocated a
gradual to Confucian cultivation and criticized the suggestion of sudden
awakening in Zhu Xi's paragraph on "investigating things to attain knowledge" in the *Daxue* for its resemblance to the Chan Buddhist doctrine
(Wang 1996: 6:811–812).[3] But, we should keep in mind that Wang con-

---

[3] In *Tropically Arranged Conversations of Master Zhu* (*Zhuzi Yulei* 朱子語類) Volume 44,
Zhu Xi said, "When (Confucius) achieved the marvelous realm of penetrating heavenly principle, he suddenly achieved it" (Li 1994: 1138). Wang Fuzhi understood "sudden achievement" as similar to sudden awakening in the Chan Buddhism.

tinued to deny the Buddhist notions of emptiness, karmic retribution, and undifferentiated love that also appear in the *Dharmalaksana*. Some scholars have proposed that while Wang was critical of scholastic Buddhism (*shi da fu fojiao* 士大夫佛教), he respected monastic Buddhism (*seng ren fojiao* 僧人佛教). The former was disseminated among scholars and bureaucrats while the latter practiced by serious Buddhist monks (Liu and Tian 2009), which would help explain why Wang wrote a commentary on the *Dharmalaksana*. This view was probably also based on the monks' criticisms of the wild Chan that Li Zhi 李贄 (1527–1602) and other Ming scholars had supported; however, it lacked textual support from Wang's overall body of writings in which he criticized Buddhism as a whole. In summary, Wang's commentary on *Dharmalaksana* reflected his sympathy with its gradualism and his dialogue and friendship with some Buddhist monks,[4] but it cannot support the conclusion that he admired or wished to transform Buddhism.

6.4 Wang Fuzhi's Criticism of Daoism

In general, Wang Fuzhi attacked Daoism on three levels, that is, ontology, methodology, and social influence. With respect to ontology, Wang made the patently false accusation that Laozi and Zhuangzi regarded the imperceptible as nothingness. He also made the false assumption that Laozi and Zhuangzi had severed Dao (道) from yin and yang and did not realize that Dao was fundamentally one with yin and yang. He said:

> Some people think that yin and yang divide evenly, and thus do not dominate each other. They believe that yin stays in the yin position and yang stays in the yang position while Dao stands between them. Thus, they deny that yin or yang is Dao, but affirm that Dao wanders the empty space between them. This sort of conception gave rise to Laozi's teaching. He observed the hole of yin and the marvelous function of yang, severed yin and yang, and thought that Dao stayed in the space between them. (Wang 1996: 1:1003)

Wang Fuzhi probably proposed this argument based on Chap. 1 of the *Laozi*, replacing being (*you* 有) and nonbeing (*wu* 無) with yin and yang.

---

[4] Wang Fuzhi cooperated with Buddhist monks all his life, and interacted with more than a dozen monks, debating and exchanging views with them (Wu and Xu 1992: 25). He used Buddhist temples as the place to plan his attack of the Manchus in 1648. He hid his family in Buddhist temples during the Wu Sangui 吳三桂 rebellion in 1673.

There, Laozi says, "Always conscious of nonbeing, you can observe the marvel of Dao [to produce things]. Always conscious of being, you can observe the manifestations of Dao [i.e., the proliferation of things]. These two outcomes emerge from the same origin, but have different names. However, they are both called mysteries" (Laozi 1). Laozi meant that being and nonbeing were different manifestations of Dao, and thus offered different angles for grasping Dao. To Laozi, being, nonbeing, and Dao were one and inseparable. But, Wang understood the two quoted sentences in terms of observing the hole of yin and the marvels of yang and insisted that Laozi not only separated Dao from yin and yang but also separated yin from yang.

With this faulty understanding of Laozi's conception of Dao, Wang Fuzhi criticized Laozi's view that "There was something undifferentiated and yet complete, which existed prior to Heaven and Earth" (Laozi 25). He thought that Laozi had separated Dao from Heaven and Earth just as he had severed it from yin and yang. He contended that "Dao is the function of the fine parts of Heaven and Earth, and operates together with them without precedence. Had Dao existed prior to Heaven and Earth, there would be a time that Dao existed but Heaven and Earth did not. In that case, where would Dao reside? Who would call it Dao?" (Wang 1996: 1:823). Regrettably, Wang had failed to realize that "the undifferentiated and complete thing" referred to the flux mass of *qi*, which ceaselessly transformed Heaven, Earth, and the myriad things. This fluctuating mass of *qi* subsumed substance and function, and surpassed the functions of Heaven and Earth. When Wang Fuzhi interrogated Laozi's conception of Dao in this way, he only revealed that he did not understand Dao in the context of the *Laozi*.

Because Wang Fuzhi assumed that Laozi's Dao existed in the space between yin and yang, he inferred that Laozi's Dao existed beyond Heaven, Earth, and human beings. Thus, he denied the proposition that "Man models himself after Earth; Earth models itself after Heaven; Heaven models itself after Dao" (Laozi 25). He questioned how Dao could be modeled, since, according to the *Laozi*, Dao was an illusory object, which existed beyond the ken of human beings. He accepted that Dao ran through human beings at every moment and human beings could not block it; thus, he held that since human beings possessed Dao from birth, there was no need for them to investigate things to discern Dao and consciously emulate it (Wang 1996: 6:736). Again, he criticized the very idea of "modeling Dao" in the *Laozi*'s sense, since that would be to model "an illusory object beyond human beings."

Wang Fuzhi's problem lay in his limited grasp of Laozi's Dao. Dao in the *Laozi* has two meanings. First, Dao refers to the undifferentiated mass of *qi*, or the fluctuating mass of *qi* as described by Zhuangzi. All things rise and fall in step with the transformation of this mass of *qi*, and each thing is a phase or a stage of the transformation of this *qi*. Second, Dao also refers to the principle of the fluctuating mass of *qi*, which guides the alterations of yin and yang. That is, this principle guides the transformation of *qi* to form the myriad things, in each of which it is embodied as their nature. A thing will unite with Dao spontaneously if it follows its own nature. As to human beings, "Modeling after Dao" would mean that a person abandons their artificial calculations and deliberations, and begins to follow their original nature. Therefore, Wang Fuzhi had unconsciously appealed to Laozi's own ideas in criticizing a strawman of Laozi based on his faulty interpretation.

Besides his criticisms of Laozi's Dao, Wang Fuzhi criticized the notion of the One (*yi* 一) in the *Laozi*. As to the propositions that "The One gives rise to two, the two give rise to three, and the three give rise to all things" (Laozi 42), Wang assumed the One was a concrete object whose division would produce the myriad things and overflow the space between Heaven and Earth (Wang 1996: 2:343). He insisted that Laozi's view was that the One sacrificed itself to produce the two, and the two sacrificed themselves to produce the three, which would parallel the situation that "The loss of Dao leads to the emergence of virtue (*de* 德); the loss of virtue leads to the emergence of righteousness and humaneness" (Wang 1996: 6:559). He concluded, "Once virtue emerges, it is the antithesis of Dao; once humaneness and righteousness arise, they remain separate from Dao and cannot unite with it. Preserving the One precludes the emergence of the two. Consequently, [in Laozi's view], there must be no humaneness or righteousness, so the One can be preserved from loss" (Wang 1996: 6:559).

To evaluate Wang Fuzhi's comments, it is necessary to understand the meaning of "Dao gives rise to the One, while the One gives rise to the two" in the *Laozi*. Here, we follow Zhuangzi's and Wang Bi's 王弼 (226–249) explanation. In *Making All Things Equal* (*Qi Wu Lun* 齊物論), Zhuangzi understood "giving rise to (*sheng* 生)" in terms of nomination. The two arose when the Dao (the One) was called "one" because the Dao and its name formed the two. The three arose when the Dao, its name, and the unity of them were counted together (Guo 1961: 79). Wang Bi continued Zhuangzi's idea. He regarded the Dao or the One as the Unnamable (*wu* 無), and said, "Now that the Unnamable is called the One, there will arise the word 'one'. The One and the word 'one' form the two. With the One and the two, there comes forth the three" (Lou 1980: 117). Hence, Dao and the One were identical and substantial. The return to the One meant that all things proceeded back and forth along with the transformation of *qi*. This was not illusory arising. Hence, Wang misunderstood the term "*sheng* 生" in the *Laozi*, and thus his criticism of Laozi was based on a misunderstanding.

Moreover, because Dao referred to the Way according to which all things naturally grew and died and was consolidated as the nature of each thing; therefore, by following Dao or one's own nature, one would realize virtue and unite with Dao spontaneously. When people recommended promoting virtue, it meant that they had departed from Dao, just as when one values good health, one may have already lost it. Because humaneness and righteousness were achieved by human deliberation and effort, Laozi saw them as departures from Dao. However, Wang regarded Dao as humaneness and righteousness, which required human effort, so he accused Laozi of dividing Dao from humaneness and righteousness.

Wang Fuzhi's own understanding of Dao led him to disapprove of Laozi's and Zhuangzi's approaches to Dao. As to Dao in the sense of the wholeness of the cosmos, it was unnamable and indescribable; for any description would refer to a concrete object and thus fail in its purpose. As to Dao in the sense of the nature of each thing, it was easy to follow but hard to express in words. For this reason, Laozi said, "If Dao could be described in words, it would not be the universal Dao" (Laozi 1). Zhuangzi said, "Those who know (the Way) do not speak; those who speak do not know (the Way)" (Watson 1968: 152). However, from his Confucian standpoint, Wang insisted that Dao as humaneness must be expressed in words for the purpose of education, so he accused Laozi and Zhuangzi of conceiving Dao as existing beyond the common people's comprehension and condemned them for being obstinate and inflexible (Wang 1996: 6:809).

As to methodology, Wang Fuzhi accused that Laozi and Zhuangzi had resorted to trickery, such as their tactics of feigning weakness and keeping to the rear in order to be strong and occupy the front, as well as their acting carefree so as not to arouse the envy of others. He also criticized them for presenting their positions and possessions as undesirable (*lou* 陋), to avoid the competition of others. "Before they are in power, they show their humbleness and undesirability to avoid the requests of others. When they are in power, they stay humble to take advantage of others before others see through them" (Wang 1996: 5:553). He cited two examples of this in the *Zhuangzi*. "When Laozi and Zhuangzi said their minds were unperturbed (*yutai* 宇泰), they actually could not be genuinely unperturbed, but only pretended to be at ease and unfathomable to others. When they said they had wiped out the envy of others (*ling ren zhi yi ye xiao* 令人之意也消), they actually could not wipe it out, but depended on the fact that others did not know them and thus did not feel envy" (Wang 1996: 5:552). Wang here committed the error of taking these two examples out of the context. When Zhuangzi mentioned the unperturbed state of one's mind, he was talking about the tranquility one achieved by transcending life and death, gain and loss. It had nothing to do with showing others one's unfathomable depth by pretending to be carefree. When Zhuangzi wrote "*ling ren zhi yi ye xiao*," it meant "making others feel not being coerced," and had nothing to do with eliminating the envy of others. While Wang had grasped Laozi's and Zhuangzi's devotion to the life attitude of humbleness, he misconstrued it as a ruse to deceive others and pursue profit, which ran counter to the magnanimity and respect for the individuality of others that the *Zhuangzi* supported and promoted.

For further examples, **first**, Wang Fuzhi regarded Laozi as sly and crafty in proposing "To be last in order to be first, to forget oneself in order to be preserved" (Laozi 41). Wang accused Laozi of manipulating the world by "shrinking from taking precedence over others." He thought this was a tactic for securing minor selfish interests, which was just the opposite of Laozi's intended meaning. On this false presumption, Wang condemned Laozi as petty minded (Wang 1996: 3:450). For this, we must question whether Wang understood Laozi's sentence or whether he was grasping at straws. In the *Laozi*, the sentence was intended to question people's petty concerns about loss and death and recommend that they be single-minded. If people discarded their fears of loss and death and became single-minded, they could harness their full potential and have more opportunities to gain and survive. This showed Laozi's magnanimity and unselfishness by forgetting self, too, just as Confucius instructed "to establish oneself, one establishes others first" (Analects 6.30). Hence, it was absurd for Wang to accuse Laozi of being concerned about selfish interest while praising Confucius as humane.

Chapter 43 of the *Laozi* reads, "The softest thing in the world dashes against and overcomes the hardest." This describes the corrosive power of soft things on hard things, of softness over hardness. Based on observations of dripping water penetrating stone, the *Laozi* suggests that people persevere in their efforts. However, given his prejudice against Laozi, Wang criticized that this chapter just revealed Laozi's craftiness and cruelty. Referring to the *Book of Changes*, Wang claimed that yang stood for hardness and life while yin stood for softness and killing, and advocated promoting yang and hardness while restraining yin and softness. Laozi had taught the opposite. Hence, "while Laozi had temporarily strengthened his life by promoting yin and softness, he did not realize that he was on the verge of killing others" (Wang 1996: 1:917). In fact, Wang's disagreement with Laozi stemmed from their different views of the role of yin and softness. Wang followed the *Book of Changes* in associating yang with life and yin with killing, while Laozi valued yin and softness as signs of life while taking hardness as a sign of death. They both could muster empirical support for their respective interpretations of natural phenomena; by the same token, neither one could disprove the other.

Second, Wang Fuzhi disapproved of Laozi's fondness of water. In Laozi's view, water was perfect in manifesting weakness, humbleness, and altruism; he regarded the highest excellence to resemble the perfection of water, which was close to Dao (Laozi: 8). Laozi also valued water's corrosive power, writing, "There is nothing softer and weaker than water. And yet, there is nothing better than water for attacking hard, strong things" (Laozi: 78). Laozi drew these conclusions because water was the basic element that sustained all things but requested nothing for itself, nor did it contend for fame or position. Wang concluded, however, that "Nobody in the world is more dangerous and craftier than water" (Wang 1996: 1:898), based solely on his reading of the Kan 坎 trigram from the *Book of Changes*. He offered that the Kan trigram stood for water, with two yin strokes on its two surfaces and one yang stroke at its core. As yang represented the hard and yin the soft, the trigram depicted water as having a soft and flexible appearance but a hard core. With a soft and flexible appearance, water attracted and then drowned hapless people and animals. "Yin is vacuous and good at compliance; yang is concrete and unbending. With its concrete core and vacuous appearance, water displays softness and pliancy to other things and feigns retreat while keeping firm and tough within. Therefore, water cannot avoid being called tricky and penetrating in the world" (Wang 1996: 1:897).

Wang Fuzhi's premise was just an assumption based on the Kan trigram with yang (hard) at the core and yin (soft) on the two surfaces, and made his arguments on this basis. Because his premise was hypothetical, Wang's conclusions were merely hypothetical, as well. Moreover, when Wang described water as "displaying softness and pliancy to other things, pretending to retreat but keeping firm and tough," Wang did not explain how water could hold firm and tough. In this way, Wang merely attached some negative characteristics to water, to justify his attack on Laozi.

Third, Wang Fuzhi criticized Laozi for predicting the incipient signs of Heaven (*tian zhi ji* 天之幾) to defeat others. He commented:

> An unscrupulous petty person, such as Laozi, who uses his self-assuming knowledge to surmise the incipient signs of Heaven and Earth, ghosts, and spirits, will depend on the likes and aversions of human beings, contract deliberately so as to expand, and overcome the firmest with the softest. He will feign retreat as things approach, then suddenly rise up to destroy them when they reach the point of no return, beyond the limits of common sense. Laozi declares such stratagems are the marvelous way, commencing with humbleness but always culminating in cruelty. (Wang 1996: 1:169)

In this paragraph, Wang Fuzhi summarized several of Laozi's strategies and attacked them altogether. These strategies included surmising the incipient signs of Heaven, contracting so as to expand, overcoming the hardest with the softest, showing humbleness and weakness to mislead and destroy the enemy, and finally grasping the time or opportunity to strike a deadly blow. Wang criticized all such strategies as tricks and cruelties from the Confucian standpoint of humaneness.

Wang Fuzhi, however, contradicted himself when he praised some historical heroes for achieving great feats by surmising the insipient signs of Heaven. He stated that Han Emperor Wen 漢文帝 knew the insipient signs of Heaven and achieved peaceful and prosperous rule (Wang 1996: 13:15). In his comments on Tang Emperor Gao 唐高祖, he defined *ji* 幾 as timeliness (*shi* 時), saying, "The Tang emperor must have grasped the proper timeliness (*ji* 幾) when he united the empire and established a reign that would last for three hundred years. Grasping the timeliness of Heaven, he did not go against the trend; responding to the people in timely fashion, he pacified their will. Timeliness is what the sages cannot ignore" (Wang 1996: 10:733).

Wang Fuzhi's contradiction showed that Laozi's grasp of the insipient signs of Heaven could be used to either pursue self-interest or put the world in order. It was just a tool or a means and could be enlisted to serve good and evil ends alike. Wang mistook the tool for the criminal who used it to kill; thus, his criticism of Laozi was no different from another case he described, when a clod of dirt struck the ground near an angry dog, the dog attacked the clod, not knowing it should attack the person who had thrown the clod.

As to the negative influence of Daoism, Wang Fuzhi first accused Daoism of opening the door to the introduction and spread of Buddhism. He held that because from the Jin dynasty (265–412), such Buddhist scholars as Zhi Dun 支遁, Xu Xun 許詢, Dao Sheng 道生, Seng Zhao 僧肇, and others had adorned and introduced Buddhism with Laozi's and Zhuangzi's ideas; Laozi's and Zhuangzi's ideas became merged with Buddhism for a long time in China. He also pointed out that Heir Apparent Zhaoming 昭明太子 had interpreted Buddhist teachings according to the Daoism of Wang Bi and He Yan 何晏, particularly in his understanding of the Buddhist theory of two truths. Wang concluded that only after the empty, mysterious teachings of Daoism had been purged would Buddhism no longer prevail in China (Wang 1996: 10:651).

Second, Wang Fuzhi criticized Daoism for corrupting social customs and leading scholars and officials to be irresponsible. In his view, the detached mental state cultivated in Daoism caused people to be indifferent to both their own affairs and those of the state, including such catastrophes as regicide and fall of a dynasty. Specifically, he read Zhuangzi's "keeping to the mean (*yuan du* 緣督)" as not aiming for either good or evil, and understood Laozi's "preserving the female (*shouci* 守雌)" as shirking from one's responsibilities. In his view, both of these tenets were evil and contrary to humaneness (Wang 1996: 10:614). When seeking the origin of the degenerate social ethos of the late Ming, he traced it to Laozi, Zhuangzi, and their like:

> Truly inhumane are those who do not strive for good or evil but maintain indifference to themselves and the world and live at ease, just as water flows freely. These people are like corpses, unaffected by joy and sorrow. These arts were advocated by Laozi, Zhuangzi, and Yang Zhu 楊朱, and promoted unrestrainedly by Wang Yan 王衍 (256–311), Xie Kun 謝鯤 (280–323), and their like since the Cao Wei 曹魏 and the Jin dynasties. The Daoist arts have destroyed many people's sense of loyalty and filial piety and led them to abandon the distinction between good and evil. (Wang 1996: 10:613–614)

Wang Fuzhi was principally concerned about humaneness and social order. He requested that everyone accept their duties to serve the ruler and maintain peace in the empire. However, Wang should have realized that in chaotic times, an individual can do nothing about a worsening political situation. At times when people could do nothing to change the situation, their best option would be to avoid the dangers to themselves and their families by following the teachings of the *Laozi* and the *Zhuangzi*. This was why people during the Cao Wei and Jin dynasties were indifferent to the downfall of the royal families. Wang should have reflected on the evils of the imperial rule instead of placing blame on the spread of Daoism.

Third, Wang Fuzhi blamed Laozi's thought for undermining the Confucian Way from the perspective of trickery. When Laozi wrote, "The great Dao extends everywhere, whether left or right" (Laozi 34), he meant that Dao was immanent in everything, guided the formation and actions of men and women, and bridged the gap between right and wrong. However, Wang assumed that Dao was a concrete object and argued, "Provided that Dao might go left or right, then going left would not be harmonious with right, and vice versa" (Wang 1996: 2:303). He went on to criticize the sentence, "Dao is empty. It may be used but its capacity is never exhausted" (Laozi 4; Chan 1963: 141). He ignored Laozi's ontological description of Dao, but viewed it as simply a gimmick to oppress others. He said, "Provided Dao were empty but inexhaustible in use, one would keep the middle empty and roam between two ends, giving oneself space but others cramped quarters, in that case the virtues under Heaven would not be true virtues anymore" (Wang 1996: 2:303). He concluded that Laozi's teachings had been a disaster for the Confucian Way, which had devolved into legalist measures, tricks, the military arts, and the origin of evils.

In summary, Wang Fuzhi criticized Laozi and Zhuangzi from his prejudiced Confucian perspective, and often launched his attacks before grasping their writings and ideas well. He understood nonbeing (*wu* 無) as nothingness and accused Laozi of "being inhumane and rejecting truth, and roaming in falsehood delightedly." He assumed that Laozi had detested his own body and human life based on the sentence "I face great disaster because I have a body" (Laozi 13). But, Wang failed to realize that Laozi was persuading people not to be attached to material pursuits and human desires, for Laozi continued, "One's body will be preserved if one puts it beyond consideration" (Laozi 13). When Laozi said, "Reversal is the movement of Dao, and weakness is the function of Dao" (Laozi 40), he elucidated the truth that there was a life cycle for everything, and that the young and weak had the greatest potential to develop. But, Wang misquoted it as "reversal is used and weakness is followed" (反以為用, 弱以為動) (Wang 1996: 1:886). As to Laozi's propositions that "Heaven and earth are not humane but regard all things as straw dogs; the sage is not humane but regards the people as straw dogs" (Laozi 5), Wang condemned them as inhumane, not realizing that Laozi was rejecting Confucian meddling and interference in people's lives and was advocating the doctrine of letting things be, later championed by Zhuangzi.

Based on above analysis, it is apparent that Wang Fuzhi attacked Laozi unfairly and often contradicted himself from his Confucian standpoint. For instance, if Wang had insisted that Laozi thought that disasters had resulted from human body and life was false, it would be ridiculous that he again criticized Laozi for seeking longevity (Wang 1996: 1:886).

6.5   Wang Fuzhi's Criticism of Legalism

The appellation Legalism, or the Legalist School (*Fajia* 法家), was coined by Sima Tan 司馬談 in the Han dynasty when he classified the pre-Qin masters. The basic assumption of this school was that human beings were inclined to do wrong rather than right because their primary motivation was self-interest. It thus argued that strong government depended not on the moral qualities of the ruler and his officials, but on establishing effective institutional structures. Legalist thought was first innovated by Shang Yang 商鞅 (died 338 BCE), then developed by Shen Buhai 申不害, and finally completed by the philosopher Han Fei 韓非 (c. 280–233 BCE). These advisors aimed at imposing order, security, and stability, and advocated that the surest means to prevent conflict and maintain social order was to implement strict laws and impose harsh punishments. To evaluate high officials' performance, they assessed whether their work achievements matched their position and functions. If their work performance matched their functions, they would be promoted; otherwise, they would be banished, even if their performance exceeded their prescribed functions. For this, Legalism was also called the teaching of names and punishments (*xingming* 刑名). Legalism was opposed to Confucianism, which held that human beings were capable of moral transformation, especially Mencius' lineage, which advocated that human nature was good.

As a Confucian scholar, Wang Fuzhi criticized Legalism mainly for its approach to governance. He maintained that the strictness of Legalist law and the harshness of the punishments would have a detrimental effect on positive customs that had been established in the spirit of humaneness and righteousness, and thus would cause the people to be more hypocritical and the officials more corrupt. He supported this view by citing the negative consequences associated with Wang Anshi's 王安石 (1021–1086) reform and governance by a new law code. Wang Fuzhi maintained that during the early years the Song dynasty, the governance was quite good. However, from 1068 when Wang Anshi administered the empire with his "new law" policy, "people throughout the empire felt distressed and bandits and rebels arose in bands." Wang Fuzhi concluded, "Any ruler who hopes to pacify the empire must know the people's needs and how to help them in order to satisfy them, and he should know that the policy of names and punishments is not well suited to achieve this" (Wang 1996: 11:93).

Unfortunately, Wang Fuzhi's argument is specious and self-contradictory. First, he praised Wang Anshi as a Confucian scholar who promoted the testing of students on the Confucian classics (Wang 1996: 12:489). Thus, he knew that Wang Anshi was not a Legalist even though he reformed old institutions and governed the people with a new law code. So, it was improper for Wang Fuzhi to use the term Legalism to slander Wang Anshi and his reform. If Wang Fuzhi had argued he was criticizing Legalist measures Wang Anshi had adopted, this argument would not have been persuasive, for there was no clear-cut distinction between Legalist measures and Confucian measures in governance. Second, Wang Fuzhi claimed there were no disturbances, bandits, or rebellions before 1068 and ascribed their appearance to Wang Anshi's reform. In fact, in 993, Wang Xiaobo 王小波 and Li Shun 李順 rebelled against the heavy taxes imposed by the Song court. Moreover, Wang was not clear as to how the Song regime managed to order the empire in the beginning or how the chaos and rebellions arose later. The temporary peace and order at the beginning of the Song Dynasty had resulted from the emperors' non-interference measures and the people's expectation of a peaceful life after the long period of chaos and conflict that characterized the Five Dynasties period (907–960). So, it was not simply Confucian governance that had brought about good order. But, by 1068 AD, the people had forgotten the bitterness of the previous chaos and were more incensed about the inequality of wealth and the harshness of governance, so Wang Anshi had to resort to reform measures to deal with this new situation.

Wang Fuzhi mainly criticized the overly harsh, strict, and cruel character of Legalist measures on the basis of his presumptions about them. He imagined that with Legalist measures in place, an official would set a standard and force the people to abide by it. If the people did not obey, he would angrily say, "These unruly people think their crimes are not deserving of the death penalty and so do not follow my orders. I will make them suffer deeply in muscle and skin and feel more misery than death; afterwards, my orders will prevail" (Wang 1996: 11:323). He imagined that Legalist officials would accept evidence of minor misdemeanors in private chambers and kitchens to accuse people of violating norms and betraying righteousness, or seize upon people's mistakes in chess and play to discipline their conduct in even their spare time. Wang considered that this approach to governance would not be effective. Indeed, it would arouse the people's indignation and defiance, causing them to grow fearless and evasive (Wang 1996: 11:323).

Wang Fuzhi committed two mistakes in this argument. On the one hand, he did not acknowledge that the Legalist laws clearly defined the limits of the people's and officials' conduct and thereby set a limit on the burden an official could impose on the people. In that sense, a clear standard would restrict not just the people but the official, as well. If the official did not abide by the standard but requested the people to do so, he would be violating basic Legalist tenets. On the other hand, Wang blamed the harsh governance of the Neo-Confucian scholar-officials on the Legalists because, as he said at the end of the previous quotation, "The Song noble persons disciplined themselves strictly, and then disciplined the stupid and low people by the same standards; they thus unconsciously committed the evil of strict Legalist measures" (Wang 1996: 11:323). The truth was that the harsh governance that the Song noble persons implemented had originated in the strictness of their own moral cultivation and practice, not from their adoption of Legalist measures.

As is well known, the Neo-Confucian officials of the Song governed the people with their moral sense instead of specific rules. When they detested a person and condemned them as immoral, they would overlook their good points and try to incriminate them even if they had observed the social rules and obeyed the law. When they found that the people did not heed them, they would become angry and complain that people had become degenerate. Then, they would start to exact their revenge and try to force the people to behave morally. Because they did not have clear standards for people's behavior, they would made impossible demands on the people. For example, some Song Neo-Confucian scholars would condemn a person of great principle for a trivial misdemeanor and found fault with the private lives of others. Cheng Yi 程頤 (1033–1107) reputedly criticized the nine-year-old emperor, Song Emperor Zhezong 宋哲宗 (1076–1100), for breaking a willow branch in the spring, accusing him of harming the harmonious *qi* of Heaven and Earth (Cheng and Cheng 2000: 400). By contrast, when Legalist officials governed the people, they set clear rules and seldom went beyond them. In this way, the officials had no chance to find trivial faults in others and punish them beyond the standard. Moreover, the people would feel no fear of officials if they knew they had not broken any laws. As a result, when an emperor ruled the empire with clear laws, the empire generally would be orderly, peaceful, and strong. Regrettably, Wang was obsessed with the harshness and cruelty of Legalist measures, and turned a blind eye to their positive side.

Wang Fuzhi further criticized the notion of rule by law from the perspective of its negative influence on social ethos. He feared that rule by law would empower the petty officials by giving them more space to abuse the law and squeeze the people. He argued, "The more detailed the law, the more powerful the petty officials. The more the death penalty is invoked, the more prevalent bribery becomes" (Wang 1996: 10:74). "The stricter the law, the more likely the emperor's authority is to be desecrated. Once a defiant mood has taken root among the common people, they will have few scruples in vying with their superiors" (Wang 1996: 12:641). He found that petty officials and runners could manipulate legal cases to the extent of exchanging the sentences for small infringements and death penalty cases with the motivation of bribes. They would deliberately let a criminal remain at large, or extend the scope of arrest for a crime, and allow the real criminal to remain in the clear with a tacit understanding between superior and inferior (Wang 1996: 10:75).

Truly, Wang Fuzhi witnessed the perverse social ethos of the late Ming under which the cruel, corrupt government inclined people to sue each other, and petty officials to manipulate laws. He did not accept the adoption of new legal measures that would restrict the petty official's space for manipulating laws because he did not believe that laws and penalties alone would put an end to bribery and corruption. Rather, he advocated improving the moral sense of the people through the practice of ritual propriety and music. He asserted, "Previous rulers worried that people would easily lose their loyalty and switch their allegiance, so they attracted them with the teaching of virtue but without demanding them to have merit or achievements; they thus transformed them with ritual propriety and music but did not regulate them with punishment and names" (Wang 1996: 10:476).

As to how to prevent the law enforcers from being corrupted, Liao Qichao 梁啟超 (1873–1929) made the case 200 years later that it was human beings who framed and implemented laws and regulations. If the implementers themselves were evil, then rule by law would only cause more chaos and disasters. Moreover, laws and regulations were considered dead things, unable to respond to changes in the will and desire of the people. As such, moral education was deemed preferable to rule by law (Liang 1984: 190, 195). In fact, Shang Yang and Han Fei had already responded to these questions long before Liang Qichao. Han Fei claimed that laws should be adapted to suit the times and be responsive to situations (Han 2000: 1178–1179). Shang Yang advocated severely punishing law enforcers who broke the law; such people would be executed and their extended families would be harshly punished, as well (Gao 1974:130).

Moreover, based on observation of modern democratic government, to dispel Wang Fuzhi and Liang Qichao's concerns, it would be necessary to set up an independent supervisory system to balance the powers of the administrative heads and to enact the separation of the powers of the legislative, administrative, and judicial branches of government. When every official is under the same restraints of law, any evil law-implementer would be removed and punished, and the new law-implementers would dedicate themselves to their mission and strive to maintain an orderly society.

Unsurprisingly, Wang Fuzhi did have the socio-political conditions needed to come up with the principle of the separation of powers. Rather, he opted for a Daoist policy of accommodation and non-stimulation to contain wicked officials. First, he proposed that laws be few and simple. "Few laws would lead to good compliance; simple regulations would lead to the peace of the state. If a fish were so huge that it could swallow a boat but the meshes of net still allowed it to escape, it would dare not touch fishing dam or basket again. Why? Laws are established by the one king, and petty officials cannot change them" (Wang 1996: 10:75). Truly, if laws were simple and loose, it would be easy for people to understand and obey them, but this would not mean that petty officials still could not distort them. It was even more absurd to think that criminals would be fearful of breaking laws if they had luckily escaped judgment for their past crimes. The truth may be the opposite: loose and simple laws only provide criminals more space to avoid getting caught and punished. Moreover, when such laws are interpreted and implemented, the petty officials will enjoy even more chances to manipulate them.

Wang Fuzhi's naivety became even more apparent when he proposed letting treacherous officials go unpunished. Inspired by the story of Zong Jun 宗均, a Han dynasty official, Wang suggested fighting corrupt officials in the same way as fighting tigers. To avoid tiger attacks on human settlements, Zong Jun requested that the people remove their traps and snares and not compete with tigers for game. Afterward, there were few tiger attacks, so his approach was deemed successful in saving people's lives. Similarly, Wang said, "If we regard wicked persons as chickens and pigs (and neglect them), they will become discouraged. This is the way to stop tricky measures in governing the people, for the people would then cease their tricky ways, as well" (Wang 1996: 10:256). In his view, if a lawman tried to compete with wicked and cunning people by appeal to the law, he would be unable to win because the wicked would always find loopholes. Moreover, this approach would incline even more people to circumvent the law. The best way would be to leave the wicked people alone; without contention and lawsuits, these people would recover their simplicity and honesty.

In this way, Wang Fuzhi approved of Laozi's tactic of accommodation, but he did not know how to implement it. Laozi's method was to accommodate and contain the wicked, without stimulating them or letting them influence others (Laozi 49). But, Wang was like an ostrich hiding its head in the sand and thinking the danger had passed. If a ruler heeded Wang's suggestion to view the wicked as chickens and pigs and not pay attention to their trickery, he would only encourage them to do evil more brazenly and create even more troubles. If upright administrative officials were to cease using laws and morality to punish wicked persons because they were not always successful, then the wicked would soon regard themselves as the rulers of city and village and do even more brazen evils.

Because Wang Fuzhi had turned a blind eye to the positive features of rule by law, he was perplexed that many rulers in previous dynasties had governed with laws rather than Confucian rituals. He asked, "Why have Shen Buhai's 申不害 (420–337 BC) and Shang Yang's 商鞅 (395–338 BC) teachings not yet perished from the Earth? Even righteous, upright personages, such as Zhuge Liang 諸葛亮 (181–234), had adopted them; and, knowledgeable, open-minded ministers, like Wang Anshi 王安石, had accepted their gist" (Wang 1996: 10:72). His explanation was that "when governing by law, the ruler rests at ease while the people are harassed; when governing by the Confucian Way, the ruler gets exhausted while the people are idle" (Wang 1996: 10:72). Regretfully, Wang over-simplified the issue. To govern by law is never easier than to govern by ritual propriety and music. People prefer rule by law because clear law gives the people a specific code of conduct and brings the state into order more easily. After witnessing many successes and failures in governance, people have begun to realize that the Confucian Kingly Way is utopian and know it is better to solve problems according to the facts of the situations.

Moreover, Wang Fuzhi and his Confucian colleagues fabricated a positive image of kingly governance based on the assumption that human beings preferred morality and humaneness to selfish desires, and thus forced the people to follow their Way. On the grassroots level, the Confucians dared not face the reality that most people put their selfish interests above public welfare and morality, so their moral teachings did not affect the people's thought or conduct but only succeeded in making them hypocritical; on the rulership level, the Confucians misled officials and rulers to adopt ineffective administrative measures and caused the state to become ever more chaotic. After the state became chaotic, the Confucians would shamelessly blame the officials for not implementing the Confucian teachings earnestly or correctly.

Based on his assumption that imperial courts implemented rule by law in keeping with the emperor's preference for leisure and idleness, Wang Fuzhi condemned Legalism, Daoism, and Buddhism as the three great disasters (*san da hai* 三大害) of the history of China, and held that they complemented each other in harming the social ethos and leading the people astray. He insisted that the teachings of Buddhism and Daoism inevitably led to the adoption of Legalist measures in governance because when the rulers cherished utmost emptiness and quietude, they would abandon all active approaches and handle state affairs according to passive Legalist regulations, demanding that the people obey them while they themselves enjoyed a free and leisurely life. Wang also supposed that if the ruler adopted stern Legalist measures, the people would adopt Buddhism and Daoism, shirk their duties and responsibilities, and justify their guilt and crimes with the doctrine of no-mind (Wang 1996: 10:653).

This could be considered the definitive explanation as to why Wang Fuzhi criticized Buddhism, Daoism, and Legalism with such venom. Apparently, he drew a connection between these three schools based on his own study and reflection; this linkage did bear considerable insight. Assuredly, the non-action and non-interference of Daoism and Buddhism would conduce to rule by law. Nevertheless, it should be noted that the over-interference of Confucianism could stir reaction and lead to the adoption of Legalist measures, too. Confucian officials are particular about the implementation of Confucian rules, intensely subjective regarding their ideals and goals, and tend to be increasingly demanding on the people. When Mao Zedong 毛澤東 (1893–1976) read this paragraph by Wang Fuzhi, he commented, "Confucius' and Mencius' teachings will also lead to the promotion of Shen Buhai and Han Fei's laws and punishments" (Mao 1993: 344).

6.6 CONCLUSION

Wang Fuzhi believed that the degenerate social ethos at the late Ming had led to the fall of the Ming and the conquest of the Manchus. He did not trace the cause of this degenerate social ethos to the misrule of the emperor, high officials, and bureaucrats, but placed most blame on the heretical schools and the misleading interpretations of the Confucian classics by previous Neo-Confucians. He hoped to improve the people's social ethos by criticizing the heretical teachings and reinterpreting the Confucian classics. In his efforts to do so, he analyzed the Channist essence of Wang Yangming's teaching of inborn knowledge of the good and the Buddhist elements with which Zhu Xi and his followers adulterated Confucianism. He indicated that Wang Yangming had regarded the mind as a perceptive mind only and sought a Channist sort of empty realm by "cutting off the path of language and ceasing mental functions." He criticized the quiet-sitting and purging of the desires instructed by Zhu Xi, and ridiculed his sage as "the sage of heresy." He then concentrated his energy on attacking Buddhism and denouncing all Buddhist teachings. He sought to replace Buddhist emptiness with true Being (*shi you* 實有), Buddhist interdependent causation with self-so-ing (*ziran* 自然), and universal love with graded love. And, he rejected the Buddhist teachings of reincarnation and karmic retribution. He blamed the tales of shamanic retribution in the *Zuo Commentary Tradition* for inclining people to be receptive to Buddhist karmic retribution, criticized the Daoist thought for providing a vehicle for the spread of Buddhism in China, and condemned the teachings of Daoism for prescribing tricky and irresponsible tactics. Based on the Confucian Way of humaneness and righteousness, he also attacked Laozi and Zhuangzi for following natural processes and letting the people be. He believed this detached, indifferent Daoist attitude toward the people and affairs had given rise to the loose, irresponsible social ethos of the late Ming.

Wang Fuzhi implicitly criticized Zhu Yuanzhan's strict and harsh rule in the name of Legalism. He thought that with its strict and harsh approach to governance, Legalism would cause the people to be hypocritical and circumvent the law, and was not good for the construction of a good social ethos. He was not confident that evil could be prevented by laws and punishments, but proposed accommodating and transforming the wicked. Yet, he was at his wits end when trying to prescribe way to contain or accommodate them.

Wang Fuzhi took great pains to reinterpret the Confucian classics and boldly reconstructed Confucianism, but he was much too biased regarding the heretical doctrines in his criticisms. First, he did not realize that Confucian ritual propriety, rules, and norms formerly had played the same role as laws and regulations in antiquity, so he was apt to scapegoat Legalism for Confucian misrule. Second, he borrowed accommodation and leniency from the *Laozi*, but misconstrued them as "leaving the wicked alone." He elevated his Confucian moral cultivation to the cosmological level by assimilating the notion of "assisting Heaven (*xiangtian* 相天)" from the *Zhuangzi*. But he still criticized Laozi and Zhuangzi for the rise of the tricky and irresponsible social ethos in the late Ming, which showed that he had not truly understood them. Third, he asked his students to steer clear of Buddhism as a spiritual contagion. He regarded Buddhism as a spiritual contaminant of Neo-Confucianism, especially the teachings of Zhu Xi and Wang Yangming. Still, his understanding of Buddhism was shallow. Although he sought to refute and replace the Buddhist doctrines of reincarnation and karmic retribution with his theory of life and death, his theory did not offer the people with spiritual comfort in facing existential suffering and death and thus could not prevent the spread of Buddhism, which offered spiritual solace. Nevertheless, by reinterpreting the Confucian classics and criticizing the heretical teachings, Wang bequeathed a comprehensive new Confucian system to posterity, which has been a precious resource for understanding and evaluating the Ming culture and promoting traditional Chinese virtues and values.

BIBLIOGRAPHY

EARLY CHINESE TEXTS

Cheng, Hao & Cheng, Yi 程颢, 程颐, *Er Cheng YiShu* 二程遗书 (*The Extant Works of the Two Chengs*), Shanghai: Shanghai Guji Chubanshe 上海古籍出版社, 2000

Gao, Heng 高亨, *Shang Jun Shu Zhu Yi*商君書注譯 (*An Annotation and Interpretation of Marquis Shang's Works*), Beijing: Zhonghua Shuju 北京:中華書局, 1974

Guo, Qingfan 郭慶藩, *Zhuangzi Jishi* 莊子集釋 (*Collected Commentaries on the Zhuangzi*), Beijing: Zhonghua Shuju 北京:中華書局, 1961

Han, Fei 韓非, *Han Fei Zi Xin Jiaozhu* 韓非子新校注 (*A New Proofreading and Annotation to the Hang Fei Zi*), Chen Qiyou陳奇猷 Annotated. Shanghai: Shanghai Guji Chubanshe, 2000

Huang, Zongxi 黃宗羲, *Huang Zongxi Quanji* 黃宗羲全集 (1–22 冊) (*The Complete Works of Huang Zongxi*), Volume 1–22, Hangzhou: Zhejiang Guji Chubanshe 杭州:浙江古籍出版社, 2012

Li, Jingde, ed. 黎靖德, *Zhu Zi Yu Lei* 朱子語類 (*Conversations of Master Zhu, Arranged Topically*), Beijing: Zhonghua Shuju 北京: 中華書局, 1994

Li, Zhi 李贄, *Fen Shu & Xu Fen Shu* 焚書續焚書 (*The Book to be Burned & The Successor of the Book to be Burned*). Beijing: Zhonghua Shuju 北京: 中華書局, 1975

Liang, Qichao 梁啟超, *Liang Qichao Xuanji* 梁啟超選集 (*Selected Works of Liang Qichao's Writings*), Shanghai: Shanghai Renmin Chubanshe 上海: 上海人民出版社, 1984

Lou, Yulie 樓宇烈, *Wang Bi Ji Jiaoshi* 王弼集校釋 (*An Exegesis of Wang Bi's Works*), Beijing: Zhonghua Shuju 北京: 中華書局, 1980

Wang, Yangming 王陽明, *Chuan Xi Lu Zhushu* 傳習錄注疏 (*Instructions for Practical Living*), annotated by Deng Aimin 鄧艾民, Shanghai: Shanghai Guji Chubanshe 上海: 上海古籍出版社, 2012

Wang, Yu 王敔, *Daxing Fujun Xingshu* 大行府君行述 (*A Brief Biographical Sketch of my Diseased Father*), in *Chuanshan Quanshu* 船山全書16 (*The Complete Works of Chuanshan*), Volume 16, Changsha: Yuelu Shushe 長沙: 岳麓書社, 1996

Zhou, Mi 周密, *Zhi Ya Tang Za Chao* 志雅堂雜鈔 (*Various Records in Zhi Ya Hall*) in *Zhou Mi Ji* 4 周密集第四冊 (*Zhou Mi's Complete Works*) Volume 4, Hangzhou: Zhejiang Guji Chubanshe 杭州: 浙江古籍出版社, 2015

SECONDARY SOURCES

De Bary, Wm. Theodore, ed., *The Unfolding of Neo-Confucianism*, New York and London: Columbia University Press, 1975

Liu, Lifu 劉立夫, & Tian, Yan 田艷, The Research Center of Chuanshan Buddhist Culture is Established in Changsha, Hunan 船山佛教文化研究中心在湖南長沙成立. *Studies in World Religion* 世界宗教研究, 2009, No. 1

Mao, Zedong 毛澤東, *Mao Zedong Du Wenshi Guji Piyu Ji* 毛泽东读文史古籍批语集 (*Mao Zedong's Comments on His Reading Classical Chinese Literature and History*), edited by the Central Literature Research Centre of the PRC, 中共中央文献研究室主编, The Central Literature Publishing House 中央文献出版社, 1993

Mao, Zedong 毛澤東, *Mao Zedong Xuanji* 毛澤東選集, 第二版 (*Selected Readings of Mao Zedong's Works*, second edition), Beijing: People's Publishing House 北京: 人民出版社, 1991

Watson, Burton, *The Complete Works of Chuang Tzu*, New York: Columbia University Press, 1968

Wu, Han 吳晗, *Du Shi Zha Ji* 讀史劄記 (*Notes on Reading the History of the Ming Dynasty*), Beijing: Shenghuo, Dushu, Zhishi San Lian Shudian 北京: 生活讀書知識三聯書店, 1956

Wu, Limin & Xu, Sunming 吳立民, 徐蓀銘, *Chuanshan Fo Dao Sixiang Yanjiu* 船山佛道思想研究 (*A Research on Chuanshan's Thought of Buddhism and Daoism*), Changsha: Hunan Publishing House 長沙: 湖南出版社, 1992

Xu, Sunming 徐蓀銘, Several Questions Pertaining to Wang Chuanshan's Thought on Buddhism and Daoism 船山佛道思想研究的若干問題, *Chuanshan Journal* 1991, no.1

CHAPTER 7

Conclusion: Assessment of Wang Fuzhi's Thought

In his writing and scholarly activity, Wang Fuzhi sought to provide solutions for the crises of his time, reinterpret the Six Classics, and provide an orthodox Confucian teaching so the Chinese would have the trust and cohesion to ward off future invasions. After several decades of effort, Wang established an orthodox Confucian system, purging heterodox elements from earlier interpretations of the Confucian classics. However, the question remains, would Wang's orthodox Confucian system effectively help the Chinese have the cohesion and trust to ward off subsequent invasions? Since his works were not published until 1866, the world had changed considerably since the conditions of his lifetime. His readers in the late Qing and early Republican period could not derive the sorts of knowledge or wisdom they needed to fend off the European powers or the Japanese invaders. The reason for this is not just that the conditions had changed. More deeply, in analyzing the fall of the Song and Ming dynasties, Wang laid too much blame on the common people and too little on the emperors, ministers, and their policies. He focused on the alleged impact of scholars' teachings but overlooked or rationalized the imperial and official misrule. In this way, he blamed the horse but not the driver, failed to grasp the crucial problem in dynastic China, and did not offer an effective strategy for building a strong China. In contrast, Huang Zongxi discovered that the cycle of dynastic China was driven by the selfishness and cruelty of imperial regimes and advocated balancing imperial power with the moral suasion of the scholar-officials.

M. Tan, *Wang Fuzhi's Reconstruction of Confucianism*, https://doi.org/10.1007/978-3-030-80263-9_7

While Wang Fuzhi criticized the common people for their ingratitude to the Ming emperor and easily switching loyalty to the Manchus, he ignored the serious imperial misrule in the late Ming. He praised the Ming emperors for their lenient policy toward the people, in particular the reduced agricultural taxes. For example, he reported that from 1368 to 1498 the area of cultivated land had increased while taxes on agricultural production were reduced. Despite the emperors' generosity in this regard, the common people disregarded these benefits and betrayed their superiors. To Wang, the people had brought the fierce wrath of the Manchus on themselves (Wang 1996: 12:623). But, the question arises, Why didn't Wang mention the misrule of the Ming regime between 1500 and 1644, which drove the people to desperation and rebellion? Since Wang had avoided the important issues and focused on minor ones in his account of the fall of the Song and Ming, how could he offer effective measures to prevent another dynastic collapse?

Wang Fuzhi was overly concerned about the negative impact of heterodox teachings on the people's thinking and social ethics, but he ignored the harsh, corrupt rulers that caused the people to seek solace in these teachings. Wang blamed the popularity of Lu Jiuyuan's and Wang Yangming's teachings for the collapse of the Song and Ming dynasties because he thought that these teachings had misled the people and inclined them to be disloyal and inhumane. However, he should have first considered why the people would be willing to accept these teachings. Wang also said, "A good way to regulate mind is to let it rest in a spacious place, a good way to govern the people is to pacify them by improving their livelihood. When the people have a certain livelihood, they do not pity each other but stabilize their minds. They are immune to the seduction of lewd fashions and music and consider them as dross to be cast aside" (Wang 1996: 3:351). If Wang really believed that the people's loyalty and humaneness were determined by their enjoying a certain livelihood, he should not have stressed the negative impact of heterodox teachings; for what had caused the people to be disloyal and inhumane was the regime's misrule and heavy taxes, not the heterodox teachings themselves. Indeed, the heterodox teachings were just an expression of the people's frustration, protest, or simply sense of helplessness in coping with the harsh government and heavy taxes.

At this point, it should be noted that the cycle of dynastic China often took the following form: the rise of misrule led to political discussions (qingyi 清議) and remonstrations. The political discussions are then repressed and devolve into the scholar-official's pure talk (*qingtan* 清談) and self-indulgence. When the scholar-officials engage in pure talk and self-indulgence, they put aside state affairs and enjoy themselves with lectures, beautiful scenery, and women to avoid political persecution. This cycle occurred in the late Han, the Three Kingdoms, the Southern Song, and the late Ming. Wang Fuzhi also noted the people's weakening loyalty and sense of responsibility while suffering from harsh government, such as evidenced in the Ming emperor's having a minister flogged at court. In other words, the Ming emperors' harsh government and persecution inclined the scholar-officials to shirk political affairs and social responsibility and indulge in pure talk, parties, and women. Moreover, heavy taxes and concentration of land ownership drove the people to hate and rebel against the Ming simply in hope of having a peaceful ordinary life. To justify such responses, Wang Gen 王艮 and Li Zhi offered naturalistic teachings: "The patterns and lines of the common people's ordinary life are identical with the sage's principle" (Wang 2001: 72). "In dressing and eating lie the human relationships and moral principle" (Li 1975: 4). Wang and Li did not care about the sacred principles of loyalty to the ruler and filial piety to the father. Later, people further doubted the reality of such principles when they witnessed the collapse of the Ming and the Manchu occupation of Nanjing. *The Fan with Peach Blossoms (Tao Hua Shan* 《桃花扇》), a drama of the late Ming vividly depicted the common people's mood of despair about the Ming government: "Bah! You two silly creatures (Hou Fangyu 侯方域 and Li Xiangjun 李香君). You see, where is your state? Where is your home? Where is your ruler? Where is your father" (Kong 1997: 192)? After this, Hou and Li converted to Buddhism, reflecting the public's indifference to and disappointment in political affairs at the time.

Such indifference and disappointment about political affairs and the noble families were typical phenomena of late imperial China. Such sentiments inclined the scholar-officials to be ineffectual and even unfamiliar with state affairs and take up Daoism and Buddhism, or use Daoist and Buddhist teachings in interpreting Confucian texts. A conversation between the Gu brothers, Gu Xiancheng 顧憲成 (1550–1612) and Gu Yuncheng 顧允成 (1554–1607), reflected the scholars' general indifference about the future of the Ming.

> One day, Gu Yuncheng drew a long breath, and sighed. His brother asked him what was wrong. He replied, "I sigh with regret that scholars today care

only about their lectures, regardless of the fall of Heaven and the quake of Earth." (Huang 2012: 17:1600)

What was the topic of such lectures? Gu Yanwu 顧炎武 provided a good answer: "The subject of scholarly pure talk in ancient times was the *Laozi* and the *Zhuangzi* while in the present it is Confucius' *Analects* and the *Mencius*." The task of pure talk at the time was, in Gu Yanwu's view, to interpret Confucius' and Mencius' teachings by using Buddhist ideas, ignoring their discussions on political affairs and academic studies. "They replaced the practical studies of cultivating the self and governing the people with empty words about finding the true self" (Gu 1997: 339). As a result, the scholar-officials became ineffectual and lazy, leading in part to the collapse of Ming dynasty.

Dismayed by the collapse of the Ming, the Manchu conquest of China, and the people's indifference to this dynastic change, Wang Fuzhi dedicated himself to reinterpreting the Six Classics while Gu Yanwu declared, "To protect the peace of the world, even those as inferior as farmers have a responsibility" (Gu 1997: 594). They both aimed to change the weak and irresponsible social ethics of the late Ming and promoted practical learning. Perhaps, they made such efforts out of youthful idealism, unaware of the insignificance and weakness of individual scholars in the face of a vast, corrupt imperial bureaucracy. As Ray Huang put it, "But soon, he (Wan-li 萬曆) was to discover that the freedom of action he had anticipated was as illusory as ever. After all, to become Son of Heaven was to fulfill an institutional requirement only" (Huang 1981: 40). If the emperor could not change the corrupt bureaucracy, how would it be possible for a handful of scholars to do so, armed only with their moral teachings and righteous indignation?

In short, while Wang Fuzhi dared not challenge the imperial system or take on the political and cultural crises of his time by seeking to limit the regime's power and influence, he still anticipated the appearance of future sage emperors and enlightened ministers, such as Liu Xiu, Zhao Kuangyin, Song Jing 宋璟, Zhang Jiuling 張九齡, and Li Mi 李泌, who would govern the people properly by ritual and music. Although Wang registered the destructive impact of harsh government on the morale of the Ming scholar-officials, he downplayed the emperors' cruelty, scapegoated some officials, and attributed much of the negative effects to "heterodox teachings." He dared not criticize the selfishness, suspiciousness, stinginess, or cruelty of the Ming founder, Zhu Yuanzhang, but he blamed Liu Ji and

Song Lian for their ignorance to the restoration of ritual propriety. He condemned Lu Jiuyuan and Wang Yangming for the collapse of the Song and Ming dynasties, respectively, but he did not register that their teachings offered the people relief from the pressures of imperial tyranny. Hence, Wang could only beat about the bush when he advocated purifying the people's mind with an orthodox Confucian teaching, for he ignored the root cause of the problems: the imperial tyranny that gave rise to perverse social ethics and caused the collapse of the dynasties. For this reason, Cai Shangsi 蔡尚思 (1905–2008) regarded Wang Fuzhi as a petty Confucian scholar, quoting Huang Zongxi's *Waiting for the Dawn*:

> It is right that the people in the world today hate the ruler and view him as their enemy and declare him a tyrant. But, a petty Confucian scholar still obediently claims a subject has nowhere to escape his duty to his ruler between Heaven and Earth. Though the ruler be as cruel as King Jie 桀 and King Zhou 紂 of old, he nonetheless declines to overthrown him. (Cai 1996)

Wang Fuzhi should be classified as one of the petty Confucian scholars Huang Zongxi condemned.

Nevertheless, Wang Fuzhi did exert some positive influence on the history of modern China. First, his voluminous works act as a reservoir of traditional Chinese culture, and his extensive commentaries provide plentiful inspirations and stimulations for later readers. In particular, his anti-Manchu stance was highly appreciated by Zhang Binglin and Hu Shi. His discourse on the relationship between Heaven and humanity was developed into Mao Zedong's doctrine of the mass line, because Mao's "collecting views from the masses (*cong qunzhong zhong lai* 從群眾中來)" corresponded to Wang's "Finding the evidence of Heaven (Truth) from popular opinion (*zheng tian yu min* 徵天于民)," while "Going back to the masses for testing (*dao qunzhong zhong qu* 到群眾中去)" corresponded to Wang's "Guiding and using the people with Heaven (truth) (*yi tian jian min* 以天鑒民)" (Wang 1996: 2:327; Mao 1991: 899). As opposed to Wang's dismay about the harmful effect of popular opinion on the emperor, Mao Zedong optimistically discovered and utilized popular opinion to subvert the ROC regime and to strengthen his own power. Unlike Wang's disdain and passivity regarding popular complaints during the period of dynastic crisis, Mao Zedong paid attention to individuals' and small groups' incipient complaints and opinions, and discerned their truth inductively.

Moreover, Wang Fuzhi built the most comprehensive Confucian system; incorporated cosmology, personal morality, and political governance; and synthesized the School of Principle, the School of Mind, and the School of *Qi* of the Neo-Confucian tradition. His originality lay in his ability to connect moral cultivation with the Great Harmony and the Kingly Way, which made his model of Confucianism more consistent. This comprehensive Confucian system will provide a treasure-trove for the restoration of traditional Chinese culture in the twenty-first century. In particular, by continuing his promotion of humaneness, ritual propriety, and harmony, people today could be inspired to improve social harmony and lessen ecological disasters. If everyone were to moderate their desires and cultivate their virtue by observing ritual propriety and practicing righteousness, they would increase the amount of harmonious *qi* in the universe and contribute to curbing modern people's insatiable material desires and healing the stultifying alienation of human relations. To a certain extent, this is the exactly sort of wisdom and guidance that people around the world need and are looking for at present. It also confirms Wang Fuzhi's bold claim that the seeds of humaneness and righteousness he was preserving would one day be planted and nurtured by later generations to realize the mind of Heaven and Earth and the principle of Heaven.

Bibliography

Early Chinese Texts

Gu, Yanwu, *Record of Daily Accumulated Knowledge (Ri Zhi Lu* 日知录), Lanzhou: Gansu Minzu Chubanshe, 1997, p339
Huang, Zongxi 黃宗羲, *Huang Zongxi Quanji* 黃宗羲全集 (1–22 冊) (*The Complete Works of Huang Zongxi*), Volume 1–22, Hangzhou: Zhejiang Guji Chubanshe 杭州:浙江古籍出版社, 2012
Kong, Shangren 孔尚任, *Tao Hua Shan* 桃花扇 (*The Fan with Peach Blossoms*), Changchun: Jilin Wenshi Chubanshe 長春: 吉林文史出版社, 1997
Li, Zhi 李贄, *Fen Shu & Xu Fen Shu* 焚書續焚書 (*The Book to be Burned & The Successor of the Book to be Burned*). Beijing: Zhonghua Shuju 北京: 中華書局, 1975
Wang, Gen 王艮, *Wang Xinzhai Quanji* 王心齋全集 (*The Complete Works of Wang Xinzahi*), Nanjing: Jiangsu Jiaoyu Chubanshe 南京: 江蘇教育出版社, 2001

Wang, Yu 王敔, *Daxing Fujun Xingshu* 大行府君行述 (*A Brief Biographical Sketch of my Diseased Father*), in *Chuanshan Quanshu* 船山全書16 (*The Complete Works of Chuanshan*), Volume 16, Changsha: Yuelu Shushe 長沙: 岳麓書社, 1996

SECONDARY SOURCES

Cai, Shangsi 蔡尚思, *Cong Zhongguo Xueshu Sixiangshi Kan Wang Chuanshan de Jizhong Tuchu Diwei* 從中國學術思想史看王船山的幾種突出地位 (*On Wang Chuanshan's Several Important Roles in Chinese Intellectual History*), in Chuanshan Quanshu 船山全書 (The Complete Works of Chuanshan), Volume 16, Changsha: Yuelu Shushe, 1996

Huang, Ray, *1587: A Year of No Significance*, New Haven and London: Yale University Press, 1981

Mao, Zedong 毛澤東, *Mao Zedong Xuanji* 毛澤東選集, 第二版 (*Selected Readings of Mao Zedong's Works*, second edition), Beijing: People's Publishing House 北京: 人民出版社, 1991

BIBLIOGRAPHY

EARLY CHINESE TEXTS

Ban, Gu 班固, *Han Shu* 漢書 (*The History of the Han Dynasty*), Beijing: Zhonghua Shuju 北京: 中華書局, 1962

Chen, Li 陳立, Gongyang Yishu 公羊義疏 (*Commentary and Annotation on the Gongyang Tradition of the Spring and Autumn Annals*), Beijing: Zhonghua Shuju, 2017

Cheng, Hao & Cheng, Yi 程顥, 程頤, *Er Cheng YiShu* 二程遗书 (*The Extant Works of the Two Chengs*), Shanghai: Shanghai Guji Chubanshe 上海古籍出版社, 2000

Dai, Zhen 戴震, *Mengzi Ziyi Shuzheng* 孟子字義疏證 (*Correction of Exegesis on the Mencius*), Beijing: Zhonghua Shuju 北京: 中華書局, 1961

Fan, Ye 范曄, *Hou Han Shu* 后漢書 (*The History of the Later Han*), Beijing: Zhonghua Shuju 北京: 中華書局, 1965

Gao, Heng 高亨, *Shang Jun Shu Zhu Yi*商君書注譯 (*An Annotation and Interpretation of Marquis Shang's Works*), Beijing: Zhonghua Shuju 北京:中華書局, 1974

Gu, Yanwu 顧炎武, *Record of Daily Accumulated Knowledge* (*Ri Zhi Lu* 日知录), Lanzhou: Gansu Minzu Chubanshe 甘肅民族出版社, 1997

Guo, Qingfan 郭慶藩, *Zhuangzi Jishi* 莊子集釋 (*Collected Commentaries on the Zhuangzi*), Beijing: Zhonghua Shuju 北京:中華書局, 1961

Han, Fei 韓非, *Han Fei Zi Xin Jiaozhu* 韓非子新校注 (*A New Proofreading and Annotation to the Hang Fei Zi*), Chen Qiyou陳奇猷 Annotated. Shanghai: Shanghai Guji Chubanshe 上海： 上海古籍出版社, 2000

© The Author(s), under exclusive license to Springer Nature
Switzerland AG 2021
M. Tan, *Wang Fuzhi's Reconstruction of Confucianism*,
https://doi.org/10.1007/978-3-030-80263-9

Huang, Zongxi 黃宗羲, *Huang Zongxi Quanji* 黃宗羲全集 (1–22 冊) *(The Complete Works of Huang Zongxi)*, Volume 1–22, Hangzhou: Zhejiang Guji Chubanshe 杭州:浙江古籍出版社, 2012

Kant, Immanuel, *Critique of Practical Reason*, trans. by Werner S. Pluhar, Hackett Publishing Co., 2002a

Kong, Shangren 孔尚任, *Tao Hua Shan* 桃花扇 *(The Fan with Peach Blossoms)*, Changchun: Jilin Wenshi Chubanshe 長春: 吉林文史出版社, 1997

Laozi 老子. *The Laozi* 老子, annotated by Wang Bi王弼注, Shanghai: Shanghai Guji Chubanshe 上海: 上海古籍出版社, 1989

Li, Jingde, ed. 黎靖德, *Zhu Zi Yu Lei* 朱子語類 *(Conversations of Master Zhu, Arranged Topically)*, Beijing: Zhonghua Shuju 北京: 中華書局, 1994

Li, Zhi 李贄, *Fen Shu & Xu Fen Shu* 焚書續焚書 *(The Book to be Burned & The Successor of the Book to be Burned)*. Beijing: Zhonghua Shuju 北京: 中華書局, 1975

Li, Zhi 李贄, *De ye Ru Chen Hou Lun* 德業儒臣后論 *(A Post Comment on Confucian Scholars' Virtue and Achievements)*, in *Li Zhi Quanji Zhu* 李贄全集注 (第六冊) *(An Annotation to the Complete Works of Li Zhi, Volume 6)*, Beijing: Social Sciences Academic Press北京: 社會科學文獻出版社, 2010

Li, Xiangfeng 黎翔鳳, *Guanzi Jiaozhu* 管子校注 *(A Correction and Annotation of the Guanzi)*, Beijing: Zhonghua Shuju北京： 中華書局, 2004

Liang, Qichao 梁啟超, *Liang Qichao Xuanji* 梁啟超選集 *(Selected Works of Liang Qichao's Writings)*, Shanghai: Shanghai Renmin Chubanshe 上海: 上海人民出版社, 1984

Liu, Xiang 劉向, *Guanzi Jiaozheng* 管子校正 *(A Correction and Compilation of the Guanzi)*, in *Zhuzi Ji Cheng* 諸子集成 (6) *(A Collection of the Philosophers)* Volume 6, Shanghai: Shanghai Shudian 上海: 上海書店, 1986

Lou, Yulie 樓宇烈, *Wang Bi Ji Jiaoshi* 王弼集校釋 *(An Exegesis of Wang Bi's Works)*, Beijing: Zhonghua Shuju 北京: 中華書局, 1980

Lu, Jiuyuan 陸九淵, *Lu Jiuyuan Ji* 陸九淵集 *(A Collection of Lu Jiuyuan's Writings)*, Beijing: Zhonghua Shuju 北京: 中華書局, 1980

Ouyang, Xiu 歐陽修, *Xin Wudai Shi* 新五代史 *(New Version of the History of the Five Dynasties)*, Beijing: Zhonghua Shuju 北京: 中華書局, 1974

Qu, Wanli 屈萬里, Shangshu Jishi 尚書集釋 (Collected Notes on the Book of Documents), Shanghai: Zhongxi Shuju 上海: 中西書局, 2014

Quan, Zuwang 全祖望, *Ji Qi Ting Ji* 鮨琦亭集 *(Collection in Jie Ji Pavilion)* Taipei: Taiwan Shangwu Yinshuguan 台北: 台湾商务印書館, 1965

Ricci, Matteo, *Tianzhu Shiyi* 天主實義 *(The True Meaning of Catholicism)*. Zheng Ande 郑安德, ed. Beijing: Institute of Religions, Beijing University, 2000

Shang, Binghe 尚秉和, *Zhou Yi Shangshi Xue* 周易尚氏學 *(Shang's Commentary on the Book of Changes)*, Beijing: Zhonghua Shuju北京： 中華書局, 2016

Wang, Fuzhi 王夫之 *Chuanshan Quanshu* 船山全書 (1–16 冊) *(Complete Works of Wang Chuanshan*, Volume 1–16), Changsha: Yuelu Shushe 长沙: 岳麓書社, 1996

Wang, Gen 王艮, *Wang Xinzhai Quanji* 王心斋全集 (*The Complete Works of Wang Xinzahi*), Nanjing: Jiangsu Jiaoyu Chubanshe 南京: 江蘇教育出版社, 2001

Wang, Xianqian 王先謙, *Xunzi Jijie* 荀子集解 (*Collected Exegesis of the Xunzi*), Beijing: Zhonghua Shuju 北京: 中華書局, 1988

Wang, Yangming 王陽明, *Chuan Xi Lu Zhushu* 傳習錄注疏 (*Instructions for Practical Living*), annotated by Deng Aimin 鄧艾民, Shanghai: Shanghai Guji Chubanshe 上海: 上海古籍出版社, 2012

Wang, Yu 王敔, *Daxing Fujun Xingshu* 大行府君行述 (*A Brief Biographical Sketch of my Diseased Father*), in *Chuanshan Quanshu* 船山全書16 (*The Complete Works of Chuanshan*), Volume 16, Changsha: Yuelu Shushe 長沙: 岳麓書社, 1996

Xu, Yuangao 徐元誥, *Guo Yu Jijie* 國語集解 (*Collected Notes on the Records of States*), Beijing: Zhonghua Shuju北京: 中華書局, 2002

Yan, Yuan 顏元, *Xi Zhai Si Cun Bian* 習齋四存編 (*The Collection of the Four Preservations at Xizhai*), Shanghai: Shanghai Guji Chubanshe 上海: 上海古籍出版社, 2000

Yan, Yuan 顏元, *Yan Yuanji* 顏元集 (*A Collection of Yan Yuan's Writings*), Beijing: Zhonghua Shuju 北京: 中華書局, 1987

Yang, Bojun 楊伯峻, *Chunqiu Zuozhuan Zhu* 春秋左傳注 (*Annotations on the Zuo Commentary Tradition on the Spring-Autumn Annals*), Beijing: Zhonghua Shuju 北京: 中華書局, 1981

Zhang, Zai 張載, *Zhang Zai Ji* 張載集 (*A Collection of Zhang Zai's Works*), Beijing: Zhonghua Shuju 北京: 中華書局, 1978

Zhou, Mi 周密, Zhi *Ya Tang Za Chao* 志雅堂雜鈔 (*Various Records in Zhi Ya Hall*) in *Zhou Mi Ji* 4 周密集第四冊 (*Zhou Mi's Complete Works*) Volume 4, Hangzhou: Zhejiang Guji Chubanshe 杭州: 浙江古籍出版社, 2015

Zhu, Xi 朱熹, *Sishu Zhangju Jizhu* 四書章句集注 (*A Collected Commentary on the Four Books*), Beijing: Zhonghua Shuju 北京: 中華書局, 1983

Zhu, Xi 朱熹, *Huian Xiansheng Zhu Wengong Wenji* 晦庵先生朱文公文集 (Master Huian Zhu's Literary Works), In *Zhuzi Quanshu* 朱子全書, 第 23 冊(*The Complete Works of Master Zhu*) Volume 23, edited by Zhu Jieren, Yan Zuozhi, Liu Yongxiang et al. 朱傑人, 嚴佐之, 劉永翔等編訂, Shanghai: Shanghai Guji Chubanshe; Hefei: Anhui Jiaoyu Chubanshe, 2010 上海: 上海古籍出版社, 合肥: 安徽教育出版社, 2010

SECONDARY SOURCES

Black, Alison Harley, *Man and Nature in the Philosophical Thought of Wang Fu-chih*, Seattle: University of Washington Press, 1989

Cai, Shangsi 蔡尚思, *Cong Zhongguo Xueshu Sixiangshi Kan Wang Chuanshan de Jizhong Tuchu Diwei* 從中國學術思想史看王船山的幾種突出地位 (*On Wang Chuanshan's Several Important Roles in Chinese Intellectual History*), in

Chuanshan Quanshu 船山全書 (The Complete Works of Chuanshan), Volume 16, Changsha: Yuelu Shushe長沙： 岳麓書社, 1996

Chan, Wing-tsit, *A Source Book in Chinese Philosophy*, Princeton: Princeton University Press, 1963

Chen, Lai 陳來, *Quanshi yu Chongjian: Wang Chuanshan de Zhexue Jingshen* 詮釋與重建: 王船山的哲學精神 (*Interpretation and Reconstruction: The Spirit of Wang Chuanshan's Philosophy*). Beijing: Peking University Press, 2004

Chen, Que 陳確, *Chen Que Ji* 陳確集 (*A Collection of Chen Que's Writings*), Beijing: Zhonghua Shuju 北京: 中華書局, 1979

De Bary, Wm. Theodore, ed., *The Unfolding of Neo-Confucianism*, New York and London: Columbia University Press, 1975

Gadamer, Hans Georg, *Hermeneutics, Religion and Ethics*, trans. Joel Weinsheimer, New Haven: Yale University Press 1999

Hu, Shi 胡适, *Zhi Qian Xuantong* 致錢玄同 (*A Letter to Qian Xuantong*) in *Chuanshan Quanshu* 船山全書 (*The Complete Works of Chuanshan*), Volume 16, Changsha: Yuelu Shushe長沙： 岳麓書社, 1996

Huang, Ray, *1587: A Year of No Significance*, New Haven and London: Yale University Press, 1981

Ji, Wenfu 嵇文甫, *Wang Chuanshan Xueshu Luncong* 王船山學術論叢 (*A Discussion on Wang Chuanshan's Academics*), Beijing: Sanlian Bookstore, 北京: 三聯書店, 1962

Kant, Immanuel, *Critique of Practical Reason*, trans. by Wemer S. Pluhar, Hackett Publishing Co., 2002b

Ke, Shaomin 柯劭忞, *Chunqiu Guliang Zhuan Zhu* 春秋穀梁傳注 (*Annotation of the Guliang Tradition of the Spring and Autumn Annals*), Beijing: Zhonghua Shuju 北京: 中華書局, 2020

Liang, Qichao 梁啟超, *Zhongguo Jin Sanbainian Xueshu Shi* 中國近三百年學術史 (*Chinese Intellectual History from 1623 to 1923*), Beijing: Dongfang Chubanshe 北京: 東方出版社, 2004

Liu, Jeeloo, Wang Fuzhi's Philosophy of Principle (li)Inherent in Qi, in *Dao Companion to Neo-Confucian Philosophy*, J. Makeham ed., Springer Science and Business Media B.V., 2010

Liu, Lifu 劉立夫, & Tian, Yan 田艷, The Research Center of Chuanshan Buddhist Culture is Established in Changsha, Hunan 船山佛教文化研究中心在湖南長沙成立. *Studies in World Religion* 世界宗教研究, 2009, No. 1

Liu, Yusong 劉毓崧, *A Chronicle of Mr. Wang Chuanshan* (*Wang Chuanshan Xiansheng Nianpu* 王船山先生年譜), in *Complete Works of Chuanshan* (Chuanshan Quanshu 船山全書 16), Volume 16, Changsha: Yuelu Shushe長沙： 岳麓書社, 1996

Mao, Zedong 毛澤東, *Mao Zedong's Comments on His Reading Classical Chinese Literature and History* (*Mao Zedong Du Wenshi Guji Piyu Ji* 毛泽东读文史古籍批语集), edited by the Central Literature Research Centre of the PRC, 中共中央文献研究室主编, The Central Literature Publishing House 中央文献出版社, 1993

Mao, Zedong 毛澤東, *Mao Zedong Xuanji* 毛澤東選集, 第二版 (*Selected Readings of Mao Zedong's Works*, second edition), Beijing: People's Publishing House 北京: 人民出版社, 1991

McMorran, Ian, The Patriot and the Partisans: Wang Fuzhi's Involvement in the Politics of the Yongli Court. In *From Ming to Qing: Conquest, Region and Continuity in the Seventeenth Century China*, ed. Jonathan D. Spence and John E. Wills, Jr., New Haven and London: Yale University Press, 1979

McMorran, Ian, Wang Fuzhi and the Neo-Confucian Tradition, In Debary, Wm. Theodore, ed., *The Unfolding of Neo-Confucianism*, New York: Columbia University Press, 1975

McMorran, Ian, Late Ming Criticism of Wang Yangming: The Case of Wang Fuzhi, *Philosophy East & West*, 1973, vol.23, no.1&2, pp91–102

Moore, G.E. *Principia Ethica*, Cambridge: Cambridge University Press, 1929

Wang, Fansen 王汎森, *Ten Essays on the Scholar's Thought at the Late Ming* and *Early Qing* (*Wanming Qing Chu Sixiang Shi Lun* 晚明清初思想十論), Shanghai: Fudan University Press, 2004

Watson, Burton, *The Complete Works of Chuang Tzu*, New York: Columbia University Press, 1968

Wu, Han 吳晗, *Du Shi Zha Ji* 讀史剳記 (*Notes on Reading the History of the Ming Dynasty*), Beijing: Shenghuo, Dushu, Zhishi San Lian Shudian 北京: 生活讀書知識三聯書店, 1956

Wu, Limin & Xu, Sunming 吳立民, 徐蓀銘, *Chuanshan Fo Dao Sixiang Yanjiu* 船山佛道思想研究 (*A Research on Chuanshan's Thought of Buddhism and Daoism*), Changsha: Hunan Publishing House 長沙: 湖南出版社, 1992

Xia, Jianqin 夏劍欽, Shi Lun Wang Fuzhi Sixiang, Xingxing dui Tansitong de Shenke Yingxiang 試論王夫之思想、行性对谭嗣同的深刻影响 (On Wang Fuzhi's Influence on Tang Sitong's Nature and Action), *Chuanshan Journal* 船山学刊, 1995, no.1

Xu, Sunming 徐蓀銘, Several Questions Pertaining to Wang Chuanshan's Thought on Buddhism and Daoism 船山佛道思想研究的若干問題, *Chuanshan Journal* 1991, no.1

Zeng, Zhaoxu 曾昭旭, *Wang Chuanshan Zhexue* 王船山哲學 (*Wang Chuanshan's Philosophy*) Taiwan: Liren Chubanshe 台湾: 里仁出版社, 2008

Zhang, Binglin 章炳麟, *Chong Kan Chuanshan Yishu Xu* 重刊船山遺書序 (*A Preface for the Second Edition of Chuanshan Extant Book*), in Chuanshan Quanshu 船山全書 16 (Complete Works of Chuanshan), Volume 16, Changsha: Yuelu Shushe長沙: 岳麓書社, 1996

Zhonggong Zhongyang Wexian Yanjiushi, ed., 中共中央文献研究室主编, *Mao Zedong's Comments on His Reading Classical Chinese Literature and History* 毛泽东读文史古籍批语集, The Central Literature Publishing House 中央文献出版社, 1993

Zhou, Zhiping 周質平 & Peterson, Willard J., eds., *Guoshi Fuhai Kaixin Lu* 國史浮海開新錄 (*A New Collection of Chinese History in Overseas*), Taipei: Lian jing Chuban Shiye Youxian Gongsi 臺北: 聯經出版事業有限公司, 2002

Index[1]

[1] Note: Page numbers followed by 'n' refer to notes.

CPSIA information can be obtained
at www.ICGtesting.com
Printed in the USA
LVHW081339240922
729069LV00011BA/326